PRESENTED

TO

BY

189

AN INNOCENT VICTIM.
S. SEYMOUR THOMAS' MASTERPIECE.

ANGELS

OF THE

BATTLEFIELD.

A History of the Labors of the Catholic Sisterhoods in
the Late Civil War.

BY GEORGE BARTON.

...1897...

THE CATHOLIC ART PUBLISHING COMPANY.
PHILADELPHIA, PA.

ISBN-0: 0-6153103-3-8
EAN-13: 9-7-80615-31033-6

Printed and bound in the United States of America.
Published by Nine Choirs Press

Distributed by:
IHS Enterprises
PO Box 796
Lake Katrine, NY 12449

www.NineChoirsPress.com

AUTHOR'S PREFACE.

————◆◆————

The object of this volume is to present in as compact and comprehensive form as possible the history of the Catholic Sisterhoods in the late Civil War. Many books have been written on the work of other women in this war, but, aside from fugitive newspaper paragraphs, nothing has ever been published concerning the self-sacrificing labors of these Sisterhoods. Whatever may have been the cause of this neglect or indifference, it is evident that the time has arrived to fill this important gap in the literature of the war.

"The Sisters," to quote an army chaplain, "do not have reunions or camp-fires to keep alive the memories of the most bloody lustrum in our history, but their war stories are as heroic, and far more edifying, than many the veterans tell."

That genuine humility so characteristic of the Sisters has made the collection of the necessary data for this work very difficult. Most of the stories embodied in the pages that follow have been gathered by personal interviews, through examinations of various archives and records, and by an extensive correspondence with Government officials, veterans of the war and the superiors of convents and communities. It is impossible to enumerate all those who have aided in the work, but the writer desires to thank especially the Sisters to whom he is indebted for the chapters relating to the Sisters of Mercy who were with the Irish Brigade in the West, and to the Sisters of St. Joseph who were at Camp Curtin, in Harrisburg, Pa.

Of course, there has been no intention of presenting a history, or even a sketch, of the war itself and the merest thread of its events has been introduced solely for the purpose of making the narrative of the Sisters as consecutive as the scattered data permitted. The aim has been constantly to present facts in an impartial manner. How far the writer has succeeded remains for the reader to judge.

The chivalrous men wearing both the Blue and the Gray, who caused American manhood and valor to be known and respected the world over, have on many occasions, and in various ways, given expression to the esteem and affection in which they hold the women who devoted their lives to the care of the sick and wounded. The ranks of the war Sisters have been gradually thinned out by death until but a handful of them remain. These survivors rest in their convent homes, tranquilly awaiting the final summons to a land where conflict is unknown. They may die, but the story of their patriotic and humane work will live as long as love for loyalty, regard for duty and admiration for self-sacrifice exist in the hearts of the American people.

G. B.

TABLE OF CONTENTS.

LIST OF ILLUSTRATIONS.

————◆◆————

TABLE OF CONTENTS.

CHAPTER I.

THE ORDERS THAT PARTICIPATED.

One of the effects of the war. The productive force of the nation deprived by death, disease and disability of one million men. The task of caring for the sick and wounded. Four notable orders— The Sisters of Charity, Sisters of Mercy, Sisters of St. Joseph and Sisters of the Holy Cross. Their history and the discipline, experience and self-sacrifice brought to bear upon their work during the war.

CHAPTER II.

ARCHBISHOP HUGHES AND THE SISTERS.

The problem of how to provide the necessary nurses for both the Union and Confederate Armies. Sisters not able to volunteer without the approval of their superiors. An interesting epistle from Archbishop Hughes to Archbishop Kenrick, The New York prelate appointed by President Lincoln as a peace commissioner to France. A characteristic letter from the martyred President to the great Archbishop. Quelling the draft riots in New York city.

TABLE OF CONTENTS.

TABLE OF CONTENTS.

TABLE OF CONTENTS.

CHAPTER IX.

LABORS IN FREDERICK CITY.

CHAPTER X.

WHITE HOUSE.

CHAPTER XI.

MANASSAS AND ANTIETAM.

TABLE OF CONTENTS.

TABLE OF CONTENTS.

TABLE OF CONTENTS.

TABLE OF CONTENTS.

CHAPTER XXI.

PAGE

THE NORTH CAROLINA HOSPITALS.

CHAPTER XXII.

LABORS IN THE WEST.

CHAPTER XXIII.

THE STANTON HOSPITAL.

TABLE OF CONTENTS.

TABLE OF CONTENTS.

CHAPTER XXVII. PAGE

A LESSON IN CHARITY.

An incident of the war in which a gentle Sister of Charity and a stern military commander played the leading parts. "What do you do with your beggings?" The Red River campaign and its fatal results. The general in the hospital. "Did you get the ice and beef?" A grateful patient and his appreciation of the real worth of the Sisters.

241

APPENDIX.

CHAPTER I.

THE ORDERS THAT PARTICIPATED.

———◆◆◆———

One of the effects of the war. The productive force of the nation deprived by death, disease and disability of one million men. The task of caring for the sick and wounded. Four notable orders — The Sisters of Charity, Sisters of Mercy, Sisters of St. Joseph and Sisters of the Holy Cross. Their history and the discipline, experience and self-sacrifice brought to bear upon their work during the war.

———◆◆◆———

On the twelfth day of April, 1861, the first shot fired upon Fort Sumter, formally inaugurated the civil war in the United States. On the ninth of April, 1865, Grant and Lee were the principals in the historic meeting at  Appomattox Court House, by which hostilities were virtually terminated. The interval between those two memorable dates presents the greatest ordeal in the history of the Republic.

As a result of these four momentous years of conflict the nation was deprived by death and disease of one million men. The total number of enlisted soldiers in the Union Army during the whole of the war amounted to 2,688,523. As many of these men were mustered in twice, and as a certain percentage deserted, it is reasonable to estimate that 1,500,000 men were actively engaged in the Northern armies.

Of this number 56,000 died on the field of battle, 35,000 expired in the hospitals from the effects of wounds received in action, and 184,000 perished by disease. It is probable that those who died of disease after their discharge from the army would swell the total to 300,000. If inferior hospital service and poor sanitary arrangements are added to the other results of war, it is safe to assume that the loss of the South was greater than that of the North. But, considering the Southern loss equal to that of the North, the aggregate is 600,000. Add to this 400,000 men crippled or permanently disabled by disease, and the total subtraction from the productive force of the nation reaches the stupendous total of 1,000,000 men. These figures seem almost incredible, but they come from what, in this particular at least, must be regarded as a trustworthy source [1].

The task of caring for such an army of dead and wounded was no light one. In the beginning of the war this feature of military life was conducted in an uncertain and spasmodic manner. As time wore on, it became evident that the war was not to consist of a few skirmishes, but was likely to be a protracted struggle between two bodies of determined men[2]. Then the necessity of a systematic sanitary and hospital service made itself apparent. As a result of the pressing needs of the hour the Sanitary Commission and the Christian Commission were organized. The meritorious nature of the work of these great charities has been made known by reports and books

---

[1] Greeley's "American Conflict".

[2] There were 2261 known battles, engagements and skirmishes during the war.

published since the war. The details of the good deeds of both organizations in supplying nurses and in caring for invalids generally are too well known to need repetition.

But the story of the labors of the Catholic Sisters is not so well known. To begin with, the Sisters brought to their aid in caring for the sick and wounded soldiers the experience, training and discipline of the religious bodies with which they were identified. Self-denial was a feature of their daily life, and the fact that they had taken vows of poverty, chastity and obedience peculiarly fitted them for a duty that demanded personal sacrifices almost every hour of the day and night.

From the data obtainable it appears that the members of four Catholic Sisterhoods participated in the merciful work incident to the war. These included the Sisters of Charity, the Sisters of Mercy, the Sisters of St. Joseph and the Sisters of the Holy Cross[3]. The soldiers, like many people in civil life, made no distinction between the orders, and to them the dark-robed angels of the battlefields were all "Sisters of Charity."

There are now three orders of the Sisters of Charity in the United States. The "black caps," or Mother Seton Sisters, who have establishments in New York, Cincinnati and other places; the "white caps," or Cornette Sisters, of Emmitsburg, Md., and the Sisters of Charity, of Nazareth, Ky. There are probably 5000 members of these three orders of Sisters of Charity in this country today. The Nazareth community was founded in 1812 by a few pious American ladies near Nazareth, Ky., under

---

(3)It is probable that scattering members from one or two other orders did praiseworthy work during the war, but diligent inquiry has failed to bring forth any specific facts concerning their labors.

Bishops Flaget and David. Mother Catherine Spalding, a relative of the late Archbishop of Baltimore, and of the present Bishop of Peoria, Ill., was the first Superioress. The members of all these three branches of the Sisters of Charity did good work during the war.

The Congregation of the Sisters of Mercy was founded by Miss Catherine McAuley, in Dublin, Ireland, September 24, 1827. Seven Sisters, who came from Carlow, Ireland, established the order in the United States, locating in Pittsburg, Pa. The Sisters of the Holy Cross have a Mother House at Notre Dame, Ind., and conduct establishments in a large number of dioceses.

The Congregation of the Sisters of St. Joseph was founded in France, in 1650. In the general ruin incident to the French Revolution, near the close of the last century, the convents of the order were destroyed. The body was subsequently reorganized, and six Sisters from the Mother House at Lyon came to St. Louis in 1836, at the request of Bishop Rosati, and founded a house at Carondelet, Mo. This became the Mother House in this country. A number of independent houses of the order have since been established, notably the one at Chestnut Hill, Philadelphia.

CHAPTER II.

ARCHBISHOP HUGHES AND THE SISTERS.

The problem of how to provide the necessary nurses for both the Union and Confederate Armies. Sisters not able to volunteer without the approval of their superiors. An interesting epistle from Archbishop Hughes to Archbishop Kenrick, The New York prelate appointed by President Lincoln as a peace commissioner to France. A characteristic letter from the martyred President to the great Archbishop. Quelling the draft riots in New York city.

Very early in the war the question of providing nurses for the sick and wounded soldiers of both armies became a serious problem, not only to the civil authorities, but also to the Church officials. In every great emergency questions of this kind generally solve themselves. It proved so in this instance. The first shot had hardly been fired, the first battle fought and the first improvised hospital put into service, before volunteers from all sections of the country had placed themselves at the disposal of generals of the contending armies. These offers came both from lay women and from members of the various Sisterhoods connected with the Catholic Church in the United States. The Sisters, of course, being under certain rules and discipline, were not able to volunteer until they had obtained the consent and approval of their Superiors.

LINCOLN.

In the beginning the nurses for the armies were taken

from all walks of life. While they were zealous and entered upon their work with the desire of alleviating suffering, they did not have the disposition or training necessary to carry on the work with the ease and thoroughness essential to complete success. As the war progressed and battles occurred more frequently, and the number of sick and wounded became alarmingly large, the medical directors in both the Union and Confederate armies began to recognize and appreciate the real value of the Sisters.

The following letter[1], written by Archbishop Hughes, of New York, to Most Rev. Francis Patrick Kenrick, D. D., Archbishop of the See of Baltimore, shows that the subject was a live one in Church circles at that time:

To the Archbishop of Baltimore.   May 9, 1861.

Most Reverend and Dear Sir: —

The Superior of the Jesuits here called upon me more than a week ago to state that their society would be prepared to furnish for spiritual necessities of the army, North and South, as many as ten chaplains, speaking all the civilized languages of Europe or America. I heard him, but did not make any reply. For myself I have sent but one chaplain with the Sixty-ninth Regiment, and to him I have already given the facilities which you had the kindness to confer upon me for such an occasion.

There is also another question growing up, and it is about nurses for the sick and wounded. Our Sisters of Mercy have volunteered after the example of their Sisters toiling in the Crimean war. I have signified to them, not harshly, that they had better mind their own affairs until their services are needed. I am now informed indirectly that the Sisters of Charity in the diocese would be willing to volunteer a force of from fifty to one hundred nurses. To this last proposition I have very strong

(1) Life of Archbishop Hughes, by John R. G. Hassard.

objections. Besides, it would seem to me natural and proper that the Sisters of Charity in Emmitsburg should occupy the very honorable post of nursing the sick and wounded. But, on the other hand, Maryland is a divided community at this moment, whereas New York is understood to be all on one side. In fact, as the question now stands, Maryland is in America, for the moment, as Belgium has been the battlefield of Europe. As I mentioned several days ago, Baltimore must be destroyed or it must succumb to Northern determination.

On these several points I would like much to know what your Grace thinks and would advise.

Sincerely your devoted brother and servant in Christ.

JOHN, Archbishop of New York.

While, as the Archbishop stated in his letter, Maryland might have been a divided community, the same could not be said of the Sisters of Charity of Emmitsburg. They were united in occupying "the very honorable post of nursing the sick and wounded" on both sides of the great conflict. It is interesting to note that as time went on the Bishop changed some of his views regarding the Sisters, as expressed in the above letter. Both the Sisters of Charity and the Sisters of Mercy in the Diocese of New York served in the camps and the hospitals. To begin with, the Archbishop withdrew his "strong objection" to the one hundred Sisters of Charity who desired to volunteer in the early stages of the war. After that all those who were willing to undertake the humane work went into it with his blessing and best wishes.

There are conflicting opinions regarding the propriety of the "war stand" taken by the Archbishop, but it is generally agreed that he was one of the heroic figures of war times. He had the absolute confidence of President Lincoln, and on the 21st of October, 1861, was sent abroad with Thurlow Weed on a "peace commission." The Archbishop went to France, while Mr. Weed confined his work To England. At the same time Messrs. Mason and Slidell were in Europe on a mission in the interests of the Confederacy. The late Bishop McNierny, of Albany, then a young priest in New York City, accompanied the Archbishop to France, acting in the capacity of private secretary.

These two rival "missions" to Europe were covered with all sorts of honeyed diplomatic terms, but their real purpose was well known. Messrs. Mason and Slidell went to induce one or more of the powerful nations of the old world to throw the weight of their influence with the Southern Confederacy. The mission of the Archbishop and Mr. Weed was to prevent that result.

The following letter from President Lincoln to Archbishop Hughes is of interest. It was the beginning of a warm personal friendship between two strong men—a friendship ended only by death.

Washington, D. C., October 21, 1861.

Archbishop Hughes.

Rt. Rev. Sir:—I am sure you will pardon me if, in my ignorance, I do not address you with technical correctness.

I find no law authorizing the appointment of chaplains for our hospitals, and yet the services of chaplains are more needed, perhaps, in hospitals than with the healthy soldiers in the field. With this view I have given a sort of quasi appointment (a copy of which I enclose) to each of three Protestant ministers, who have accepted and entered upon the duties.

If you perceive no objection I will thank you to give me the name or names of one or more suitable persons of the Catholic Church to whom I may with propriety tender the same service.

Many thanks for your kind and judicious letters to Governor Seward, and which he regularly allows me the pleasure and profit of perusing.

With the highest respect. Your obedient servant,

A. LINCOLN.

A letter written by Archbishop Hughes to Cardinal Barnabo, at the time of his appointment by President Lincoln, goes to show that the Archbishop accepted the mission with the very highest motives. After explaining that he had refused it once and only reconsidered his refusal at the earnest request of the President, he adds: "My mission was and is a mission of peace between France and England on the one side, and the United States on the other. The time was so brief between my visit to Washington and my departure from New York that I had no opportunity of writing to your Eminence upon the subject, or of consulting any of the other Bishops in regard to it. I made it known to the President that if I should come to Europe it would not be as a partisan of the North more than of the South; that I should represent the interests of the South as well as of the North; in short, the interests of all the United States just the same as if they had not been distracted by the present civil war. The people of the South know that I am not opposed to their interests. They have even published that in their papers, and some say that my coming to Europe is with a view to bringing about a reconciliation between the two sections of the country. But in fact no one but myself, either North or South, knows the entire object of my visit to Europe."

Archbishop Hughes was one of the great men of his day. He was on terms of friendship with several of the

Presidents who preceded Mr. Lincoln, and also enjoyed the confidence and respect of the leading statesmen of the nation. As early as 1847 he preached before Congress upon the invitation of such men as John Quincy Adams, John C. Calhoun and Thomas H. Benton. His subject was: "Christianity, the Only Source of Moral, Social and Political Regeneration."

In July, 1863, Archbishop Hughes was instrumental in quelling the draft riots in New York City. The mob was beyond the control of the local authorities, and the Archbishop finally consented to say a few words in the interest of law and order. The venerable prelate was fast approaching his end. He was so weak at this time that he had to be conveyed to the balcony of his residence in an arm chair. He spoke briefly, and succeeded in inducing the rioters to return to their homes for the time being. It was his last public appearance, and soon after this he peacefully passed away, surrounded by friends and relatives and the ever faithful Sisters of Charity.

In the chapters that follow it is proposed to deal with the labors of the Sisters of Charity, taking up first the Cornette or Emmitsburg Sisters, then the "Sisters of Charity of Nazareth," and finally the "black caps" or Mother Seton Sisters. The concluding chapters deal with the Sisters of Mercy, the Sisters of St. Joseph and the Sisters of the Holy Cross in the order named.

CHAPTER III.

IN AND AROUND RICHMOND.

Sisters of Charity inaugurate their labors in the Confederate Capital. St. Anne's Military Hospital begins with three hundred patients. A zealous Sister makes her colleague prisoner in the pantry. An odor of death, and how it was caused. The Union soldier who was "shot at Manassas." Nurses who first got "a puff and then a buff."

In the early part of June, 1861, Dr. Gibson, who was in charge of the Military Hospital at the Confederate capital, Richmond, Va., called upon the Sisters of Charity of Emmitsburg to come to the relief of the sick and wounded soldiers in that neighborhood. The late Rt. Rev. John McGill, the Bishop of the Diocese of Richmond, did not object to having the Sisters engage in a work of mercy, but he was opposed to any hospital or infirmary which might prove to be an obstacle to or impair the prosperity of the church hospital of St. Francis de Sales. The civil authorities did not make any impression upon the prelate, but when the Sisters themselves called at the episcopal palace and begged to be assigned to the work, the Bishop could not resist, and the coveted consent was obtained.

LEE.

It was announced that the Sisters would begin their work on the following Saturday. Two physicians called at the convent, and conducted them to the institution, which afterwards became known as St. Anne's Military Hospital. The structure was in an unfinished state, and

the walls were not plastered. But it was thoroughly venti-
lated and free from dampness, and that meant much in a
building designed for the care of the sick.

The house contained altogether about three hundred
patients. Each ward held from twelve to fourteen men,
and the rooms opened into one another. It was noon
when the Sisters arrived, and they were shocked to find
that many of the wounded men had not yet broken their
fast. The first care of the newcomers was to relieve the
hunger of the patients. To effect this they went to the
kitchen, making the acquaintance of "Nicholas," the cook;
"Black George," his assistant, and other occupants of this
section of the house. While these employees were good
men and were doing their very best, they succeeded but
poorly in having an orderly kitchen, or in providing the
soldiers with the sort of food adapted to their weakened
condition.

One Sister among those who had volunteered to work
in the hospital was detained a little later than the others. She felt remorseful at the unavoidable delay, but determined to compensate for it by unusual activity. The
first thing that caught her alert eye on her arrival was a
pantry with the door wide open. Burning with zeal to be
useful she closed and locked the door. Suddenly there
was a rapping from the inside. The zealous Sister was not
superstitious, nor could she be called nervous, but these
strong noises frightened her, and she became pale as the
rappings continued to grow in volume and number.

"Open the door and let me out," came in sepulchral
tones from the pantry.

The key was applied and the door hastily opened,
and out walked another frightened Sister, who had been

imprisoned while searching for supplies.

After many little incidents of a trivial character order was restored from chaos. Some of the soldiers declared that the first meal they received from the Sisters was better than anything they had eaten since entering the army. The Sisters, that first night, got no sleep, for the wants of the sufferers were pressing.

One of the patients called a Sister to his bedside and in a low voice said: "You know the doctors think I may not live over night, therefore I have a great favor to ask that I hope you will not refuse. I have a mother." Here tears checked his utterance. The Sister said: "I understand; you want me to write to her." "Yes," he said; "say that her child is dead, but do not tell her how I have suffered; that would break her heart."

This delicate mission, like many similar ones entrusted to the Sisters, was faithfully fulfilled.

The wounded men came from the battles and skirmishes that had taken place in the vicinity of Richmond, notably Phillippi, Big Bethel, Romney, Rich Mountain, Carrick's Ford and Manassas, Va. The last engagement, which is also known as the first battle of Bull Run, ended disastrously for the Union forces. It occurred on the 21st of July, 1861, and the Sisters silently going the rounds in their infirmary could almost hear the reverberating sound of the shot and shell.

Toward night about fifty wounded soldiers, prisoners from Manassas, were brought into the hospital, some dying and others wounded, and until better accommodations could be provided they had to be laid on the floor.

One of the Sisters was called by the doctor, who said:

"Sister, get something for this poor man's head; he has just asked for a log of wood."

The Sister went out, but where to get a pillow was a mystery; everyone was engaged. At last a pillow case was found, and the bright idea came to the Sister: "I will stuff it with paper." She brought it to the man, who was a down-East Yankee, thinking the invention suited the individual for whom it was destined. The poor fellow, despite his suffering, smiled as it was given him.

It was very late when the Sisters finally prepared to retire from a hard day's work. They were not settled in their room before Sister Blanche remarked:

"I cannot sleep; there is such an odor of death about this apartment."

Nevertheless they composed themselves as best as they could. In the morning the secret of the strong odor was revealed. A pair of human limbs amputated the week before had been carelessly thrown in the adjoining room. It was a great trial for the Sister to visit that room. She covered her nose and mouth with her handkerchief and threw open the windows. Under her directions the limbs were at once interred. One of the Sisters writing in her diary at this time says: "Yesterday a man was buried with three legs."

On a Sunday morning an addition of eleven Union officers was received to the number of the wounded. They were given accommodations in the garret. In the officers' quarters were found captains, majors, lieutenants and sergeants, all wounded. One fellow blessed with a fine voice had a guitar loaned him, and he could always be seen in a corner whiling away the dull hours. Sometimes these invalid officers were annoyed by visitors who were untiring in their questions.

"Where were you shot at?" asked one inquisitive individual, meaning in what part of the body.

"Shot at Manassas," was the laconic reply.

As one of the Sisters was crossing the porch a tall, brawny soldier cried out: "You ladies have a sight of work to do, but I tell you what, you get high pay."

"None at all," was the quiet answer.

"What!" said he, starting back with surprise; "you don't tell me you do all this work for nothing?"

"Precisely," was the quiet response.

One of the nurses or hands about the place being sadly put out about something that went wrong exclaimed that he was "neither an angel nor a Sister of Charity," and that he would not put up with it at all. Sister Mary Ann, in speaking of the varied dispositions of the men, said that the Sisters "first got a puff and then a buff."

Five of the Union officers who were in the garret clubbed together after their departure and sent the Sisters a check for fifty dollars for the benefit of the orphanage in Richmond.

The Infirmary of St. Francis de Sales had been in operation by the Sisters for the sick in general when the war commenced, but after that it was utilized for the wounded soldiers. On May 16, 1861, the Sisters in this institution were appealed to by the medical authorities. Very soon the building was too much crowded for the patients. The Government then took a large house, which was transformed into a hospital. It was thought that male nurses would answer the purpose. In a few days, however, the surgeon and officers in charge went to the Sisters at the Infirmary, begging them to come to their assistance at the new hospital, ass the sick were very much in need of their services. The Sisters went to this hospital on June 26, 1861.

Other hospitals in and around Richmond were built, and as rapidly as they were made ready for use the surgeons applied for Sisters to take charge of them. All of the Sisters outside of the blockade which existed at that time were at military posts, except those engaged in caring for the orphans. The schools and academies controlled by the Sisters had been closed for some time. As the Sisters were sent to many different hospitals the number that could be assigned for each one was small. The hospitals were often without the necessaries of life. For the Sisters' table rough corn bread and strong fat bacon were luxuries; as for beverages, they could rarely tell what was given to them for tea or coffee, for at one time it was sage and at another herbs.

Soon after going to one of the new hospitals in Richmond the surgeon in charge said to one of the Sisters: "I am obliged to make known our difficulties to you that you may enable me to surmount them, for you ladies accomplish all you undertake. Until now we have been supplied with the delicacies necessary for our patients from Louisiana, but the blockade prevents this at present and I fear to enter the wards, as the poor men are still asking for former refreshments, and they cannot be quieted. We dislike to inform them of the strait we are in, though this state of affairs may be of short duration."

The Sister hardly knew what to do, but proposed that wagons be sent among the farmhouses for the purpose of gathering in fowl, milk, butter and fruit. This was done, but in the meantime complaints had been made to headquarters that since the Sisters had come to the hospital all delicacies had been withheld from the poor sick. The surgeon and Sisters knew nothing of this complaint until a deputy Government official arrived to learn the truth of the charges. He visited the wards during meal time, after which he entered the room where the Sisters dined. Then he told the surgeon the motive of his visit. The surgeon was glad to explain to the deputy the cause of the complaints. The deputy informed the soldiers that the nurses were not in any way responsible for their sufferings, and that the fare of the Sisters was always worse than that furnished to the soldiers.

The men soon became convinced that they had been too hasty in their judgment of the Sisters, and that the stoppage of the delicacies was for unavoidable causes. They found before long that the "Angels of the Battle-field," as they came to call the Sisters, had but one desire, and that was to add to their comfort, as much as the limited supplies would permit.

CHAPTER IV.

HARPER'S FERRY.

———◆◆———

The adventures of three Sisters who were detailed from the mother
house at Emmitsburg. Their offer to retire in the interest of the
ladies of Winchester. A night's "repose" with foreheads resting
upon umbrella handles. A journey homeward by car and stage,
and then across the Potomac River in a flat canoe. Received at
the convent as one from the grave.

———◆◆———

Nearly all of the Sisters that could be spared had
been sent from the mother house at Emmitsburg, and
were engaged in performing works of charity on the bat-

tlefields and in the various camps
and hospitals. On June 7, 1861, a
telegram was received from the
authorities asking that a number of Sisters be detailed to serve
the sick and wounded soldiers at
Harper's Ferry.

In spite of the severe strain
that it entailed upon their available assignments, the Superiors
made the sacrifice of sending
three Sisters. These brave women

GRANT.

left Emmitsburg on June 9 for Frederick City. Mother
Ann Simeon cautioned them to act with prudence, lest
they meet with trouble, as they had the Northern Army
and its sentinels to pass in order to reach their destination. An orderly had been sent to escort them, but the
Sisters passed their intended guide without knowing it,
by going by them on the road to Emmitsburg.

An expected engagement kept villagers and farmers quietly at home. Many cautiously whispered their fears or opinions, and the sight of people bold enough to travel just then was a matter that occasioned mild surprise. For this reason the Sisters tried to huddle in the rear of the stage coach, hoping to pass unobserved. During a brief halt for the mail in one little town the driver opened the stage door and handing in a letter said in a loud voice:

"Sisters, a gentleman in Emmitsburg desires you to put this letter in a Southern post office after you have crossed the line."

The eyes of the curious and astonished people were on them in a moment. The Sisters were not aware that the driver knew of their destination, but they remained quiet and made the best of the incident. The heat was excessive. One of the horses gave out on the way, and another had to be hastily substituted. After some delay the party arrived in Frederick City. A few sentinels stood here and there, but no one paid much attention to the new arrivals. Before they started again, however, a number of men gathered around their carriages, saying: "Why, ladies, where are you going?" Several of the men asked questions at the same time, but the Sisters stared at them blankly, and civilly answered anything except what the gossips most desired to know.

As hostilities had stopped the railway cars the pilgrims had to continue their journey in a stage-coach. Almost sick with heat they journeyed on until another horse succumbed. This meant more trouble and suspense, but it was borne with heroic patience.

The most exciting adventure was yet to come. The rocks of the Maryland Heights on one side, and the Potomac River on the left, came in view. Just as the carriage was, seemingly, proceeding smoothly on its way there came a sudden grating sound and then an abrupt stop. "We're stuck!" ejaculated the driver, with more force than elegance. The carriage was so tightly fastened that it was feared the vehicle would have to be abandoned and the remainder of the journey made upon foot. The driver swore and stormed about, while the Sisters meekly looked on in silence, fearing to further irritate him with suggestions. Finally the carriage was extricated and the pilgrimage proceeded upon its way.

About twilight the Southern pickets were seen, for the South still held a portion of Maryland. The first soldier inquired where the Sisters were going, and with what intent. He then passed them on to the next guard, and so on until they came to the last, who said: "We have just received such strict orders regarding persons crossing in or out, that it is not in my power to pass you on." The captain of the guards was sent for, however, and the Sisters were transferred over the Potomac Bridge. Great cargoes of powder had already been placed on this bridge, so that, in the event of the enemy's approach it might be destroyed.

Harper's Ferry is at the junction of the Potomac and Shenandoah Rivers, the Potomac separating Maryland and Virginia. A summit above the town, standing between the two rivers, is called Bolivar Heights. On this elevation was located the military hospital where the Sisters were to labor. A neat little Catholic church was located about midway between the valley and the town.

The hospital was filled with the sick, and around the town lay thousands of men just arrived from the most remote Southern States. A cold wet spell had preceded the present heat, and many of the men were ill and lay in their tents until vacancies opened for them in the badly sheltered houses in the town. The men in one regiment had contracted measles on their march; this spreading among others with the exposure incidental to army life thinned their numbers before the ball and the sword had begun their quicker work.

On reaching their lodgings the Sisters found supper prepared, and after disposing of this they soon retired to rest. The stillness and darkness of the town was frightful. No sound but the Sisters' voices or footsteps was to be heard. Not a light gleamed from the fastened windows for fear of discovery by the hidden enemy. The whole army had been sleeping or resting on their arms since their arrival, expecting an early attack.

The medical director, who had sent for the Sisters, came early in the morning and took them to the hospital. With his assistant he escorted them from room to room, introducing them and saying to the patients: "Now you will have no cause to complain of not getting nourishment, medicine and attention at the right time, for the Sisters of Charity will see to all these things."

The town had been by turns in the possession of the North and South, and was therefore completely drained of provisions and necessary conveniences for the sick. Notwithstanding these difficulties things were beginning to look more comfortable, when a telegram was received from Winchester ordering the whole Confederate Army to repair to that town immediately. The Northern Army, it was announced, would attempt to cross the Potomac above and below Harper's Ferry, thus surrounding the

BOMBARDMENT OF FORT SUMTER.

Southern Army and cutting off all supplies.

The soldiers moved at once, with the exception of those who served the sick, and those who were to collect the tents and finally destroy bridges and tracks. Provisions were cast into the river by the wholesale, in order to deprive the enemy of benefit. Then came new orders to wait a while, but the invalids had already been removed to the depot, to await the return of the cars from Winchester. Arrangements were now being made for the destruction of the bridges and tracks, and the Sisters were sent to remain with a worthy Catholic family far away from these structures. During the night one explosion after another shook the grand bridge and seemed to shake the mountains. The little Catholic church, the only one that had not been applied to military purposes, was filled and surrounded by the frightened people. The worn-out pastor was their only consoler.

The Sisters looked at the awful destruction around them, and felt encompassed with desolation. All the next day they hourly expected to be called to the cars, but no word came. They now learned that the ladies of Winchester had written to the medical director requesting him not to let the Sisters of Charity serve the sick, as they themselves would wait on them. The Sisters knew that the ladies had been enthusiastic in caring for the Confederate sick and, thinking the delay was owing to the embarrassment the doctors might experience in regard to this, one Sister, acting as spokeswoman, said to them:

"Gentlemen, we are aware of the ardor with which the Winchester ladies have labored for your poor men, as also of their desire to serve them alone—that is, without any aid of ours; therefore be candid enough to allow us to return to our home. In case you feel any difficulty respecting the ladies of Winchester the Sisters consider it reasonable that they should wish to serve their own people, and will not be offended, but rather feel grateful for your friendly candor."

The physicians replied that they did not care for the objections that had been made to the Sisters; that the ladies of Winchester could never do for the sick what the Sisters of Charity would do, and therefore unless the Sisters insisted on returning home the doctors would hold them to their undertaking.

The physicians then begged the Sisters not to leave the town, but to await the signal for departure. Expecting all day and even until 11 P. M. to be sent for, and feeling that rest was absolutely necessary, the Sisters were preparing for bed when the kind lady of the house came into their room, saying: "My dear, poor Sisters, a wagon and your baggage are at the door for you." They soon left their benevolent hostess, who wept to see them pursing such hardships. It was a genuine farm wagon, with two negroes as drivers. The worthy pastor of Harper's Ferry, who was determined not to leave the Sisters entirely to strangers, attended to their trunks and found seats for them. The heavy spray from both rivers was thick in the air. Here and there a star appeared between broken clouds, giving barely light enough to see the sentinels at their posts. One of these, advancing, asked the countersign, which the pastor gave him. The wagon, running on the high terrace edge of the Potomac River, made, with the darkness, a gloomy prospect for the Sisters.

On reaching the depot an officer met them and offered to find them a shelter until the cars would arrive.

He took them across two boards that formed a temporary bridge. By the aid of his lantern they could see water on either side of them, so that they had to watch carefully and pick their steps lest they slip off the boards. At last he opened the door of a little hut, which was almost washed by the river. Here they entered and sat down, resting their foreheads on their umbrellas until between 3 and 4 o'clock, when a rumbling outside announced the arrival of the cars. The train reached Winchester five hours later. Almost the entire town was occupied by soldiers, so that accommodations at hotels were not to be had for any consideration. The zealous priest, who was still with the Sisters, took them to the church, and afterwards went in search of lodgings for them.

The church, which was of stone, and was one of the poorest old buildings in the place, was located in the suburbs. A crowd of ignorant and curious men and children followed the Sisters as they walked to the edifice. As they entered the church the bystanders crowded in and about the door. When the Sisters went by turns to the confessional the village men and boys hurried outside and peeped through the cracks at the penitents, peering into their very faces. Soon the priest went out and as he did so he shut and locked the door after him. After some time he returned, although the Sisters feared that it was just possible he had lost his mind and would not come back. They knew his hardships had been excessive, because, besides being sick and without food or sleep, he had many other inconveniences to contend with. But he returned and took them to a plain, worthy Catholic family.

The following morning being Sunday they walked to the church, and just as the gate had to halt to let a company of soldiers, on their way to Mass, enter the church.

About twenty or thirty Catholics constituted the congregation usually, but on this day the soldiers and Sisters made quite a crowded assembly. After that the Sisters waited patiently for the doctors to take them to the scene of their labors. The Reverend Dr. Costello had called on them from time to time, informing the authorities that the Sisters were ready to go to work among the sick. The medical director finally asked them if they must remain in one hospital, or whether each Sister could take charge of a separate one. He was informed that their number was too small to divide and they would remain at one of the hospitals.

The heads of families in the city of Winchester remained in town, while grown-up daughters and children were sent to country seats, the mothers of these staying at their houses, receiving and serving as many sick soldiers as they could. The Sisters received much kindness from these ladies, for they knew that the common rations of the soldiers were very rough. Indeed, one of the greatest distresses of the Sisters at this time was that they had not more for the poor sick.

The Sisters began their labors in one of the largest hospitals in Winchester. They worked incessantly day and night, frequently not pausing long enough to take necessary food and nourishment for themselves. Such labor began to show on them, especially as they were only three in number. The doctors said while more nurses were needed there would be no way of sending for more Sisters except by one of them going home and returning with the others. Affairs had reached such a crisis that only the Sisters of Charity could travel now. One of them finally started off for the mother house, going by car, then by stage, and then crossing the Potomac in a flat canoe. Then she went on as fast as possible, and after running for a mile reached the railroad car before it left the station.

The evening of the next day she reached St. Joseph's at Emmitsburg, where she was received as if from the grave. The anxious Superiors had heard nothing from or of the Sisters except what meagre news was published of the movements of the two armies. Sister Euphemia, afterwards Mother Superior, then left St. Joseph's with three companions for Winchester, to relieve the Sisters there. At the same time a telegram was sent to Sister Valentine at St. Louis instructing her to go immediately and replace Sister Euphemia in Winchester, who was to proceed farther southward, for in Richmond, Va., the Sisters were almost overcome with continuous duty. The Sisters, now six in number continued their labors in Winchester until very few remained in the hospitals. The convalescent members of the army had been leaving Winchester for some days, going towards Richmond. The Sisters themselves finally proceeded towards Richmond.

CHAPTER V.

ST. LOUIS MILITARY HOSPITAL.

The border State of Missouri the scene of some of the most dramatic events of the war. Soldiers ask the nurses if they are Free Masons. The Chaplain obtains a pardon for a prisoner of war. Archbishop Ryan and his work among the sick and wounded. The young Confederate who declined to express sorrow for his course in the war. Amusing and pathetic incidents.

In the meantime operations in the great civil conflict were beginning in the Southwest. The fact that Missouri was a border state made it the scene of some of the most dramatic events of the war. Thousands of the sick and  wounded of both armies were cared for in St. Louis. It was on the 12th of August, 1861, that Major-General Fremont, commanding the Department of the West, established a military hospital in the suburbs of St. Louis.

General Fremont desired that every attention should be paid to the wounded soldiers. He visited them frequently, and perceiving that there was much neglect on the part of the attendants, applied to the sisters of st. Philomena's school for a sufficient number of them to take charge of the hospital. He promised the sisters, if they would accept, to leave everything to their management. There was no delay in acceding to this request. Rev. James Francis Burlando, the Superior of the Sisters of Charity, during a visit made to St. Philomena's School a few months previous, had foreseen the probability of such an occurrence and given the Sisters directions to guide them in such a case.

The Sisters had the superintendence of everything relating to the sick in the hospital. Some of the soldier attendants at first looked with wonder on the strange dress and appearance of the new nurses, asking them if they were Free Masons. The Sisters were, however, treated with the greatest respect, so much so that not an oath or disrespectful word was heard in the hospital during the three years that they were there.

The hospital was visited every other day by the ladies of the Union Aid Society, who could not help admiring the almost profound silence observed in the wards. They could not understand the influence the Sisters exercised over the patients, both sick and convalescent, who were as submissive as children. The Archbishop of St. Louis, the late Most Rev. P. R. Kenrick, D. D., was pleased when he learned that the Sisters had been asked for at the hospital. The prelate provided a chaplain, who said Mass every morning in the oratory arranged in their apartment. After the Mass the chaplain visited every ward instructing, baptizing and reconciling sinners to God. There were hundreds of baptisms during the time the Sisters were in the hospital, the greatest number of the persons thus baptized dying in the hospital. The institution was closed at the end of the war, and the Sisters returned to their former homes.

Father Burke was one of the priests who did a great deal of work in the hospital, and he bears testimony to the fact that the patients thought there were no persons like the Sisters. They would often say: "Indeed, it was not the doctor that cured us; it was the Sisters." When returning to their regiment they would say: "Sisters, we may never

see you again, but be assured you will be very gratefully remembered." Others would say: "Sisters, I wish we
could do something for you, but you do not seem to want
anything; besides, it is not in the power of any poor soldier to make you anything like recompense. All that we
can do for you is to fight for you, and that we will do until
our last breath."

They would rather apply to the Sisters in case where
they could do so than to the doctors, and as a result the
Sisters had a difficult task in encouraging them to have
confidence in the doctors. Every evening the Sisters were
accustomed to visit a tent a few yards distant from the
hospital, where the badly wounded cases were detained.
One night a Sister found a poor man whose hand had
been amputated from the wrist, suffering very much,
the arm being terribly inflamed. He complained that the
doctor had that morning ordered a hot poultice and that
he had not received it. The Sister called the nurse and
wound-dresser and inquired why the doctor's orders had
not been attended to. They told her that there were not
hops in the hospital; that the steward had gone to town
that morning before they knew it, and they had no other
opportunity of sending to obtain any that day. The Sisters immediately sent across the yard to a bakery and
got some hops and had the poultice put on. The poor
man was gratified and surprised. "The Sisters," he said,
"find ways and means to relieve everyone, but others who
make a profession of the work do not even know how to
begin it."

When a new doctor came to the hospital it was from
the patients that he would learn to appreciate the value of
the Sisters. When the patients returned to their regiments
they would say to their sick companions: "If you go to

St. Louis try to get to the House of Refuge Hospital; the Sisters are there and they will soon make you well." Late one evening a Sister went to see that nothing was wanting for the sick. She found one poor man suffering intense pain in his forehead and temples. He had taken cold in camp and the inflammation went to his eyes, so that he became entirely blind. The pain in his forehead was so intense that he thought he could not live until morning. The Sister asked him to let her bind up his forehead with a wide bandage.

"Oh, Sister," he said, "it is no use. The doctor has been bathing my forehead with spirits of ether and other liquids, and nothing will do me any good. I cannot live until morning; my head is splitting open. But you may do what you like."

She took a wide bandage which, unknown to him, was saturated in chloroform, bound up his head and left him. Early in the morning she went to ask him how he spent the night. He said: "Oh, Sister, I have rested well; from the moment you put your hands on my forehead I experienced no pain." He never thought of attributing the relief to the chloroform, because he did not know of it, and the Sister, feeling that in his case ignorance was bliss, did not enlighten him.

The patients had the best of feeling toward the Sisters, and when the medical doctor visited the hospital he would stand in the middle of the ward and tell the patients to whom they owed their comfort, the good order, cleanliness and regularity that reigned there. He told them that all these things came through the Sisters. It is a notable fact that the respect with which they were treated in the beginning never diminished, but went on increasing while the hospital lasted.

Two of the prisoners of war, as the result of a court-martial, were to be executed, but the worthy chaplain who daily attended the prison obtained the pardon of one, while the Sisters obtained that of the other. On one occasion a soldier who was accused of desertion was sentenced to be hanged, and the Sisters attended him until all was over.

There was an elderly man confined to the prison hospital who always found great pleasure in seeing to the wants of his companions. He told the Sisters it made him happy to see them get what they most desired. Toward the close of the war he obtained his release, and afterwards sent fifty dollars to the Sisters to supply the wants of the suffering sick. His son, some time later, was charged with some military offense, tried by court-martial and afterwards executed. The young man became a Catholic, and in his last moments received the consolations of the Church. His remains were given up to his family, and his father requested the clergyman who attended him before his execution to preach the funeral sermon, which the priest did in a Baptist church, where his hearers were all Baptists.

One of the priests who was untiring in his work among the soldiers in St. Louis during those heart-breaking days was Father Patrick John Ryan, now the Archbishop of the great Archdiocese of Philadelphia. Early in the war he was appointed a chaplain of the Government, but resigned his position, feeling that he could do better work among the Southern prisoners of war if he appeared among them simply as a priest. The rector of one of the Protestant Episcopal churches in St. Louis succeeded him as chaplain. Father Ryan is authority for the statement that there were probably more baptisms in this military hospital than on any of the battlefields or in any other hospital of the Civil War.

He was a witness to many pathetic and humorous incidents in the daily routine of hospital service. On one occasion he was attending a poor drummer boy who was only too surely approaching the end of his life of warfare. He spoke to him gently of the things necessary to do under such circumstances, instructed him to glance over his past life and try and feel a genuine sorrow for all of his sins and for anything he had done against his fellow-man.

The boy listened meekly for a while, but when he was told to be sorry for all his wrong-doing a new light flashed upon him. He half rose in bed and defiantly declared that if this contemplated the serving of his allegiance to the Southern Confederacy and an admission that the "Yankees" were right he would have none of it. Half-amused at this outburst, and not entirely unmoved at this flash of spirit in what the lad no doubt deemed a righteous cause, the good priest soon assured him that his mission was not of the North or the South, but of God. The young sufferer died soon after this with most edifying sentiments upon his lips.

Sister Juliana, a sister of Bishop Chatard, of Vincennes, who did good service in this and other hospitals, was the witness of many affecting death-bed scenes and many wonderful death-bed conversions. Fervent aspirations to heaven went up from the lips of men who had never prayed before. Soldiers from the backwoods who had known no religion and no God were in a few hours almost transformed. It is estimated that priests and Sisters baptized between five and six hundred persons at this one hospital.

Archbishop Ryan tells the following incident that came under his personal observation, and which John Francis Maguire, Member of Parliament from Cork, has incorporated in one of his works: ([1])

"A Sister was passing through the streets of Boston with downcast eyes and noiseless steps when she was suddenly addressed in a language that made her pale cheeks flush. The insult came from a young man standing on a street corner. The Sister uttered no word of protest, but raising her eyes gave one swift, penetrating look at the brutal offender.

"Time passed on; the war intervened. The scene changed to a ward in a military hospital in Missouri. A wounded soldier, once powerful but now as helpless as an infant, was brought in and placed under the care of the Sisters of Charity. It was soon evident that the man's hour had arrived; that he was not long for this world. The Sister urged the man to die in the friendship of God, to ask pardon for his sins, and to be sorry for whatever evil he might have done.

'I have committed many sins in my life,' he said to the Sister, 'and I am sorry for them all and hope to be forgiven; but there is one thing that weighs heavy on my mind at this moment. I once insulted a Sister of Charity in the streets of Boston. Her glance of reproach has haunted me ever since. I knew nothing of the Sisters then. But now I know how good and disinterested you are and

---

(1) "The Irish in America."

how mean I was. Oh! if that Sister were only here, weak and dying as I am, I would go down upon my knees and ask her pardon.'

"The Sister turned to him with a look of tenderness and compassion, saying: 'If that is all you desire to set your mind at ease you can have it. I am the Sister you insulted and I grant you pardon freely and from my heart.'

"'What! Are you the Sister I met in Boston? Oh, yes! you are—I know you now. And how could you have attended on me with greater care than on any of the other patients?—me who insulted you so.'

"'It is our Lord's way,' replied the Sister gently. 'I did it for His sake, because He loved His enemies and blessed those who persecuted Him. I knew you from the moment you entered the hospital. I recognized you from the scar over your forehead, and I have prayed for you unceasingly.'

"'Send for the priest!' exclaimed the dying soldier, 'the religion that teaches such charity must be from God.'

"And he died in the Sister's faith, holding in his failing grasp the emblem of man's redemption, and murmuring prayers taught him by her whose glance of mild rebuke had long filled him with remorse through every scene of revelry or of peril."

CHAPTER VI.

IN AND AROUND WASHINGTON.

———◆◆◆———

Dilapidated frame buildings serve as hospitals at the National Capital. A convalescent patient who was "tired and vexed." A whole day spent in going from store to store in a vain attempt to purchase "one of those white bonnets" for a Sister. The soldier whose life was saved by being "shot in the U. S. A."

———◆◆◆———

When the fratricidal conflict between the sections began very few persons paused to consider its extent and consequence. But as each week passed it grew in intensity and volume. In the beginning  of the year 1862 at least 450,000 Union troops were in the field, and half of that number were under the command of General McClellan in and around Washington. Upon the breaking out of hostilities old Virginia had at once become a principal arena of the contending armies of the East. The Confederate capital being at Richmond and the Unions eat of Government at Washington, D. C., only a short stretch of country south of the Potomac River separated the armies.

A disastrous defeat at Bull Run on the 21st of July, 1861, caused the Union Army to retreat to Washington. There were various minor engagements both before and after this date, but nothing of unusual consequence occurred until February, 1862, when General U. S. Grant, commanding the land forces, and Commodore Foote the gunboats, captured Fort Henry on the Tennessee, and Fort Donelson on the Cumberland River in Kentucky. It was on this occasion, when the commander of Fort Donelson asked for terms, that Grant gave the now historic reply: "No terms except immediate and unconditional surrender can be accepted. I propose to move immediately upon your works."

Some time before this the Confederate and Union forces realized that they were insufficiently provided with trained nurses. In the early part of 1862 the Government made a formal request upon the Sisterhoods for nurses. The Sisters of Charity were requested to send a deputation to attend the sick and wounded in the temporary hospitals at Washington. These hospitals consisted of a number of rather dilapidated frame buildings and various tents which had been improvised into structures for hospital purposes.

The Sisters were promptly assigned from the mother house at Emmitsburg, Md. When they arrived at the National Capital they found the buildings and tents crowded with patients. The majority of these had been brought in from battlefields in the vicinity of Washington. The Sisters endeavored to look after the temporal needs of the men, in many instances acting in the dual capacity of doctor and nurse. There were many incidents, some of them of a humorous, most of them of a decidedly serious character.

While the nurses were rushing from one cot to another a poor man who was in a dying state cried out at the top of his voice, "I want a clergyman."

One of the Sisters hastened to him and asked: "What clergyman do you want?"

He replied: "A white bonnet clergyman; the one you

ladies have."

"But you are not a Catholic?" said the Sister.

"I know that, but I want to see a Catholic priest."

After a slight delay a clergyman reached his bedside. The poor patient reached his skeleton-like hand to the priest and began as follows: "In the Bible we read 'as the Father hath sent Me, I also send you, and whose sins you shall forgive are forgiven.' Now tell me has that order ever been countermanded in any part of the Bible"

The priest replied with a smile: "No, my son; it is the same now as it ever was and ever shall be."

"Well," said the sick man, "I have never disobeyed an order when one who gave that order had authority to command. Therefore being a good soldier I wish to fulfill that order in every respect."

As he was not in immediate danger and a man of considerable intelligence the priest told him he would come and see him again. The soldier asked for a catechism or any book that would instruct him in the white bonnet religion. Later he made a confession of his whole life and was baptized on the following Sunday morning in the chapel in the presence of the entire congregation. He said he did not wish to be baptized behind closed doors, but wished all to know that he was a Catholic. While he remained in the hospital he would go from one patient to another reading and explaining what had been explained to him. Several of the soldiers argued with him upon the subject of religion, but with the Bible in one hand and the little catechism in the other he would put them all to silence.

One dreary night a score of ambulances drove up to

the hospital grounds with sixty-four wounded men. Of this number fifty-six had been shot in such a manner as to necessitate amputation of either a leg or an arm. Indeed, a few of the unfortunates were deprived of both legs.

Some died in the short while it took to remove them from the ambulance to the ward. The Sisters went from bed to bed doing all they could to minimize the sufferings of the soldiers. Two of the patients were very disrespectful to one of the Sisters, showing anger and telling them to begone. The nurse in charge quietly walked away. After a little while another Sister went to them asked if they wished her to write to anyone for them. They did, and she wrote as they dictated, then read it to them and left. By this time they began to reflect on the kindness that had been shown them and soon appreciated the fact that the Sisters were indeed their friends.

Of the sixty-four wounded men eight died the next day. There were thirty bodies in the dead house, although it was the custom to bury two a day. For a while the patients suffered from smallpox, which added very much to the labors of the Sisters, since such patients had to be separated and quarantined from the others. Several died from the disease. One of the Sisters who waited upon them took it, but recovered. Many of the patients who seemed to dislike and fear the Sisters found they had been mistaken in the opinions they had formed of them. They often showed their confidence by wanting to place their money in the custody of the Sisters.

One day a poor fellow obtained a pass and spent the entire day in the city and returned at twilight looking sad and fatigued. A Sister of his ward asked him if he was suffering, and he replied: "No, Sister; but I am tired

and vexed. I received my pass early to-day and walked
through every street in Washington trying to buy one of
those white bonnets for you and did not find a single one
for sale."

There are amusing stories of life in the hospitals,
and on the field, and the following one is vouched for by
Mather M. Alphonse Butler:

"Every Union soldier wore a belt with the initials
'U. S. A.'—United States Army. When a wounded man
was brought to the hospital notice was given to the Sister and she would at once prepare to dress the wound.
One day a man was brought in on a litter, pale and unconscious, and the Sister rushed to give him attention.
By degrees he became conscious, and the Sister asked
him where he was wounded. He seemed bewildered at
first, but gradually his mind returned. Again the Sister
asked him where he was wounded. A smile spread over
his face.

"'It is all right, Sister,' he said; 'don't disturb yourself.'

"'Oh, no,' she said, 'they tell me you were shot.'

"'Yes,' he answered, 'I was shot, but shot in the U. S. A.'"

"The Sister understood at once the bullet had struck
the initials on his belt, and they had saved his life."

CHAPTER VII.

SISTER ANTHONY AT SHILOH.

———◆◆◆———

Terrible loss of life at the battle of Pittsburg Landing or Shiloh. Sister
Anthony wins enduring laurels. Seven hundred wounded soldiers
crowded on one boat. The deck of the vessel resembles a slaughter
house. A Sister of Charity acts as assistant surgeon. Sisters refuse
to abandon their patients. Sketch of the life of Sister Anthony.

———◆◆◆———

The battle of Shiloh, Tenn., sometimes known as the
battle of Pittsburg Landing, was one of the great combats
of the war. Shiloh cost the Union army in killed, wounded
and prisoners 14,000 men, while
the Confederates lost 10,700
men, including General Albert
Sidney Johnston, who fell in
the first day's fight. The battles
were fought on the 6th and 7th
of April, 1862, The morning of
the 6th was clear and beautiful,
with no indications of a storm;
but the day's terrific battle was
followed by a night of drenching rain. The battle of the
next day was also succeeded by a fearful storm, which in
this case consisted of rain, hail and sleet. An eye-witness
writing of this says: "And to add to the horrors of the
scene, the elements of Heaven marshaled their forces—a
fitting accompaniment to the tempest of human devastation and passion that was raging. A cold, drizzling rain
commenced about nightfall and soon came harder and
faster, then turned to pitiless, blinding hail. This storm
raged with unrelenting violence for three hours. I passed

SISTER ANTHONY.

long wagon trains filled with wounded and dying soldiers without even a blanket to shield them from the driving sleet and hail which fell in stones as large as partridge eggs until it lay on the ground two inches deep." ([1])

It was by the work that she did at and after this battle that Sister Anthony, a notable member of the Sisters of Charity, won enduring laurels. She left Cincinnati for Shiloh, accompanied by two other Sisters of Charity. Dr. Blackman, of Cincinnati; Mrs. Hatch and daughter, Miss McHugh, Mrs. O'Shaughnessy and some charitable ladies of the Queen City. This trip was made on Captain Ross' boat, under the care of Dr. Blackman. Sister Anthony, whose mind is unimpaired and whose memory is excellent, thus tells of her experience at Shiloh:

"At Shiloh we ministered to the men on board what were popularly known as the floating hospitals. We were often obliged to move farther up the river, being unable to bear the terrific stench from the bodies of the dead on the battlefield. This was bad enough, but what we endured on the field of battle while gathering up the wounded is simply beyond description. At one time there were 700 of the poor soldiers crowded in one boat. Many were sent to our hospital in Cincinnati. Others were so far restored to health as to return to the scene of war. Many died good, holy deaths. Although everything seemed dark and gloomy, some amusing incidents occurred. Some days after the battle of Shiloh the young surgeons went off on a kind of lark, and Dr. Blackman took me as assistant in surgical operations, and I must acknowledge I was much pleased to be able to assist in alleviating the sufferings of

---

(1)   From "War and Weather," by Edward Powers (c. e.), Delavan, Wisconsin, 1890.

these noble men.

"The soldiers were remarkably kind to one another. They went around the battlefield giving what assistance they could, placing the wounded in comfortable places, administering cordials, etc., until such time as the nurses could attend to the wounded and sick. I remember one poor soldier whose nose had been shot off, who had almost bled to death and would have been missed had we not discovered him in a pen, where some kind comrade had placed him before he left the field, every other place of refuge being occupied. His removal from the pen caused great pain, loss of blood, etc. The blood ran down his shirt and coat sleeves, down his pantaloons and into his very boots. He was very patient in the boat up the river. On arriving in Cincinnati he was placed in a ward in our hospital. Shortly after his arrival in the city a gentleman came to Cincinnati and called at the Burnett House, which was then used as a military hospital, inquiring for his son. After searching everywhere else he called at St. John's Hospital. I met this sorrowing father just as I was leaving the hospital to attend to some business. From the description he gave I concluded that the boy without the nose must be his son. I took him to the ward. When we reached the bed where the man lay the father did not know him.

"'Well,' said he, 'if he is my child I shall know him by his head.' Running his fingers through the boy's hair he exclaimed: 'My son! my dear boy!'

"There was one young man under the care of Sister De Sales. This Sister spoke to him of heaven, of God and of his soul. Of God he knew nothing, of heaven he never heard, and he was absolutely ignorant of a Supreme Being. He became much interested in what the Sister said and was anxious to know something more of this good God of whom the Sister spoke. This good Sister of Charity instructed him, and, no priest being near, she baptized him and soon his soul took its flight to that God whom he so late learned to know and love.

"Were I to enumerate all the good done, conversions made, souls saved, columns would not suffice. Often have I gazed at Sister De Sales, as she bent over the cots of those poor boys, ministering to their every want, in the stillness of the night. Ah! here is one to whom she gives a cool drink, here another whose amputated and aching limbs need attention, there an old man dying, into whose ears she whispers the request to repeat those beautiful words: 'Lord, have mercy on my soul!' I asked myself: 'Do angels marvel at this work?'

"Day often dawned on us only to renew the work of the preceding day, without a moment's rest. Often the decks of the vessels resembled a slaughter house, filled as they were with the dead and dying."

The following is what an eye-witness says of Sister Anthony: "Amid this sea of blood she performed the most revolting duties for those poor soldiers. Let us follow her as she gropes her way among the wounded, dead and dying. She seemed to me like a ministering angel, and many a young soldier owes his life to her care and charity. Let us gaze at her again as she stands attentive kindness and assists Dr. Blackman while the surgeon is amputating limbs and consigning them to a watery grave, or as she picks her steps in the blood of those brave boys, administering cordial or dressing wounds."

A Sister relates a sad story of a young man who was

shot in the neck. The wound was very deep. From the effect of this and the scorching rays of the sun he suffered a burning thirst. He was too weak to move, when suddenly the rain fell down in torrents. Holding out his weak hands, he caught a few drops, which sustained life until he was found among the dead and dying on the battlefield. Cordials were given which relieved him. His looks of gratitude were reward enough. Many other soldiers who were thought to be dying eventually recovered.

After the Sisters had finished their work at Shiloh they followed the army to Corinth, where the Confederates had retreated. The river was blocked by obstacles in the stream and progress by boat was necessarily slow. Finally the impediments became so thick that the boat was stopped altogether. The vessel was crowded and the situation was a critical one. The captain finally said that it was a matter of life and death and that the Sisters would have to flee for their lives. To do this it would have been necessary to abandon their patients, who were enduring the greatest misery on the boat. This the Sisters heroically refused to do. All expressed their willingness to remain with the "wounded boys" until the end and to share their fate, whatever it might be. Such heroism melted the hearts of hardened men. The Sisters fell on their knees and called on the "Star of the Sea" to intercede for them, that the bark might be guarded from all harm. And their prayer was answered. Two rave pilots came, who steered the boat to their destination and to a place of safety.

After the war Dr. Blackman became an active member of the medical staff of the Good Samaritan Hospital in Cincinnati and ever proved a sincere friend of Sister Anthony. The Sisters unite in praising the services of Mrs. Hatch and her daughter. Miss Hatch was a most es-

SISTER ANTHONY.

timable lady, who bestowed upon the soldiers the greatest of charity and kindness. Many of them called her "Sister Jennie," a rare compliment for one who was not a religious.

The groans of the soldiers on the battlefield of Shiloh still linger in the memories of many of the Sisters. Sister Anthony and her colleagues frequently picked their way through the files of the dead and wounded, and on many occasions assisted in carrying the sufferers to the boats. These floating hospitals were unique in many ways, but they will ever remain memorable as the scenes of the Sisters' greatest triumphs, where they did so much for the cause of humanity and where so many unwarranted prejudices were removed from the minds of brave men.

Among the surviving Sisters none is regarded with more affection and reverence than this same Sister Anthony, who is now living in quiet retirement in Cincinnati, surrounded with all the loving attentions and comforts that should go with honorable old age.[2] Her work for humanity has been spread over a long series of years, and the heroic labors she performed during the war form but an episode in a busy and useful career. But it was a brilliant episode, one that deserves to be handed down to history and that brought fadeless laurels to a modest and unpretending woman. Sister Anthony was born near Tipperary, Ireland, of pious Catholic parents. She came with them to this country at an early age, and, in pursuance of a long-cherished idea, renounced the world and was vested with the familiar habit of the Sisters of Charity. Her novitiate and earlier years in the order were spent at Emmitsburg, Md. Finally she was placed in charge of a

(2) September, 1897.

community at Cincinnati. According to good people in that city who have carefully watched her career, she displayed unusual devotion, business talent and self-sacrifice. Through her exertions an orphan asylum was founded at Cumminsville, where large numbers of friendless and homeless children were cared for and reared to a sense of their responsibility to God and man.

When the civil war broke out Governor David Tod issued a call for volunteer nurses. Alive to the necessities of the occasion, Sister Anthony relinquished the care of her asylum to other hands and, taking a band of Sisters with her, offered their services. Their work was in the South, most of it being in and around Nashville, Shiloh, Richmond, Ky.; New Creek and Cumberland. Colonel John S. Billings, M. D., now of the Surgeon General's office at Washington, is one of the physicians having personal knowledge of Sister Anthony, and he speaks of her in the very highest terms. "I first knew Sister Anthony," he said to the writer, "in 1859, when she was in charge of the old St. John's Hospital, on Fourth street, Cincinnati, in which I was resident physician, and I have known her ever since. I can say very cordially that she was a competent hospital manager and that I have always had the greatest respect and affection for her." (³)

Sister Anthony and her brave assistants spent many

---

(3) Dr. John Shaw Billings was born in Switzerland County, Ind., April 12, 1839. He received his degree in medicine in 1860, and the following year was appointed demonstrator of anatomy in the Medical College of Ohio. The same year he was appointed an assistant surgeon in the United States army, in which position he continued until placed in charge of the hospital at Washington, in 1863. He was later appointed medical inspector of the Army of the Potomac. In 1894 he was appointed surgeon general, and placed in charge of the division of vital statistics. In addition to this he has been medical advisor to trustees of the Johns Hopkins University.

months in Nashville. The care and attention that was bestowed upon the sick and wounded soldiers of both the Union and Confederate armies did much to dispel the thoughtless prejudices that had previously existed against the Sisters. They went about like good angels, easing many a troubled spirit and showering love upon all with whom they came in contact. Sister Anthony stood out in bold relief from all the others, and one who has knowledge of those times says: "Happy was the soldier who, wounded and bleeding, had her near him to whisper words of consolation and courage. Her person was reverenced by Blue and Gray, Protestant and Catholic alike, and the love for her became so strong that the title of the 'Florence Nightingale' of America was conferred upon her, and soon her name became a household word in every section of the North and South." Many of the Sisters with whom she worked fell upon the field of honor, but Sister Anthony lived and survived to enjoy a peaceful old age and the sweet thought and consolation of work well done.

The ending of the war, however, did not end her work. After the white wings of peace had been spread over the battlefields she returned to Cincinnati and made an effort to found an asylum that should be larger and greater than old St. John's, where she had labored before the war. For a time it looked as if this noble intention was to be frustrated. Funds were not available and the usually charitable people of the city seemed to be indifferent. They only seemed, however, for just when the effort was about to be given up in despair, John C. Butler and Lewis Worthington, two of the wealthy men of the city, came forward with sufficient money to build and equip a magnificent institution. The result of this was the establishment of the Good Samaritan Hospital. Sister Anthony was placed in charge and the work she did there equaled, if it did not exceed, her war experiences. Already a model nurse, she became a model hospital manager. In the hospital she increased her great knowledge and made a science of nursing the sick. She remained in executive control of the institution until 1882, when devoted friends finally prevailed upon her to relinquish her task and live in peace and quiet the remainder of her life. She has had several successors, the one now in charge being Sister Sebastian.

As a direct result of the good done in the Good Samaritan Hospital came the establishment of an orphan asylum at Norwood through the munificence of Joseph Butler, Sr. It is at this institution that Sister Anthony is spending the last years of her life. Her time is spent between the asylum at Norwood and the Good Samaritan Hospital, in Cincinnati. Although very venerable, indeed, she retains all her faculties to a surprising degree. She walks about unaided and takes great delight in doing little tasks about the hospital. On the last feast of the Assumption she celebrated her seventy-ninth birthday. On that occasion the event was noted in many of the churches in Cincinnati and a prayer for her went up in many parts of the country.

CHAPTER VIII.

PORTSMOUTH AND NORFOLK.

The contest between the Monitor and the Merrimac, and general
operations of the war during the seven days' battle near Richmond.
The taking of the cities of Norfolk and Portsmouth by the union
forces. Sisters narrowly escape drowning while crossing the river in
a row boat. One instance where hatred was turned to love.

In the East the Union cause had not been so successful. When the Union forces at the beginning of the
war abandoned Norfolk, with its navy yard, they blew

up all the Government vessels to prevent them from
falling into the hands of the
Confederates. One frigate,
which had been sunk, was
raised by the Confederates
and transformed into an
iron-clad ram, making her
one of the most formidable
vessels then afloat, though
now she would be considered ridiculous. This vessel, rechristened the Merrimac,
aided by three gun boats, destroyed the United States
frigate Cumberland, forced the surrender of the Congress
and scattered the remainder of the Union fleet in Hampton Roads. That night, amid the consternation which prevailed, the new Union gun boat, called the Monitor, designed by John Ericsson, arrived in Hampton Roads and
prepared to resist the Merrimac the next day. The Monitor was a turreted ironclad. The following morning, after

a severe battle, the Monitor drove the Merrimac back to Gosport Navy Yard, where she was later blown up. This was one of the turning points of the war.

In the meantime General McClellan made his advance on Richmond, going by sea to Yorktown and advancing thence on Richmond. For seven days there was tremendous fighting near Richmond, the Confederates usually getting the best of it. Finally McClellan retreated to Harrison's Landing to make a new effort. He was greatly disappointed in not getting reinforcements, and finally was ordered back with his army to Washington.

During the contest known as the "seven days' battles" the fighting commenced about 2 o'clock A. M., and continued until 10 P. M. each day. The bombs were bursting and reddening the heavens, while General McClellan's Reserve Corps ranged about three hundred yards from the door of the Sisters' house. While the battle lasted the Sisters in the city hospitals were shaken by the cannonading and the heavy rolling of the ambulances in the streets as they brought in the wounded and dying men. The soldiers informed the Sisters that they had received orders from their general "to capture Sisters of Charity, if they could," as the hospitals were in great need of them.

One night the doctors called in the Sisters to see a man whose limb must be amputated, but who would not consent to take the lulling dose without having the Sisters of Charity say he could do so. The Sisters said it was dark and the crowd was too great to think of going. The doctors left, but soon returned, declaring that the man's life depended on their coming. Two Sisters then, escorted by the doctors, went to see the patient, who said to them: "Sisters, they wish me to take a dose that will deprive me of my senses, and I wish to make my confession first, and a priest is not here." They put his fears at rest, and he went through the operation successfully. Sometimes the poor men were brought to them from encampments where rations were very scarce or from hospitals from which the able-bodied men had retreated and left perhaps thousands of wounded prisoners of war, who, in their distress, had fed on mule flesh and rats. These poor men, on arriving at the hospitals, looked more dead than alive.

Norfolk, being left undefended about this time, was soon occupied by General Wood, who swooped down upon it with a force from Fortress Monroe. The bombardment of the cities of Portsmouth and Norfolk gave notice to the Sisters of Charity that their services would soon be needed in that locality. They had a hospital, an asylum and a day school in Norfolk. The tolling of the bells on that May morning first announced the destruction of the city. Soon Portsmouth was in flames. Large magazines and powder exploding shook the two cities in a terrible manner. The hospital where the Sisters were in charge was crowded with the sick and wounded. They were cared for as well as possible with the limited means at hand. In a short time, however, Norfolk was evacuated, and both that city and Portsmouth taken by the Union troops. All of the Southern soldiers that could leave before the coming of the Northerners left, and the hospital was comparatively empty. The Union soldiers crowded into the city and great confusion ensued. The Marine Hospital in Portsmouth was prepared for the sick and wounded, and the Union authorities asked the Sisters to wait upon their men. These troops were in a deplorable condition. There was no time to be lost and the Sisters lost none. They were constantly administering by turns to soul and body. Indeed, as far as possible, the self-sacrificing Sisters subtracted from their own food and rest tin order that the suffering men might have more of both.

In a few days several more sisters came to aid those who were in charge. The newcomers met with many vexatious trials on the way. First they were denied transportation, and next barely escaped being lost in crossing a river in a small rowboat, the frail craft, through the carelessness of some one in charge, being heavily overloaded. They eventually reached their destination, however, and were enabled to effect much good among the men. Many affecting scenes took place in the wards. The Sisters were applying cold applications to the fevered men. One soldier, bursting out in tears, exclaimed:

"Oh, if my poor mother could only see you taking care of me she would take you to her heart."

A man of about 23 years saw a Sister in the distance and raised his voice and cried:

"Sister, come over to my bed for awhile."

He was in a dying state, and a Sister knelt by his bedside making suitable preparations for him in a low voice. He repeated the prayers she recited in a very loud tone. The Sister said:

"I will go away if you pray so loud."

"Ah, Sister," he said, "I want God to know that I am in earnest."

The Sister showed him her crucifix, saying: "Do you know what this means?"

He took it and kissed it, reverently bowing his head. While another man was receiving instructions he suddenly cried out at the top of his voice: "Come over and hear what Sister is telling me." She looked up and saw a wall of human beings surrounding her, attracted by the loud prayers of the poor man. In this crowd and on his knees was one of the doctors, who, being on his rounds among the patients and seeing the Sister on her knees, involuntarily knelt, and remained so until the Sister arose. The patient soon after died a most edifying death, receiving the last rites of the Church.

Another poor fellow seemed to have a deep-seated prejudice against the Sisters. He constantly refused to take his medicine, and would even go so far as to strike at the Sisters when they offered it to him. After keeping this up for some time and finding the Sisters undisturbed and gentle as ever, he said, "What are you?"

The Sister replied: "I am a Sister of Charity."

"Where is your husband?"

"I have none," replied the Sister, "and I am glad I have not."

"Why are you glad?" he asked, getting very angry.

"Because," she replied, "if I had I would have been employed in his affairs, consequently could not be here waiting on you."

As if by magic he said in a subdued tone: "That will do," and turned his face from her. The Sister left him, but presently returned and offered him his medicine, which he took without a murmur. When he recovered from his long illness he became one of the warmest friends of the

Sisters.

As the war continued the Government also made use of the Sisters' Hospital of St. Francis de Sales. Here all things were under the direct charge of the Sisters, the Government, in this particular instance, paying them a stated sum for their services. During the time their house was thus occupied about twenty five hundred wounded soldiers were admitted, of whom but one hundred died.

The Sisters had been at Portsmouth about six months when the hospital was closed. Several of the Sisters were sent to other points, while the remainder started for Emmitsburg. The cars took them to Manassas, in the midst of an extensive encampment, where they were told they could not pass the Potomac, as the enemy was firing on all who appeared.

The army chaplain celebrated Mass at this point, an old trunk in a little hut serving as an altar. The Sisters were obliged to go to Richmond, and it was too weeks before a flag of truce could take them into Maryland. They met the Judge Advocate of the army on the boat and he showed them every attention, saying: "Your society has done the country great service, and the authorities in Washington hold your community in great esteem."

CHAPTER IX.

LABORS IN FREDERICK CITY.

The Sisters quartered in a stone barracks that had been occupied by General Washington during the Revolutionary war. Patients see no necessity for "tincture of iron" from the doctors. Soldiers without food for thirteen days. Young scholastics from the Jesuit Novitiate in the capacity of nurses. Not enemies "except upon the battlefield."

On the 4th of June, 1862, a telegram was received at the Central House, in Emmitsburg, asking that ten Sisters be detailed for hospital service in Frederick City, Md. The request came from the medical authorities in charge

of the hospital, and it explained the immediate and imperative need of the Sisters. There were only three Sisters at liberty in the main house at the time, but the zeal of the Superiors managed to secure seven others from the various Catholic schools and academies in the city of Baltimore.

The ten nurses started upon their journey without any unnecessary delay and soon reached Frederick City. When they arrived at the hospital they were received by an orderly, who showed them to their room. It was in an old stone barracks, that had been occupied by General George Washington during the Revolutionary War. The room contained ten beds, so closely jammed together that there was scarcely space to walk about them. An old rickety table and two or three dilapidated chairs comprised the only furniture of the room. The chief surgeon called to welcome the Sisters and expressed the hope that they would be comfortable in their military quarters. He informed them that they were to call upon the steward for whatever they needed. The medicine was plentiful, but badly administered by the nurses, who did not attach much importance to the time or manner of giving it.

The Sisters' food consisted of the soldiers' ration. It was served to them on broken dishes, with old knives and forks, red with rust. The patients often amused their nurses by saying:

"There is no necessity for the doctors to order us the tincture of iron three times a day; don't you think we get nearly enough of it off our table service?"

On the Fourth of July an addition to the sick from the field of battle arrived at the hospital. The newcomers numbered about four hundred, and the majority were suffering from typhoid fever and dysentery. They came unexpectedly and no preparations had been made to receive them, so that many of the men had to lie in the open yard of the hospital for nearly a whole day exposed to the scorching heat of the sun. The Sisters were thus doomed to witness a most distressing scene without having it in their power to alleviate the suffering. Finally the Sister servant, who could no longer behold such a spectacle, managed to procure some wine, which, with the aid of water, she multiplied prodigiously, thereby giving all a refreshing drink. This drew from the lips of the poor sufferers many a blessing and prayer for the Sisters of Charity.

There were continual skirmishes in the Shenandoah Valley, from whence large numbers of wounded were frequently brought to the hospital, so that in a short time it

was overcrowded and the chief surgeon was obliged to occupy two or three public buildings in the city as hospitals.
At the request of the doctors eight additional Sisters were
sent from the Mother House at Emmitsburg, and they
were divided among the various hospitals that were occupied as temporary wards until accommodations could
be made at the general hospital to receive the worst cases.
The sick and slightly wounded men were transferred to
Baltimore.

A young man, a Philadelphian, was brought in one
day fearfully crushed, one hand and arm mangled to
a jelly. Opening his eyes he beheld a Sister of Charity
standing near him; a look of light succeeded the heavy
expression of weary pain and he exclaimed: "Oh, I wish
I were as good as the Sisters of Charity, then I would be
ready to die." He begged for baptism. There was no time
to lose. The Sisters hastened to instruct him in what was
necessary for him to believe and then baptized him, after
which he calmly expired.

One of the difficulties with which the Sisters had to
contend was the improper manner in which the food was
prepared. One day the chief surgeon asked for a Sister
to superintend the kitchen, and one who was qualified
for the charge was sent for that purpose. Her silence
and gentleness soon quelled the turbulent spirits of the
soldiers employed in her office, so that in a short time
they became as docile as children. On the first day an improvement was noticed in the hospital. The steward said
that for the short time the Sisters had been there their
presence in the barracks had made a wonderful change.
He said that the men were more respectful and were seldom heard to swear or use profane language. A Sister was
unexpectedly accosted one day by a convalescent patient,

FIRST BATTLE OF BULL RUN.

whom, she often noticed, viewed her with a surly countenance and would reluctantly take from her whatever she
offered him. He said:

"Sister, you must have noticed how ugly I have acted
towards you and how unwillingly I have taken anything
from you, but I could not help it, as my feelings were so
embittered against you that your presence always made
me worse. I have watched you closely at all times since
you came to the barracks, but when you came in at midnight last night to see the patient who lay dangerously ill
I could not but notice your self-sacrificing devotion. It
was then that my feelings became changed towards you.
I reflected upon the motives which seemed to actuate the
Sisters of Charity and I could not help admiring them.
I thank you, Sister, for all the kindness you have shown
me. I am happy to say that the Sisters of Charity have left
impressions on my mind that will not be easily effaced."

On the 19th of July, 1862, the feast of St. Vincent
de Paul, the Sisters received quite a treat in the shape
of an excellent dinner, sent by the director of the Jesuit
Novitiate and the Superioress of the Visitation Convent,
in Washington. Several ladies also visited them and sent
refreshments for the day.

There were many Germans in the barracks, and the
band of Sisters who were there only spoke the English
language. The Superior, however, sent a German Sister
who could speak to these men and interpret for the other
Sisters. At their request one of the clergymen from the
Novitiate, who spoke the German language, heard the
confessions of the German Catholics.

On the evening of September 5, 1862, the Sisters were
suddenly alarmed by an unusual beating of the drums.

They had all retired to bed except the Sister servant, who called to them to rise quickly and go to the barracks; that the Confederate army was in Maryland and would reach the camp in the morning. They were informed that all the patients who were able to walk, including the male attendants and men employed about the hospital, would have to leave the place in about an hour, and that all the United States army stores in the city must be consigned to the flames. Imagine their feelings at such news. The hour passed like a flash. The soldiers all disappeared except a few of the badly wounded, who could not be removed. The signal was given and in a few moments the entire city was enveloped in smoke and flames. The conflagration was so great that it illuminated all the surrounding towns. The Sisters spent the remaining part of the night with the sick who were left alone in the wards. The doctors who remained at their posts carried their instruments and other articles to the Sister servant for safe-keeping, knowing that whatever the Sisters had in their possession was secure.

The next day dawned bright and beautiful, but what a scene of desolation and ruin was presented to the view! There was no one on the hospital grounds but the steward and doctors, about four in number, and the Sisters, who were going to and from the barracks attending the helpless soldiers. It was then that these poor, helpless men exclaimed in astonishment and gratitude:

"Oh, Sisters, did you stay to take care of us? We thought you also would have gone, and then what would have become of us?

About 9 o'clock in the morning the Confederates were discovered on the top of a hill advancing rapidly towards the hospital. Suddenly the advance guards appeared in front of the Sisters' windows, which were under the doctor's office. One of the Confederates demanded without delay the surrender of the place to the Confederate army, in command of Generals Jackson and Lee. The officer of the day replied, "I surrender." The guards rode off and in about fifteen minutes afterwards the whole Confederate army entered the hospital grounds. It was then that the Sisters witnessed a mass of human misery—young and old men, with boys who seemed like mere children, emaciated with hunger and covered with tattered rags that gave them more the appearance of dead men than of living ones. After these skeleton-like forms had been placed in their respective barracks and tents the sick were brought in, numbering over 400. The majority of these were, however, half-dead from want of food and drink. They informed the Sisters that they had been without anything to eat for thirteen days, with the exception of some green corn, which they were allowed to pluck on their march into Maryland. The Sisters were delighted to find a field in which to exercise their charity and zeal on behalf of the suffering men. But, alas! a new trial awaited them. The United States surgeon called upon the Sister servant and told her that the Sisters could not at that time give any assistance to the Confederates, as they, the Sisters, were employed by the Union Government to take care of their sick and wounded, but he added that the Union army was daily expected, and as soon as it would reach the city the Confederate sick would receive the same care and attention as the Union soldiers.

The citizens were now at liberty to do as they pleased. They flocked in crowds to the hospital, distributing food and clothing at their own discretion. This proved fatal in many cases, as the diet furnished the sick men was contrary to what their condition required. The young scholastics of the Jesuit Novitiate near-by volunteered to nurse the sick soldiers, and their services were accepted by the United States surgeon, who arranged accommodations for them at the barracks. The Sisters were also allowed to give the scholastics meals in their refectory. It was truly edifying to see the zeal of those school boys. Father Sourin, the confessor of the Sisters, was likewise indefatigable in his labors. He deeply regretted the restrictions the Sisters were under, at the same time admiring the wonderful ways of God in permitting the young scholastics to gain admittance into the hospital, to fill the mission of charity of which the Sisters were so unexpectedly deprived.

On the fifth day of the invasion the Sister servant obtained a passport from General Lee for two Sisters to Emmitsburg. They were thus enabled to apprise the Superiors of their situation. These same Sisters returned to Frederick on September 12, accompanied by the Sister assistant from Emmitsburg. On re-entering the city their astonishment was great when they found that the whole Southern army had disappeared. When they reached the barracks the other Sisters informed them that the Confederates had left the city the previous night, leaving only their sick who were unable to be removed.

Frederick City was again in possession of the Union forces and the good nurses were now at liberty to exercise their duties in behalf of the sick Confederates who were prisoners at the hospital. The doctors made no distinction between them and the Union soldiers. They lay side by side, so that the Sisters had it in their power to give them equal attention. It was truly edifying to see the patience and harmony that prevailed among them. They would say: "Sisters, we are not enemies except on the battlefield."

General McClellan was at the time in command of the Union army. On one occasion he visited the barracks and was delighted with the order that reigned throughout. Before leaving he expressed a desire to have fifty additional Sisters sent to nurse the sick and wounded, but the scarcity of Sisters made it impossible to comply with his request.

A reinforcement of Sisters was now required to go to the various places occupied by the wounded. The Superiors could only send a few on account of the great demand for them throughout the different parts of the State. In Frederick City the Sisters had to divide their services between the barracks and the tents, and even then it was impossible to do justice to all. They were thus occupied for nearly six weeks without intermission except a few hours, which they would occasionally take for repose, and even that was frequently interrupted. They thought little of fatigue or bodily privation, being happy in the belief that they were not better served than the sick and wounded.

During the month of September the Sisters were recalled by their Superiors to the Central House at Emmitsburg, and this for the time being ended their labors at Frederick City.

CHAPTER X.

WHITE HOUSE.

———◆◆◆———

Sixty Sisters depart from Baltimore for the station in Virginia. Wounded
and dying men upon transport boats. Nurses who shared every
horror with their patients. Two Sisters who were martyrs to duty and
humanity. The worn-out Sister of Charity buried. Military honors
upon the banks of the Potomac. Death of a deserter.

———◆◆◆———

The many appeals for Sisters to repair to the war-
stricken sections of the country, both North and South,
had widely separated the members of the Emmitsburg

community. The venerable
Mother Ann Simeon remained
in executive charge at home.
Father Burlando visited as well
as he could the various military
hospitals where the Sisters were
stationed. His care would not ex-
tend beyond the line of hostilities,
but, fortunately, the Sister assistant had been sent to superintend the missions in the South before the blockade.

On July 14, 1862, the surgeon general at Washing-
ton wrote for one hundred Sisters to be sent to a station
called White House, in Virginia, then in possession of the
Northern forces. So many were already in service that it
was impossible to comply fully with this request. Sixty
Sisters, however, started from Baltimore for that place.
As all traveling was attended with much difficulty, the
Sisters experienced many hardships. The authorities in-
tended to make a hospital encampment in the vicinity of
White House, as many thousands of wounded had been

brought there from the recent battles. No preparations had been made for accommodating the Sisters, although the officers and doctors were rejoiced at their coming. General George B. McClellan, then chief in command, was some miles distant at the time, but sent orders that every possible care and attention should be offered to the Sisters. Father Burlando accompanied the Sisters to this place, and after receiving assurances that proper arrangements had been made for them returned home. They had only passed a few days here when suddenly all hands were ordered to leave with the greatest haste—the enemy was only two miles distant. Then began confusion and additional suffering.

The wounded and dying men were hurriedly placed upon transport boats. These vessels were so overcrowded that they seemed more like sinking than sailing. The Sisters were detailed to accompany the wounded to the several cities where they were destined, the work of transportation continuing for several weeks. The Sisters shared with their patients every horror but their bodily pains. They were in the lower cabin, the ceiling of which was low and the apartment lighted by hanging lamps and candles. The man lay on beds on the floor, with scarcely enough space to walk between them. The Sister in charge of this lower ward was so persevering in her zealous attention that even the doctor declared he did not know how human nature could endure such duties. A few months later this Sister died from the effects of overwork—a martyr to duty. The remaining Sisters not engaged with the sick returned to Baltimore, but in a few days received a summons to go to Point Lookout, situated at the southern extremity of Maryland, bounded on one side by the Chesapeake Bay and on the other by the Potomac River.

On the 14th of July, 1862, Father Burlando, with twenty-five Sisters, left Baltimore, and in twenty-four hours reached the hospital encampment of Point Lookout. The Sisters were soon destined to have another martyr in their band. They were only at Point Lookout two weeks when one of the zealous band, who had contracted typhoid fever on the transport boat, died from that disease. She gave up her whole being as generously as she had offered her zealous labors. Father Burlando had returned to Baltimore, but a good priest, who came occasionally to the encampment, heard her confession, and she received communion a day or two previous to her death. The priest being stationed twelve miles distant could not reach the encampment in time to administer the last sacraments, but arrived in time to perform the burial service. The kind doctors and officers made every effort to suitably honor the departed Sister. The men said they deemed it a great privilege to act as the pall-bearers. All of the soldiers who had died had been buried with only a sheet wrapped around them, but for the Sister a white pine coffin was procured. The authorities walked in procession, the drum corps playing a dead march. There on the banks of the Potomac rested the worn-out Sister of Charity. What a subject for the pen of the poet or the brush of the painter!

Several cottages and tents, as well as wooden wards for the accommodation of thousands of sick and wounded, made this narrow strait a thickly-inhabited place. Many of the men were in a deplorable state from the effects of their wounds and painful removals from distant battle-grounds. The priest often came on Friday and remained until Monday, constantly engaged among the soldiers, instructing, baptizing and hearing confessions. On Sunday mornings he said the first Mass at the encampment and the second in the little chapel. The first Mass was said in a tent surrounded by soldiers. The captain of the guards marched his company to Mass on that day, and at the elevation a drum was sounded and all adored profoundly.

Later on the officers gave the Sisters more cottages, and by removing the patients they had a good-sized chapel. With but few exceptions the doctors and officers were very kind to the Sisters. Removals by death and the arrival of more wounded men sometimes caused the wards to be emptied and refilled again the same day. As soon as a boat would land a horn was blown to let the Sisters know that they must go to their wards. Then they would appoint a place for each sufferer, giving the best accommodations to those who were enduring the greatest suffering. Many among the new arrivals were Confederate prisoners.

About this time orders came from Washington that no women nurses were to remain at the Point. After the Sisters had begun their work a band of young ladies arrived for the purpose of nursing the sick, and they were surprised to find the Sisters there before them. When the Sisters heard the order from Washington concerning "women nurses," they made preparations for leaving, but the chief physician said to them:

"Remain here, Sisters, until I hear from Washington, for we cannot dispense with your services at this time."

The physician telegraphed to the national capital and received this reply:

"The Sisters of Charity are not included in our orders. They may serve all alike at the Point, prisoners and others, but all other ladies are to leave the place."

About 5 o'clock on the morning of the 6th of August, 1864, the Sisters were at meditation in their chapel, when they were startled by a noise like thunder, and, looking out, saw the air darkened with whirling sand, lumber, bedsteads, stovepipes and even the roofs of houses. A raging tornado and waterspout were tearing and destroying all in their way, taking in everything from the river to the bay. The little chapel shook from roof to foundation. Doors and windows were blown down. Sick and wounded men were blown out on the ground. Wards and cottages were carried several feet from their base. Two Sisters who had not yet arisen, terrified at finding their lodgings falling to pieces, ran out and in their efforts to reach the chapel were struck down by the flying doors and as often raised from the earth by the violent wind.

The Sisters were too stunned with surprise to know what to do, though truly nothing could be done, for they would only have left one part of the chapel for another when the last part would be blown away. In one of these intermissions a Sister seized hold of the tabernacle, fearing that its next place would be in the bay, but the altar was the only spot in the chapel that the angry elements seemed to respect. Lumber and iron bedsteads were carried over the tops of the cottages. The wards were nearly all filled with patients, and several of these buildings were leveled to the ground. The men who were able to move about were running in all directions for safety, many of them only half dressed. One house was seen sailing through the air, and the bodies in at the time of the storm were not discovered until some days afterward. The storm lasted about ten or fifteen minutes, but in this time heavy mattresses were carried through the air like so many feathers. It was some time before all could be repaired. The poor patients had to be cared for in some way or other, and it was not an unusual sight to see the Sisters standing by the stove with their saucepans of broth in one hand and umbrellas in the other, only too happy thus to relieve the poor sufferers.

The Sisters going to the Provost one day were informed that a deserter was to be shot the next morning, and they would do well to visit him. They went to prison, but the man showed no desire to see them, and they sorrowfully returned home. Later the prisoner regretted not having seen the Sisters, and asked to have them sent for. The kind Provost sent an orderly, telling the Sisters of the poor man's desire. It was now very dark, and some of the authorities advised the Sisters not to go until the next morning. The orderly carried this message to his superior but was sent back again with a note from the Provost, saying:

"I will call for you on horseback and will be your pilot with the ambulance. I will guide the driver safely through the woods and will also conduct you home safely. I think circumstances require your attendance on the prisoner."

This was enough for the Sisters, and they were soon at the prison, but found a minister of the prisoner's persuasion with him. After he had finished his interview the Sisters were taken to the man, who apologized for not seeing them sooner. One of the Sisters asked him if he had been baptized. He said, "No, never." Then she informed him of its necessity, and he regretted, with much fervor, that he had not known this sooner. The Sisters remained with him some hours, giving him such instructions as his condition required. After baptizing him he expressed his desire to see a priest. The Provost, looking at his watch, replied that he could not be there in time. It was now late and the execution must take place early in the morning. The young man resigned himself fully to his fate, saying:

"I deserve death, and freely pardon anyone who will take part in it. I know I must die by the hand of one of my company, but whoever it may be I forgive him."

Then he returned to his devotions with such a lively faith the at the Sisters had no fear for his salvation. They bade him adieu and promised to assemble before the alter in his behalf when the hour of his trial drew near and to remain in prayer until all would be over with him. The kind Provost made all arrangements for the Sisters' return home, and said, when leaving the prison:

"May I have such help at my death and die with such a good disposition."

At the dreaded hour in the morning the Sisters knelt before their humble altar, most fervently imploring the Redeemer to receive the soul of the poor deserter. They continued very long after the sound of the fatal fire had told them that his destiny had been decided. The soldiers remarked afterwards that every one on the Point was present at the execution with the exception of the Sisters, who had retired to pray for the doomed man.

Peace being declared, preparations were made for a general removal. The doctors desired the Sisters to remain until all the sick and wounded had gone. After this they, too, left the Point on the 1st of August, 1865, going to their home in Emmitsburg.

CHAPTER XI.

MANASSAS AND ANTIETAM.

Five Sisters charged with the care of five hundred patients. Bodies of the dead consumed by the flames. The military hospitals at Gordonsville and Lynchburg. Boonsboro and Sharpsburg selected for hospital purposes for the men wounded at Antietam. General McClellan's kindness to the Sisters. A man who had met Sisters during the Crimean war. The brave flag bearer.

There was scarcely a time from the opening of the war until its close that some of the Sisters of Charity were not located at Richmond. This was a sort of unoffi-cial Southern headquarters for them, whence they were sent for duty on the various Southern battlefields. The section of country in which the Mother House was located was in possession of the Union army most of the time. But the house was looked upon as sacred property by the generals of both armies and was never molested by the soldiers.

Late in August, 1862, Dr. Williams, the medical director of the army of the Potomac, made a hasty summons for a detachment of Sisters to wait upon the sick and wounded at Manassas, where a severe battle had just taken place. Five of the Sisters immediately left Richmond for the scene of the conflict.

When they arrived at Manassas they found five hundred patients, including the men of both armies, awaiting them. The mortality was very great, as the wounded men had been very much neglected. The wards of the temporary hospital were in a most deplorable condition and strongly resisted all efforts of the broom, to which they had long been strangers. It was finally discovered that the aid of a shovel was necessary. One small room was set aside as a dormitory for the Sisters. They were also provided with a chaplain and Mass was said every day in one corner of the little room. Fresh difficulties and annoyances presented themselves later in the season. The kitchen, to which what was called the refectory was attached, was a quarter of a mile from the Sisters' room, and often it was found more prudent to be satisfied with two meals than to trudge through the snow and sleet for the third. These meals at the best were not very inviting, for the culinary department was under the care of negroes who had a decided aversion to cleanliness. On an average ten of the patients died every day. Most of these poor unfortunates were attended by either Father Smoulders, Father Tuling or the Sisters.

After spending a long while at Manassas the Sisters received orders from General Johnston to pack up quietly and prepare to leave on six hours' notice, as it had been found necessary to retreat from that quarter. They had scarcely left their posts when the whole camp was one mass of flames and the bodies of those who died that day were consumed.

The next field of labor for the Sisters was the military hospital at Gordonsville. There were but three Sisters, and they had two hundred patients under their charge. The sick were very poorly provided for, although the mortality was not as great as at Manassas. The Sisters had a small room, which served for all purposes. One week they lay on the floor without beds, their habits and a shawl loaned by the doctor serving for covering. The trunk of a tree was their table and the rusty tin cups and plates, which were used in turn by doctors, Sisters and negroes, were very far from exciting a relish for what they contained. The approach of the Federal troops compelled the Sisters to leave Gordonsville on Easter Sunday.

They retreated in good order toward Danville. Having been obliged to stop at Richmond some time they did not enter on this new field of labor until much later in the year. At Danville they found four hundred sick, all of whom were much better provided for than at Manassas or Gordonsville. The Sisters had a nice little house, which would have been a kind of luxury had it not been the abode of innumerable rats, of which they stood in no little dread. During the night the Sisters' stockings were carried off, and on awakening in the morning the meek religious frequently found their fingers and toes locked in the teeth of the bold visitors.

In November the medical director removed the hospital to Lynchburg, as there was no means of heating the one in Danville. The number of the Sisters had increased to five, as the hospital was large and contained one thousand patients, most of whom were in a pitiable condition. When the Sisters arrived they found that most of the unfortunate patients were half-starved, owing to the mismanagement of the institution. As a Sister passed through the wards for the first time, accompanied by the doctor, a man from the lower end cried out:

"Lady, lady, for God's sake give me a piece of bread!"

The doctors soon placed everything under the con-

BATTLE OF ANTIETAM.

trol of the Sisters, and with a little economy the patients were provided for and order began to prevail. Father L. H. Gache, S. J. ([1]), a zealous and brave priest, effected much good among the patients. During the three years that the Sisters remained in Lynchburg he baptized one hundred persons. The approach of the Federal troops placed the hospital in imminent danger, and it was decided to remove the sick and the hospital stores to Richmond. The surgeon general of the Confederate army begged that the Sisters would take charge of the Stuart Hospital in that city, which they did on the 13th of February, 1865.

Father Gache accompanied them and continued his mission of zeal and charity. The Sisters were then ten in number, and, as usual, found plenty to do to place the sick in a comfortable situation. They had just accomplished this when the city was evacuated, and on the 13th of April they left Richmond for the Mother House at Emmitsburg.

A terrible engagement took place near the Antietam River, in Maryland, not far from the Potomac, on the 17th of September, 1862. Not only were thousands on both sides killed, but as many more were left wounded on the battlefield, with the farmhouses and barns their

---

[1] Rev. Louis Hippolyte Gache, S. J., was born June 18, 1817, in the department of Ardeche, France. His early studies were pursued at the College of Bourg, St. Andeole. At the outbreak of the Civil War he was appointed chaplain of a Louisiana regiment in the Confederate army. Owing to losses in battle, sickness, etc., the regiment ceased to exist in two years, and Father Gache from then to the close of the war was attached as chaplain to military hospitals. At the end of the conflict he returned to Grand Coteau, remaining there a year He was then transferred to the new province of Maryland, now that of New York-Baltimore, becoming a professor in Loyola College. He has occupied various posts of responsibility since that time, and only last year (1896) celebrated his golden jubilee or fiftieth year in the Society of Jesus, at the Church of the Gesu, in Philadelphia.

only prospective shelter. As the fighting had been from twelve to fifteen miles in space, the towns of Boonsboro and Sharpsburg were selected for hospital purposes. The general in charge of the Maryland division requested the people to aid the fallen prisoners, as the Government provided for the Northern soldiers and would have cared for all if it had enough for that purpose.

The Superior of the Sisters of Charity, with the people of Emmitsburg, collected a quantity of clothing, provisions, remedies, delicacies and money for these poor men. The overseer of the community drove in a carriage to the place, with Father Smith, C. M., and two of the Sisters. Boonsboro is about thirty miles from Emmitsburg, and the wagon containing the supplies reached the town by twilight. Two officers of the Northern army saw the cornettes by the aid of the lighted lamps, and, pointing to the carriage, one said to the other:

"Ah, there come the Sisters of Charity; now the poor men will be equally cared for."

The Sisters were kindly received at the house of a worthy physician, whose only daughter had previously been their pupil. They were in the town four hospitals. The morning after their arrival they set out for the battlefield, having Miss Janette, their kind hostess, as a pilot. They passed houses and barns occupied as hospitals, fences strewn with bloody clothing, and further on came to the wounded of both armies. The poor men were only separated from the ground by some straw for beds, with here and there a blanket stretched above them by sticks driven into the earth at their head and feet to protect them from the burning sun. The Sisters distributed their little stores among the men, although their wretched condition seemed to destroy all relish for food or drinks.

Bullets could be gathered from the small spaces that separated the men. They were consoled as much as possible, but the Sisters scarcely knew where to begin or what to do. If they stopped at one place, a messenger would come to hastily call them elsewhere. In a wagon shed lay a group of men, one of whom was mortally wounded.

An officer called the Sisters to him, telling them how the mortally wounded man had become a hero as a flag-bearer in the bloody struggle just ended. The poor fellow seemed to gain new strength while the Sisters were near him.

They were about to move away when the officer recalled them, saying: "I fear the man is dying rapidly; come to him. He has been so valiant that I wish to let his wife know that the Sisters of Charity were with him in his last moments."

Father Smith was summoned and hastily prepared the man for death. The thought of having the Sisters near him seemed to fill the poor man with joy and gave him the confidence and courage to die with a smile upon his lips.

Two wounded Protestant ministers lay among the wounded soldiers, and with one of these Father Smith spoke for a long time while preparing the man for his end. The steward, who seemed delighted to see the Sisters, informed them that he had met members of their order during the Crimean War.

A Northern steward and a Southern surgeon became involved in a personal dispute, which ended by one challenging the other to meet him in mortal combat in a retired spot near the battlefield. Both withdrew towards an old shed, at the same time talking in a loud voice, threatening each other in angry tones. No one interfered and the duel would have taken place had not one of the Sisters followed them. She spoke to both of them firmly and reproachfully, taking their pistols from them, and the affair ended by their separating like docile children, each retiring to his post.

Nightfall drove the Sisters to their lodgings in the town, but they returned early in the morning. The medical director met the Sisters, saying: "You dine with me to-day," and added: "If you will remain I shall make arrangements for your accommodations." But he was ordered elsewhere a few hours later and the Sisters saw no more of him.

The Sisters were requested by one of the officers to attend the funeral of the brave flag-bearer. It was about dusk and eight or ten persons followed the body to the grave, besides Rev. Father Smith and the Sisters. Presently they saw about two hundred soldiers on horseback galloping towards them. A few of the horsemen approached the group of mourners and taking off their caps and bowing one of them said:

"I am General McClellan and I am happy and proud to see the Sisters of Charity with these poor men. How many are here?"

"Two," was the reply. "We came here to bring relief to the suffering, and we return in a day or so."

"Oh," he replied, "why can we not have more here? I would like to see fifty Sisters ministering to the poor sufferers. Whom shall I address for this purpose?"

Father Smith gave him the address of the Superior at Emmitsburg. Then he asked:

"Do you know how the brave standard-bearer is doing?"

He was informed that the flag-bearer was just about to be buried, whereupon he joined the procession and remained until after the interment.

General McClellan at this time was in the full flush of a vigorous manhood, with the added prestige of a West Point education. His command was considered the finest body of men in either the Union or the Confederate army. Just prior to the battle of Antietam General McClellan had ordered a review of his troops before the President and the members of his Cabinet. It was a magnificent sight to see 70,000 well-drilled and well-dressed soldiers keeping step to the tune of martial music. What a difference between then and now. The finest blood in the nation lay spilled upon the field of Antietam; the dread hand of death had broken up and demoralized the Army of the Potomac.

General McClellan was the idol of his men and was affectionately styled "Little Mac." Upon his staff were two volunteers from France, the Compte de Paris and the Duc de Chartres. They were grandsons of King Louis Philippe, were commissioned in the Union army and served without pay as aides-de-camp to General McClellan. The Compte de Paris has written what is considered to be the best and most impartial history of the civil war extant. Both of these distinguished volunteers were with General McClellan at the time of his conversation with the Sisters.

About this time the work of removing the wounded soldiers to Frederick City and Hagerstown began. During the time the Sisters remained on the battlefield they went from farm to farm trying to find those who were in most danger. The Sisters were in constant danger from bomb shells which had not exploded and which only required a slight jar to burst. The ground was covered with these and it was hard to distinguish them while the carriage wheels were rolling over straw and dry leaves. The farms in the vicinity were laid waste. Unthreshed wheat was used for roofing of tents or pillows for the men. A few fences that had been spared by the cannon balls were used for fuel. The quiet farmhouses contained none of their former inhabitants. Stock in the shape of cattle and fowl seemed to have disappeared from the face of the earth. Even the dogs were either killed or had fled from the appalling scene. It was very remarkable also that on none of the battlefields during the war were there any carrion birds, not even a crow, though piles of dead horses lay here and there. Some of these animals were half burned from the efforts made to consume them by lighting fence rails over them, but this seemed rather to add to the foulness of the atmosphere than help to purify it. Long ridges of earth with sticks here and there told "so many of the Northern army lie here" or "so many of the Southern army lie there." General McClellan's army was encamped in the neighborhood, with arms stacked, shining in the sun like spears of silver.

A Northern soldier was rebuking a sympathizing lady for her partiality towards the fallen Southerners and said: "How I admire the Sisters of Charity in this matter. When I was in Portsmouth, Va., they were called over from Norfolk to serve their own men, the Southerners, in their hospitals and labored in untiring charity. When, a few weeks later, our men took the place and the same hospital was filled with the Northern soldiers, these good Sisters were called on again, when they resumed their kind attention the same as if there was no sectional change in the men. "This," he continued, "was true Christian charity, and would not fear for any human misery when the Sisters have control. This, young lady, is what all you young ladies ought to do."

The following day Father Smith celebrated two Masses in the parlor of the house at which he was stopping. The Sisters left this place on the 8th of October, having spent six days among the wounded soldiers, who had nearly all been removed at this time from the neighborhood.

CHAPTER XII.

NEW ORLEANS.

———◆◆◆———

———◆◆◆———

On the 25th of April, 1862, a fleet under the famous
Admiral Farragut, together with a land force under General Benjamin F. Butler, captured the city of New Orleans.
Butler assumed charge of the "commercial metropolis of the Southwest,"
as it was then called, while the gun
boats proceeded up the Mississippi
River, subjugating other cities and
towns along its banks. One of these
was Donaldsonville. In shelling this place Admiral Farragut injured some of the property under the charge of
the Sisters of Charity. The Superior entered a complaint
with General Butler and in return received the following
chivalrous letter:

"Headquarters Department of the Gulf, New Orleans, La.,
September 2, 1862

"Santa Maria Clara, Superior and Sister of Charity.

"Madame: I had no information until the reception of your
note that so sad a result to the Sisters of your community had
happened from the bombardment of Donaldsonville.

"I am very, very sorry that Rear Admiral Farragut was
unaware that he was injuring your establishment by his shells.
Any injury must have been entirely accidental. The destruc-

tion of that town became a necessity. The inhabitants harbored a gang of cowardly guerrillas, who committed every atrocity, amongst others that of firing upon an unarmed boat crowded with women and children going up the coast, returning to their homes, many of them having been at school in New Orleans.

"It is impossible to allow such acts, and I am only sorry that the righteous punishment meted out to them in this instance, as, indeed, in all others, fell quite as heavily upon the innocent and unoffending as upon the guilty.

"No one can appreciate more fully than myself the holy, self-sacrificing labors of the Sisters of Charity. To them old soldiers are daily indebted for the kindest offices. Sisters to all mankind, they know no nation, no kindred, neither war nor peace. Their all-pervading charity is like the boundless love of 'Him who died for all,' whose servants they are and whose pure teachings their love illustrates.

"I repeat my grief that any harm should have befallen your society of Sisters and will cheerfully repair it, so far as I may, in the manner you suggest by filling the order you have sent to the city for provisions and medicines.

"Your Sisters in the city will also further testify to you that my officers and soldiers have never failed to do to them all in our power to aid them in their usefulness and to lighten the burden of their labors.

"With sentiments of the highest respect, believe me your friend,   Benj. F. Butler."

Some time after this General Blanchard, who was in command of the military in Monroe, La., made a request for Sisters to care for the sick and wounded under his charge. A deputation of Sisters was at once sent from St. Mary's Asylum in Natchez.

The Sisters were obliged to leave in the night in consequence of a dispatch announcing the approach of the Federal gun boat Essex, which might have prevented their departure had they remained until the next day. Hence they were compelled to cross the Mississippi River shortly before the midnight hour. The good Bishop of Natchez, now Most Rev. W. H. Elder, Archbishop of Cincinnati, alarmed for their safety, determined to accompany them to the post to which they were destined, and he did so. The pastor of the church at Monroe was also one of the party. The Sisters and their friends crossed the river in a skiff, and, reaching the other side, found an ambulance awaiting them. They traveled the remainder of that night and the following two days over a very rough and dangerous road. General Blanchard had a matron and nurses employed in the hospital. He dismissed these and arranged with the Sisters to take charge the day after their arrival.

Sister E—— had in her ward a convalescent patient who, deeming himself of more consequence than the others, was somewhat piqued at her for not showing him special attention. The Sister kept him in his place and treated him precisely as she did the others. One day she went as usual to administer the medicines, and as she was passing the ward in which he was located she heard him utter most terrible oaths. She passed on quietly, but on her return showed her displeasure at his disorderly conduct. He made every apology for his misbehavior. The Sister proceeded on her way, having a bottle in each hand. At a very short distance from where the man was standing she stopped to say a few words to another patient. She happened to look back and noticed the convalescent man put his hand in his coat pocket, and at the same instant the crack of a pistol shot was heard. The ball passed through the front of the Sister's cornette, within an inch or two of her forehead. The poor man with whom the Sister had been talking thought he was wounded again, jumped up and clapped his hands on his old wound, as if to assure himself of its escape from harm. The Sister, pale, but with perfect presence of mind, still held her bottles and made her way through the cloud of smoke and the crowd that had gathered at the report of the pistol. The man was arrested and would have been dealt with in a summary manner, but at the request of the Sister he was released. He claimed that it was an accident. It was afterwards discovered that he was a gambler and had loaded the pistol to shoot an enrollment officer in town.

In the meantime things were reaching a crisis in the city of Natchez. One morning the sound of a shell bursting over the town filled the people with consternation. The scene that followed is beyond description. Women and children rushed through the streets screaming with terror. The asylum was thronged by persons of every description, who begged to be admitted within its walls. One of the Sisters speaking of this says: "I can never forget the anguish I felt at the sight of mothers with infants in their arms begging us to preserve the lives of their little ones, without a thought for their own safety. At the sound of the first shell our good Bishop hastened to the asylum to assist us in placing the children out of danger of the shells. The Bishop was surrounded as soon as he appeared and nothing could be heard but cries of 'Oh, Father, hear my confession,' and 'Bishop, baptize me. Do not let us be killed without baptism.' The Bishop kindly went into the confessional, but soon perceived that he would be detained there too long; therefore he requested the Sisters to assemble all in the chapel and he would give a general absolution, as the danger was so imminent. Immediately their cries and sobs were suppressed. The

Bishop, after a few touching words, bade us remember that no shell could harm the least one among us without the Divine permission. He then gave a general absolution to all present."

Shells passed over the building in rapid succession while the Sisters were kneeling in the chapel. Some of the bombs fell in the adjoining yard, yet not one of those in the asylum was injured. Within the silence of death reigned. No sound was heard but the fervent aspirations of the Bishop and the suppressed sobs of the smaller children. Giving the final blessing the Bishop said: "Tell the Sisters to take the children away as soon as possible." When all were in readiness each of the orphans, with a bundle of clothing, passed out of the asylum with the thought that they were never again to enter its loved walls. Five of the Sisters accompanied them, and the others, with two sick children, followed in a market wagon, the only vehicle that could be procured. While the Sisters were placing the smaller children in the wagon a shell passed over the horse's head, so near as to frighten and cause the animal to jump, but it fell some distance away without exploding. The poor children had to go five miles without resting, so great was the danger. After remaining some weeks in the country the authorities compromised, and the gunboat left the city without doing any further damages. The Bishop announced the Forty Hours' Devotion in thanksgiving.

Good work was done in the Charity Hospital, New Orleans. The Sisters of Charity had charge of this hospital and attended many hundreds of the sick and wounded on both sides. It was the same with the Marine Hospital of New Orleans. The first act of one of the Sisters on entering a ward in this hospital was to grasp a cup of water from a nurse and baptize a dying soldier.

One Sister relates how she endeavored for a long time to get a cot for a very sick patient who lay on the floor reclining on his carpet bag. She finally succeeded, and then persuaded a convalescent soldier to convey the sick man to the cot. The patient was unwilling to go without his carpet bag and his boots, fearing they would be stolen if he left them. He kept a watchful eye on them all the time, and the Sister, understanding the reluctant movements of the patient, took up the carpet bag in one hand and the boots in the other and followed. The poor man was very much struck with the humility and charity of the Sister, and said:

"The soldiers wonder how the Sisters can work so hard without pay."

The Sister replied: "Our pay is in a coin more precious than gold; it is laid up in a country more desirable than any that exists on this earth."

CHAPTER XIII.

SOUTHERN BATTLEFIELDS.

————◆◆◆————

A letter from Central Georgia begging for Sisters of Charity. -- "Are they men or women?" A cautious priest who took the good nurses for impostors. The train crashes through a bridge. The "magic" lunch basket and how it fed an unlimited number of Sisters and soldiers. The hospitals at Marietta and Atlanta.

————◆◆◆————

After the battle of Fredericksburg, in December, 1862, the Sisters who had been looking after the sick and wounded in the hospitals near Richmond soon found their labors reduced very materially. The armies on both sides were becoming more accustomed to the hardships of the camps, and as a result there was less sickness in the various regiments. There had also been a cessation of battles in the vicinity of Richmond, and as a consequence there were no wounded men to care for. The Sisters, feeling that their usefulness was at an end, called upon the officer in charge and asked for passports in order that they might return through the lines to their Emmitsburg home. The official would not consent to their going away, claiming that he knew they would be needed in other places in the near future. This being the case, they remained.

The next day a letter came from the military in Central Georgia, begging for Sisters of Charity to be sent to their hospital there. Five Sisters left for this place on the night of February 24, 1863. A fierce battle had taken place, rendering the services of the Sisters very necessary.

On the way, at many places where they stopped, there was great curiosity at the sight of their peculiar garb. Upon one occasion, having to wait two hours for a train, the curious bystanders examined the Sisters closely, saying:

"Who are they?" "Are they men or women?" "Oh, what a strange uniform this company has adopted." "Surely the enemy will run from them."

Once or twice the crowd pushed roughly against the Sisters, as though to see whether they were human beings or not. A Sister spoke to a woman at the station, and thereupon many in the crowd clapped their hands and shouted: "She spoke! she spoke!"

At one of the towns where the Sisters stopped they did not know where to look for lodgings. Acting upon the first impulse, they went to the Catholic pastor's residence and inquired where they might be accommodated. The good old priest, strange as it may seem, had never seen their costume before, and as every day had its impostures to avoid, he was reserved and cautious, even unwilling to direct them to any house. At last his pity got the better of his prudence and he said slowly: "I will show you where the Sisters of Mercy live." He took them there, where the good Mother received them with open arms, saying: "Oh, the dear Sisters of Charity. You are truly welcome to my house."

This lady had been kindly entertained some years before by the Sisters of Charity at Baltimore. The poor, abashed priest had kept near the door, fearing he had put trouble on the good Sisters of Mercy, but when he saw the reception accorded the visitors he brightened up. Approaching one of the Sisters with outstretched hands, he said: "Oh, ladies, make friends; I thought you were impostors."

Continuing the journey, one night a cry suddenly went up: "The cars have gone through the bridge and we are in the river." The greatest excitement prevailed in the train. Passengers rushed to and fro, falling over one another in their confusion. The Sisters had gone through so many exciting scenes during the war that they had learned the value of retaining their presence of mind in such an emergency. They remained still and soon learned that the accident had not occurred to their train, but to one coming in the opposite direction. Except by the help of torches very little could be done until daylight. Two of the Sisters, however, crossed to the other side of the bridge and gave suitable attention to the sufferers, washing and binding their wounds. None were killed or in serious danger. By 12 o'clock the next day they reached a town. No refreshments were to be had. The work of devastation on the part of Sherman's army had preceded them. Fortunately a little basket of lunch, originally prepared for five Sisters, offered some sustenance. The next day the number of Sisters had increased to eleven and several strangers also, with whom they shared their supplies. At 9 o'clock the same evening a poor soldier near them in the car said: "Oh, but I am hungry. I have not had one crumb of food this day."

Out came the magic basket and the sufferer was satisfied. Immediately others asked for food. The two following days the Sisters had the soldiers to supply besides themselves, and yet the generous basket was true to all demands. On the third day's journey they reached their field of labor. It was in the town of Marietta. A very fine building had been prepared for hospital purposes, and the whole place, with its wants and workings, was placed in charge of the Sisters. Their trained hands soon reduced everything to a system, and from that hour until its close the affairs of the institution went like clockwork.

The Sisters were five weeks without having the opportunity or facilities for hearing Mass. Two Sisters at last went to Atlanta, where there were two priests, and begged that they might at least have Mass at Easter, which was then approaching. This was agreed to, and not only the Sisters, but many poor soldiers made their Easter duty. An earnest appeal was also made for a chaplain, and "headquarters" appointed one. Before he arrived, however, orders were given to remove, as the enemy was advancing. The Sisters had just received many wounded soldiers, and these men grieved bitterly when the religious left them. (¹)

On the 24th of May, in response to an urgent appeal, the Sisters reached Atlanta, where nearly all the houses were filled with the sick and wounded. Only tents could

---

(1). One of the nurses who did splendid service in the South was Sister Mary Gabriel. She was the daughter of the late Henry W. and Barbara Kraft, of Philadelphia. When little more than a child she entered the novitiate at Emmitsburg, Md., an action which even then had been delayed a year in deference to her father's expressed wish. At the end of two years she was professed on the Feast of the Nativity of the Blessed Virgin, 1842.

Her first mission was the Charity Hospital, New Orleans, where she entered upon what proved to be a long life of devotion to the poor sick. Soon after her arrival she contracted the dreaded yellow fever while nursing stricken patients, and her life was despaired of. She recovered, however, and was again at the point of danger in the plague-stricken city. During the war she labored among the dying soldiers at Mobile and Holly Springs. Twice in later years she visited Philadelphia, the second visit following retirement from active duty. It was during this second visit and while she was staying at St. Joseph's Hospital that she celebrated her golden jubilee. Her superiors finding her so full of vigor and zeal, again assigned her to active duty, and at her own request she was returned to the Charity Hospital, New Orleans. This devoted Sister passed to her reward about the fall of 1896.

be raised for the Sisters. They had five hundred patients in the tents at the start, and large numbers were added daily. The Sisters were provided with a little log house, containing two small rooms. The mice ran over them at night and the rain was so constant through the day that their umbrellas were always in their hands. Two of them became very ill. The surgeon told them to keep in readiness for a move, but the patients were so happy and doing so well under their care that he could not think of their leaving at that time.

A poor man, badly wounded, had been very cross and abusive towards the Sister who served him, but she increased her kindness and on the surface did not seem to understand his rudeness. At last he became very weak, and one day when she was waiting on him she saw that he was weeping. She said: "Have I pained you? I know I am too rough. Pardon me this time and I will try to spare you pain again, for I would rather lessen than augment distress in this hour of misery."

He burst into tears and said: "My heart is indeed pained at my ingratitude towards you, for I have received nothing less than maternal care from you, and I have received it in anger. Do pardon me. I declare I am forced to respect your patience and charity. When I came into this hospital and found that the Sisters were the nurses my heart was filled with hatred. My mind was filled with prejudice—a prejudice which I confess was inherited from those nearest and dearest to me. I did not believe that anything good could come from the Sisters. But now I see my mistake all too clearly, and in seeing it I recognize the unintentional blackness of my own heart. I have seen the Sisters in their true light. I see their gentleness, their humility, their daily—aye, their hourly sacrifices, their untiring work for others; in a word, their great love for humanity. Forgive me if you can."

This man soon after expired with the most edifying sentiments upon his lips.

On May 2, 1863, General Joseph Hooker, who had succeeded Burnside, fought General Lee at Chancellorsville, but was defeated. Lee followed up this victory by crossing the Potomac at Harper's Ferry, and marching into Pennsylvania. The Union army under General Meade advanced to meet him, and then came Gettysburg.

CHAPTER XIV.

GETTYSBURG.

Twelve Sisters depart for the battlefield from the Mother House at
Emmitsburg. A white handkerchief on a stick serves as a flag of
truce. An open charnel house red with the blood of American
manhood. The little church in the town of Gettysburg filled with
the sick and wounded. A Sister saves the life of a helpless man. "I
belong to the Methodist Church."

What is now generally conceded to have been the decisive battle of the Civil War was fought on the 1st, 2d and
3d of July, 1863. It took place in and around Gettysburg,

a town located only about ten miles
north of Emmitsburg, the mother
house of the Sisters of Charity. The
Union army was under the control of
General George G. Meade, and the
Confederate forces under General
Robert E. Lee. Over 140,000 men
were engaged in that bloody struggle,
which lasted until the evening of the
third day. The contending armies by their movements
advanced more and more toward the Sisters' house in
Maryland. The scene of this historic battle covered an
area of over twenty-five square miles. The soldiers were
so close to the Sisters' house that the buildings trembled
from the fearful cannonading.

On the morning of July 1, as the head of the One
Hundred and Seventh Regiment, Pennsylvania Volunteers, Second Division, First (Reynolds) Corps was approaching St. Joseph's Academy near Emmitsburg the

soldiers were greeted with a remarkable and impressive sight. A long line of young girls led by several Sisters of Charity took their position along the side of the road and at a word from the Sister in charge all fell upon their knees and with upturned faces toward the vaulted skies earnestly prayed for the spiritual and physical safety of the men who were about to go into deadly battle. The sight was at once solemn and inspiring in the extreme. The roughest soldiers ofttimes have the tenderest hearts, and this scene affected them more than they cared to confess. In an instant the head of every soldier in the line was bowed and bared, and remained so until the prayer was finished. All instinctively felt that the prayers of those self-sacrificing women and innocent children would be answered. To many of the men it was a harbinger of coming victory as certain as the sunshine that smiled upon them on that beautiful July morning. The scene was photographed upon the mind of many a veteran and remained ever afterwards as one of the sweetest memories of the war.([1])

The night of the third day the rain fell heavily, and it continued raining all the next day. On Sunday morning immediately after Mass, Rev. James Francis Burlando, with twelve Sisters, left Emmitsburg for the battlefield, taking refreshments, bandages, sponges and clothing, with the intention of doing all that was possible for the suffering soldiers and then returning home the next evening([2]) The roads previous to the rain had been in a

---

(1). The accuracy of this story is vouched for by several persons who were eye-witnesses of the incident. One of these was Major John C. Delaney, now of Harrisburg, Pa.

(2). Father Burlando was a notable member of the Congregation of the Missions, commonly known as Lazarist Fathers. A sketch of his useful career will be found in appendix vii at the end of this volume.

bad condition and the two armies had passed over them with difficulty. But with the mighty rain the mud became so thick that they were almost impassable. The subdued Southerners having retired, their thousands of dead and wounded were left on the field and in the barns and farmhouses in the vicinity. Scouts of the North were stationed here and there, prepared to meet and cope with any eleventh hour surprises. One of these bands seeing the Sisters' carriages was about to fire on them, thinking they were the ambulances of the enemy. The Sisters had reached a double blockade of zigzag fence thrown across the road for defensive purposes. The visitors wondered whether they dare go around it by turning into the fields, for in the distance they saw soldiers, half hidden in the woods, watching them. Father Burlando put a white handkerchief on a stick and holding it high in the air, walked towards them, while the Sisters alighted and walked about, so that the concealed soldiers might see their white head-dress, known as cornettes. The men viewed the priest sharply, for they had resolved to refuse to recognize a flag of truce if it were offered, but the sight of the cornettes reassured them. They met the priest and, learning his mission, sent an escort with him to open a passage for the Sisters through the fields. The meek messengers of peace and charity soon came in sight of the ravages of grim war.

It was a sight that once seen was not soon to be forgotten. Thousands of guns and swords, representing the weapons of the living, the wounded and the dead, lay scattered about. The downpour from heaven had filled the roads with water, but on this awful battlefield it was red with real blood. The night before the unpitying stars shone down upon the stark forms of the flower of Ameri-

can manhood. Hundreds of magnificent horses—man's
best friend to the end—had breathed their last and lay
by the sides of their dead masters. Silent sentinels upon
horseback, as motionless almost as the dead about them,
sat guarding this gruesome open-air charnel.

With the first streak of gray dawn the work of interment had begun. Bands of soldiers were engaged in
digging graves and others were busy carrying the bodies
to them. There was no attempt at system. Vast excava-
tions were made and as many bodies as possible placed
in them. The dead were generally buried where they fell.
In one trench at the foot of the slope known as Culp's Hill
sixty Confederates were buried. In that three days' fight
2834 Union soldiers were killed and 14,492 wounded. On
the Confederate side there were 5500 killed and 21,500
sounded. Thousands of the slightly wounded cared for
themselves without the assistance of either doctor or
nurses. Thousands of others were shipped to the Satterlee Hospital, in West Philadelphia, where their wants were
looked after by the Sisters of Charity in that institution.
The remainder were forced to remain in Gettysburg.

This was the condition of things that confronted
the brave Sisters as they rode over the battlefield on
that scorching July day. Frightful as it may seem,, their
carriage wheels actually rolled through blood. At times
the horses could scarcely be induced to proceed on account of the ghastly objects in front of them. The sight
of bodies piled two and three high caused the animals
to rear up on their hind legs and kick over the traces in a
most uncomfortable manner. In the midst of the sicken-
ing scenes the Sisters discovered one little group sitting
about an improvised fire trying to cook some meat. The
carriage was directed to this point and here again Father

GENERAL MEADE AT GETTYSBURG.

Burlando informed the soldiers of his errand. The officers seemed well pleased and told the Sisters to go into
the town of Gettysburg, where they would find sufficient
employment for their zealous charity. Every large building in Gettysburg was being filled as fast as the wounded
men could be carried in. Within and around the city one
hundred and thirteen hospitals were in operation, besides
those located in private houses. On reaching Gettysburg
the Sisters were shown to the hospital, where they distributed their little stores and did all they could to relieve and
console the wounded soldiers.

The little band was soon disposed of by sending two
of the Sisters to return to Emmitsburg that same evening
with Father Burlando, for the purpose of sending additional nurses to relieve those already on the ground. On
arriving at the first hospital the surgeon in charge took
the Sisters to the ladies who had been attending there
and said to them: "Ladies, here are the Sisters of Charity
come to serve our wounded; they will give all the directions here; you are only required to observe them." Those
addressed cheerfully bowed their assent.

The soldiers seemed to think that the presence of the
Sisters softened their anguish. One Sister was giving a
drink to a poor dying man with a teaspoon. It was slow
work and a gentleman who entered unobserved at the
time stood near by without speaking for some moments.
This gentleman was from a distance and was in search of
the very person the Sister was serving. Standing a moment in silence, he exclaimed in a loud voice: "May God
bless the Sisters of Charity," and repeated it emphatically,
adding: "I am a Protestant, but may God bless the Sisters
of Charity."

The Catholic Church in Gettysburg was filled with sick and wounded. The stations of the cross hung around the walls, with a very large oil painting of St. Francis Xavier holding in his hand a crucifix. The first man put in the sanctuary was baptized, expressing truly Christian sentiments. His pain was excruciating and when sympathy was offered for him he said: "Oh, what are the pains I suffer compared with those of my Redeemer." Thus disposed he died. The soldiers lay on the pew seats, under them and in every aisle. They were also in the sanctuary and in the gallery, so close together that there was scarcely room to move about. Many of them lay in their own blood and the water used for bathing their wounds, but no word of complaint escaped from their lips. Others were dying with lockjaw, making it very difficult to administer drinks and nourishment. Numbers of the men had their wounds dressed for the first time by the Sisters, surgeons at that juncture being few in number. When the Sisters entered in the morning it was no uncommon thing to hear the men cry out: "Oh, come, please dress my wound," and "Oh, come to me next." To all the pain suffered by the soldiers was added the deprivations of home friends and home comforts, which in such times come so vividly to the mind.

Four of the Sisters attended the sick in the Transylvania College building, which for the time being was used as a prison for about six hundred confederate soldiers. The Sisters dressed their wounds as in other cases. Every morning when they returned, eight or ten dead bodies lay at the entrance of the college awaiting interment. Two youths lay in an outstretched blanket and a little ditch two inches deep was around the earth they lay upon, to prevent the rain from running under them.

There was quite a sensational scene in this prison one morning. One of the Sisters hearing a great noise among the patients looked to see the cause. She discovered a group of men with guns aimed at one poor, helpless man. There had been a quarrel, and no one attempted to stop the strife. The Sister promptly and with no thought of personal danger hurried over to the group and placed her hand on the shoulder of the prospective corpse. Then she pushed him back into the surgeon's room, holding her other arm out to hinder the men from pursuing him. There was a dead silence. The poor man was put safely inside the doctor's room and his tormentors retired without a word, quietly putting away their guns. The silence continued for some time. The Sister placidly resumed her duties in the mess room.

Presently the doctor came to her and said: "Sister, you have surprised me. I shall never forget what I have witnessed. I saw their anger and heard the excitement, but feared that my presence would increase it. I did not know what to do, but you came and everything was all right. Indeed, this will never die in my memory."

"Well," replied the Sister calmly, "what did I do more than any other person would have done? You know they were ashamed to resist a women."

"A woman!" exclaimed the doctor; "why, all the women in Gettysburg could not have effected what you have. No one but a Sister of Charity could have done this. Truly it would have been well if a company of Sisters of Charity had been in the war, for then it might not have continued so long."

One young man after being baptized requested the Sister to stay with him until he died. He prayed fervently until the last breath, and almost his final words were: "Oh, Lord, bless the Sisters of Charity." This brought a crowd around him, as his bed was on the floor. The Sister was kneeling by him and continued to pray for him until the last; then she closed his mouth and bandaged his face with a towel, in the usual manner. They who stood near said one to another: "Was this man her relative?"

"No," was the reply; "but she is a Sister of Charity."

"Well," said one of the company, "I have often heard of the Sisters of Charity, and I can now testify that they have been properly named."

The surgeon remarked to the religious: "Sisters, you must be more punctual at your repast. I see you are often here until 4 o'clock in the afternoon without your dinner, working for others with a two-fold strength. Where it comes from I do not know—forgetting no one but yourselves. You should, however, try to preserve your own health."

A Protestant gentleman remarked to one of the Sisters that "the Sisters of Charity have done more for religion during the war than has ever been done in this country before."

Both the Catholic church and the Methodist church tin Gettysburg were used for hospital purposes. One day a Sister from the Catholic church had ordered her supplies, as usual, from the sanitary store. Soon after this a Sister who was nursing the sick in the Methodist church called at the store and as she was about to leave the merchant said:

"Where are these articles to be sent? I believe that you belong to the Catholic church."

"No, sir," replied the Sister, with a barely suppressed smile. "I belong to the Methodist church. Send the goods there."

After the more severely wounded had been removed by friends, or had died, the officers began directing the work of transferring the remaining patients from the town hospital to a wood of tents, called the general hospital.

A Sister was passing through the streets of Gettysburg about this time when a Protestant chaplain, running several squares to overtake her, said:

"I see the Sisters of Charity everywhere but in our general hospital. Why are they not there?"

The Sister told him that when the wounded men had been removed none of the surgeons or officers had asked them to go there or they would have gone willingly.

"Well," he said, "I will go immediately to the provost and ask him to have you sent there. I feel sure that he needs you there."

In going over the field encampment one of the Sisters was pleased and saddened to find her own brother, whom she had not seen for nine years. He had been wounded in the chest and ankle and was in one of the hospitals in the town. The meeting under such circumstances was an affecting one. Both were devoted, loyal souls, each doing duty earnestly according to his or her knowledge of the right. Through the kindness of the officer of the day the wounded man was permitted to be removed to the hospital where his sister was in charge.

A few days after the battle of Gettysburg Father Burlando wrote a letter to one of his reverend colleagues in

Maryland. Some of the facts mentioned in this document have already been told in this chapter, but the fact that it was written while the echoes of that famous fight were still fresh makes it of unusual interest. It is as follows:

Emmitsburg, July 8, 1863.

Rev. and Dear Sir:—You have been informed without doubt by the papers that we have been visited by the Army of the Potomac, and that very near us has been fought a terrible battle, the most bloody since the secession. St. Joseph has well taken care of his house, and St. Vincent of his daughters; we have not been troubled, or at least we have escaped with the slight loss of a little forage and some wooden palings, which have served for the wants of a portion of the army.

The evening of the 27th of June the troops commenced to appear upon a small hill a little distance from St. Joseph's. Regiment after regiment, division after division, all advanced with artillery and cavalry, and taking possession of all the heights encamped in order of battle. The 28th, 29th and 30th we were completely surrounded. General Howard and his suite took possession of our house in Emmitsburg; General Schultz and his suite were close to St. Joseph's, in the house which served some time since for an orphanage; the other Generals took quarters in different houses along the line of army.

For the protection of St. Joseph's General Schultz gave orders that guards should be posted in its environs, and General Howard did the same for our little place in Emmitsburg. A great number of officers asked permission to visit the house, and all conducted themselves with courtesy, expressing gratitude for the services rendered the soldiers in military hospitals by the Sisters.

On Monday this portion of the army departed, and was replaced by another not less numerous, which ranged itself in line of battle as the first. A colonel of artillery, Mr. Latrobiere, with other officers quartered in the orphanage; he also visited the Institution. The Sisters distributed bread, milk and coffee.

On the 1st of July the battle commenced about seven miles from Emmitsburg. Whilst the booming of the cannon announced that God was punishing the iniquities of man our Sisters were in church praying and imploring mercy for all mankind.

On Sunday I accompanied eight Sisters bearing medicaments and provisions for the wounded. At the distance of six miles we were stopped by a barricade, and at about three hundred yards there was another to intercept all communication. At the second was stationed a company of Federal soldiers, who perceived us from afar. I descended from the carriage, and raising a white handkerchief advanced to the second barricade, and announced the purpose of our errand. Immediately several soldiers were sent to open the way, and the two vehicles continued their route without danger. At some distance we found ourselves again in face of another barricade, which compelled us to make a long circuit. Behold us at last upon the scenes of combat—what a frightful spectacle! Ruins of burned houses; the dead of both armies lying here and there; numbers of dead horses; thousands of guns, swords, vehicles, wheels, projectiles of all dimensions, coverings, hats, habiliments of all color, covered the fields and the road. We made circuits to avoid passing over dead bodies; horses, terrified, recoiled or sprang from one side to the other. The further we advanced the more abundant were the evidences presented of a terrible combat, and tears could not be restrained in the presence of these objects of horror. At last we halted in the village of Gettysburg. There was found a good portion of the Federal army in possession of the field of battle. The inhabitants had but just issued from the cellars wherein they had sought safety during the engagement. Terror was still painted upon their countenances. All was in confusion, each temple, each house, the Catholic church, the Court House, the Protestant Seminary were filled with wounded, and still there were many thousands extended upon the field of battle nearly without succor. I placed two of our Sisters in each one of the three largest improvised hospitals, offered some further consolations to the wounded and then returned to St. Joseph's.

The next day I started with more Sisters and a reinforcement of provisions. Meanwhile provisions had been sent by the Government, and the poor wounded succored, and the inhabitants having recovered from their terror have given assistance to thousands of suffering and dying. Eleven Sisters were now employed in this town transformed into a hospital. We shall send some Sisters and necessaries to-morrow if possible. Whilst I write you the sound of cannonading re-echoes from the Southwest, where another engagement takes place. My God, when will you give peace to our unhappy country?

Yours,   BURLANDO.

CHAPTER XV.

SATTERLEE HOSPITAL.

A sketch of the remarkable labors of Sister Mary Gonzaga and her work as the executive head of a hospital where 50,000 sick and wounded soldiers were cared for. The chaplain kept busy preparing men for death. Bishop Wood visits the hospital and administers the sacrament of confirmation. A soldier who was saved from the stocks. A veteran's tribute.

As stated in the previous chapter many car-loads of wounded soldiers were conveyed from Gettysburg to the Satterlee Hospital in Philadelphia. Sister Mary Gonzaga,

SISTER GONZAGA.

who was in charge of this institution, deserves special mention in connection with her work during the war. If nobility of character, earnestness and purity of purpose, great natural executive ability, together with unaffected piety and humility tell for anything, this Sister will rank high in the bright galaxy of self-sacrificing women whose lives have illumined the history of Catholic Sisterhoods in the United States. Celebrating her golden jubilee more than 20 years ago[1] she can look back over a series of years in the course of which she has been school teacher, nurse, Mother Superior, head of a large orphan asylum and the executive of a great military hospital, where nearly 50,000 sick and wounded soldiers received the self-sacrificing attention of a staff of 40 Sisters of Charity. Sister Gonzaga, just before her death, was cred-

---

(1)The interesting event took place on April 12, 1877.

ited with being the oldest living Sister of Charity in the United States. She spent the tranquil evening of a busy and eventful life as the Mother Emeritus of St. Joseph's Orphan Asylum, on e of the magnificent charities of the City of Brotherly Love.

This venerable woman's name in the world was Mary Agnes Grace. She came from a respected Baltimore family, being born in that city in 1812. She was baptized in St. Patrick's Church, and there and in a Christian home received her preliminary religious training. In December, 1823, she was sent to St. Joseph's Academy, Emmitsburg, Md., where she proved to be a most diligent pupil. The four years she spent in this institution helped to make that certain foundation upon which her subsequent successful career was built. She had early conceived the idea of retiring from the world and devoting her life entirely to the service of God. Accordingly, on March 11, 1827, she was received into the community of the Sisters of Charity of St. Vincent de Paul. In April, 1828, in company with two other Sisters, she opened a school in Harrisburg. On the 25th of March, 1830 she made her holy vows.

In May, 1830, Sister Gonzaga was sent to Philadelphia to St. Joseph's Orphan Asylum, with which her future was to be so intimately connected. The Asylum at that time was situated on Sixth street, near Spruce, adjoining Holy Trinity Church. On October 24, 1836, the institution was removed to the site of the present asylum at the southwest corner of Seventh and Spruce streets. Four Sisters and fifty-one children comprised the population then. The Sisters were Sister Petronilla, Sister Theodosia, Sister Mary John and Sister Mary Gonzaga. Sister Petronilla died on August 3, 1843, sincerely mourned, and was succeeded by Sister Gonzaga, who remained in charge until October, 1844. Here she went on with her good work, placid and calm in the midst of the worrying turbulence of anti-Catholic bitterness and persecution, which at times threatened the lives of innocent women and children. In the latter part of 1844 she was sent to Donaldsonville, La., as assistant in the Novitiate, which at that time was for the purpose of graduating Southern postulants.

In the following year Sister Gonzaga was transferred to New Orleans. On March 19, 1851, she returned to St. Joseph's Asylum in Philadelphia to re-assume her former charge. In 1855 she was sent in an administrative capacity to the mother house of the Order in France, where she remained for a year, obtaining and imparting much valuable information regarding the work and duties of Sisters. In May, 1856, she returned to the United States, going to St. Joseph's, Emmitsburg where she filled the office of Procuratrix. In January, 1857, she returned to Philadelphia, taking charge of her old love, St. Joseph's Asylum, for the third time.

The beginning of the Civil War a few years later was to mark one of the most eventful epochs in the career of Sister Gonzaga, and to develop extraordinary gifts and qualities of administration. The Satterlee Military Hospital was established in Philadelphia. Dr. Walter F. Atlee, an honored physician of the Quaker City, felt that the interests of the Government and of the soldiers would be benefited if the Sisters of Charity were installed as nurses in the army hospital. He had several interviews with Surgeon-General Hammond and with the Secretary of War, Edwin M. Stanton. As a result of this the Sisters of Charity were invited to assume charge. On June 9, 1862, Sister Gonzaga, accompanied by 40 Sisters, assembled from

all parts of the United States, entered upon the duties
in the hospital. It is difficult to estimate the good work
done by the Sisters during the period they spent in this
place, which has been aptly styled the "shadow of the valley of death." In those three momentous years the Sisters
nursed and cared for upwards of 50,000 soldiers. Only
those who have had the care of the sick can begin to estimate the amount of ceaseless labor and patience involved
in such a vast undertaking. The sick and wounded comprised both Union and Confederate soldiers. The gentleness of the Sisters soon endeared them to all under their
charge.

In securing the necessary number of Sisters a requisition was made by Surgeon-General Hammond for
twenty-five from the mother house at Emmitsburg. They
were sent to Philadelphia at once to take their places in
the new hospital. To quote one of the Sisters, the place
was so large that "they could scarcely find the entrance."
The workmen about the grounds looked at the Sisters
in amazement, thinking perhaps they belonged to some
flying artillery. At 12 o'clock they repaired to the kitchen
for dinner, and by the time this meal was finished they
found plenty of work had been planned for them. One
hundred and fifty men who had been brought in were in
the wards. All of the Sisters went to work and prepared
nourishment for the men, most of whom looked at them
in astonishment, not knowing what kind of persons they
might be, but among the number was a French soldier
named Pierre, who immediately recognized the garb of
the "Daughters of Charity." In a short time the number
of patients was increased to nine hundred.

On the 16th of August over fifteen hundred of the
sick and wounded were brought to the hospital, most of

them from the Battle of Bull Run or Manassas. Many had died on the way from sheer exhaustion, others were in a dying state, so that the chaplain was kept busy in preparing the men for death. The wards being now crowded, tents were erected in the yard to accommodate over one thousand patients, for the Sisters at that time had not less than forty-five hundred in the hospital. When they first went to Satterlee their quarters were very limited, consisting of one small room, about seven feet square, which served as a chapel. Another, somewhat larger, answered the purpose of a dormitory by night and community room by day. Dr. Hayes soon supplied four more rooms, one of which was for a chapel. The soldiers, who were very much interested, took up a collection among themselves and gave the money to the Sisters, requesting them to purchase ornaments or whatever was needed for the chapel. They did so at different times until they finally had a good supply of everything that was necessary. They even secured new seats and sanctuary carpet. The men stipulated that when the hospital was closed the Sisters should take everything for the orphans.

In April, 1863, Rt. Rev. Bishop Wood administered the sacrament of confirmation in the little chapel to thirty-one soldiers, most of whom were converts and two of whom were over 40 years of age. In February, 1864, forty-four others received the sacrament of confirmation. One man was unable to leave his bed, and the Bishop was kind enough to go to the ward in his robes to confirm the man. After the ceremony the prelate distributed little souvenirs of his visit and then asked the Catholics who were present to approach the railing of the altar. To his great astonishment as well as satisfaction all in the chapel came forward. He gave a little exhortation and then dismissed them. Mass was said at 6 o'clock in the morning, and many of the patients were in the chapel at half-past four, in order to secure seats. This was generally the case on great festivals, although some of the crippled men had to be carried in the arms of their comrades. At 3 o'clock on Sundays and festivals vespers were sung in the chapel, in which the patients felt quite privileged to join. In Lent they had the Way of the Cross, and in May the devotions of the month of Mary. The chapel was always crowded at these times. The soldiers took great delight in decorating the chapel at Christmas with green boughs, festooned with roses; indeed, it always gave them great pleasure to help the Sisters in any kind of work, and they often interfered when they found their kind nurses engaged in laborious duties. In May, 1864, a Jubilee was celebrated at the hospital with great success.

Cases of smallpox had occurred in the hospital from time to time, but the patients were removed as soon as possible to the smallpox hospital, which was some miles from the city. The poor men were very much distressed because they were compelled to leave the Sisters. It was heartrending when the ambulances came to hear the men begging to be left at Satterlee, even if they were entirely alone, provided the Sisters were near them. The Sisters offered their services several times to attend these poor men, but were told that the Government had ordered them away to prevent the contagion from spreading. At last the surgeon in charge obtained permission to keep the smallpox patients in a camp some distance from the hospital. The tents were made very comfortable, with good large stoves to heat them. The next thing was to have the Sisters in readiness in case their services should be required. Every Sister was courageous and generous enough to offer her services, but it was thought prudent to accept one who had had the disease. From November, 1864, until May, 1865, there were upwards of ninety cases. About nine or ten of these died. Two of the men had the black smallpox, and were baptized before they expired. The Sisters had entire charge of the poor sufferers, as the physicians seldom paid them a visit, permitting the Sisters to do anything they thought proper for them. They were much benefited and avoided being marked by drinking freely of tea made of "pitcher plant." The patients seemed to think the Sisters were not like other human beings, or they would not attend to such loathsome and contagious diseases.

One day a Sister was advising an application for a man who had been poisoned in the face. He would not see the doctor because, he said, he did not do him any good. The Sister told him that the remedy she advised had cured a Sister who was poisoned. The man looked astonished and said: "A Sister?" She answered, "Yes." "Why," he said, "I did not know that Sisters ever got anything like that." She told him that they were human beings and liable to take diseases as well as anyone else. "But I believe they are not," he said, "for the boys often say they must be different from anyone else, or from other people, for they never get sick and they do for us what no other person would do. They are not afraid of the fever, smallpox, or anything else." The men had more confidence in the Sisters' treatment than in that of the physicians'. The doctors themselves acknowledged that they would have lost more of their patients had it not been for the Sisters' watchful care and knowledge of medicine.

One occurrence will show the good feeling of the men towards the Sisters. One of the convalescent patients had

SISTER MARY GONZAGA.

been in town on a furlough, and while there had indulged too freely in liquor. On his return he went quietly to bed. A Sister, not knowing this, went with his medicine as usual and touched his bedclothes to arouse him. The poor man, being stupid and sleepy, thought his comrades were teasing him, and lifting up his arm gave a terrific blow, sending the Sister and medicine across the room. Several of the convalescent patients seized their comrade by the collar, and would surely have choked him to death if the Sister had not compelled them to desist. However, he was soon reported by the men and sent under an escort to the guard house, where stocks were prepared for him.

Nothing could be done for his release, as the surgeon in charge was absent. As soon as that official returned the Sister begged that the poor man might return to his ward and be also free from all other punishment, as well as from imprisonment in the guard house. The surgeon complied with the Sister's request, but in order to make a strong impression on the soldier he dispatched an order to all the wards, which was read at roll call, as follows: "This man was released only by the earnest entreaty of the Sisters; otherwise he would have been punished with the utmost severity." When the poor man came to himself and learned what he had done he begged a thousand pardons and promised never to take liquor again.

The hospital was one of the largest in the country, and everything was arranged on a generous scale. It was not the cause of any wonder, therefore, when the wounded were brought in by the car-loads. Sister Gonzaga always recalled two events in the history of the institution with particular distinctness; the first was after the battle of Bull Run and the second the day following the battle of Gettysburg. After the battle of bull Run the soldiers were brought to the hospitals by the hundreds. The time of the battle of Gettysburg there was a terrible period of suspense for the people of Philadelphia. They only knew in a general sort of way that a battle was taking place perhaps somewhere in the neighborhood of the State capital, but they had no information regarding the result, or who was the victor or vanquished. The earliest information came with the first consignment of wounded soldiers to the Satterlee Hospital. The sick and wounded from the blood-stained field of Gettysburg did not come by the dozen or by the car-load or by the hundred, but by the thousands. One careful estimate puts the number at four thousand. Such an emergency as this naturally tested the capacity of the women in charge, but Sister Gonzaga came through the ordeal with flying colors. The surgeon in chief of the hospital was Dr. Isaac Hayes, who achieved much fame by his connection with the celebrated Kane Arctic exploring expedition, and who afterwards headed an expedition of his own. The wards of the hospital were very commodious and comfortable, each one accommodating at least seventy-five beds.

Dr. Hayes was as a kind father to the Sisters, consulting them upon everything that would contribute to their comfort and happiness. Through the kind offices of Dr. Hayes and Dr. Atlee they secured a chaplain, Father Crane, who said Mass for them once a week. In the early part of the war many of the wounded soldiers were taken to St. Joseph's Hospital, where Sister Hillary was in charge. The hospital was then located in a dwelling house on Girard avenue, between Sixteenth and Seventeenth street. After the battle of Bull Run about sixty soldiers were cared for at St. Joseph's Hospital. At the same time St. Teresa's Church, of which the venerable Hugh Lane is pastor, was temporarily used as a hospital for wounded soldiers. The Sisters from Emmitsburg, as detailed in the previous chapter, did much good service after the fight at Gettysburg, going directly from their mother house in Maryland to the scene of the battle.

There is an old and very rare print of the Satterlee Hospital still in existence. From this valuable documentary evidence it is clear that the hospital occupied many acres of ground. In order to reach the building it was necessary to cross a bridge in the vicinity of South street. In crossing this at the time the hospital was opened the carriage containing a number of Sisters broke down and they were compelled to walk the remainder of the distance.

During all the time of the war Sister Gonzaga remained in charge of St. Joseph's Asylum, which she visited at regular intervals. At the close of the war she returned to give her whole time to the Asylum; the other Sisters returning to their various missions.

Sister Gonzaga has had frequent visits from grateful soldiers who were nursed back to life through her Christian devotion. One who heard of her serious illness a few years ago called, and then, as the outpouring of a grateful heart, sent the following letter to the Philadelphia Evening Star as "A soldier's tribute to the noble work of Mother Gonzaga during the war:"

"In your valuable paper dated yesterday the announcement was made that Mother Gonzaga, in charge of St. Joseph's Orphan Asylum, southwest corner of Seventh and Spruce streets, was lying dangerously ill. In reciting her many acts of charity for the young orphans under her care and protection, victims of epidemics, etc., during the many years of her life, you were not aware that the short notice touched a tender chord of affection in the breast of many a veteran of the late war.

"Mother Gonzaga was a mother of sixty thousand soldiers, as patients under treatment in Satterlee United States Army Hospital, Forty-fourth and Pine streets, from 1862 until 1865. Those who were under her care, no matter of what religion or creed, when they received the midnight visits of Mother Gonzaga, her silent steps after 'taps' and by the dim gaslight, will recognize her familiar countenance surrounded by that white-winged hood or cowl, just bending her form to hear the faint breath or whisper of some fever patient or some restless one throwing off the bed clothes; she kindly tucking them in around his body as a mother would a child; then a visit to they dying to give them expressions of comfort. Those who recall these scenes I say think of her truly as an angel of peace and sweetness.

"Administering medicine when required, loosening a bandage or replacing the same, watching a case of a sufferer in delirium—at all times annoying to those near him—was her daily duty. To see her always calm, always ready, with modesty and fidelity, faithfully performing a Christian duty as an administering angel when physicians, surgeons, friends and all human aid had failed, was a beautiful sight. No poet could describe, no artist could faithfully portray on canvas the scenes at the deathbed of a soldier, that would convey to those not having witnessed them the solemnity of the quiet kneeling, the silent prayer, a murmur faintly heard as a whisper, a Sister of Charity paying her devotion to Him on high, and consigning the spirit of the dying soldier to His care.

"As one of many thousands under her care I shall always think of Mother Gonzaga as one of a constellation of stars of the greatest magnitude—surrounded by many others that were devoted servants, among whom I would mention Dorothea Dix, Annie M. Ross, Hettie A. Jones and Mary Brady. We soldiers cannot forget the service they rendered.

"J. E. MacLane."

On the 12th of April, 1877, Sister Gonzaga celebrated the occasion of her golden jubilee in the Sisterhood. On the previous 19th of March she had attained her 50th year in the community. On that day she received the blessing of the Holy Father (Pope Pius IX), a gracious act obtained for her at the suggestion of Rev. Father Alizeri, C. M., a saintly man and a faithful missionary, who has since gone to his reward. Bishops, priests, Sisters and laymen vied with one another on this jubilee occasion in showing the reverence and esteem in which they held the simple religious woman who had gone about doing good for so many years.

Ten years later she was recalled to the mother house at Emmitsburg by her superiors, who had desired to relieve her of her responsibility as the head of such a large institution. Born to obedience she promptly responded to the order, and left the house which had become as a home; left friends who had become endeared to her, and left orphans who truly regarded her as a mother. There was not a murmur from this woman who was being taken away from associations with which she had been lovingly and intimately connected for nearly half a century.

Her Philadelphia friends, without solicitation and spontaneously and simultaneously, addressed petitions to her superiors requesting her return to the scenes of her life's labors. In the words of one who loved Sister Gonzaga, "Heaven was stormed by fervent prayers for the return of the Mother of the Poor." She remained at Emmitsburg for sixteen months and at the end of that time returned to Philadelphia. Her home-coming on the 20th of December, 1888, was made the occasion of a great demonstration. The Sisters, the orphans, the managers of the asylum and a host of friends participated.

The actual extent of the good done by Sister Gonzaga is scarcely realized by those who are around her.
Many of her charitable acts have been done quietly, even
secretly. There was one story with almost the pathos of
a tragedy in which she was concerned. The daughter of
an estimable family went astray, and the parents in the
first violence of their anger and grief turned her out of
the house. A few months passed, and then in their sober
better judgment coming to the surface they attempted to
find and forgive the child they had disowned. But they
searched in vain, and finally almost in despair turned
to Sister Gonzaga. She had not the slightest clue to the
missing girl, but she pledged herself to bring her back. In
a short time she located the erring one in the insane ward
of the Philadelphia hospital. She was a raving maniac.
The girl was restored to her remorseful parents, and by
careful nursing was gradually brought back to reason.

On another occasion when the Sister was missing for
an hour or so every day it was discovered that she was in
daily attendance on a poor woman who lay ill in a small
house in a street near by. Although this was entirely foreign to her duties she regularly called and washed and
dressed the woman.

Sister Gonzaga departed this life on the morning
of October 8, 1897, in her room in St. Joseph's Orphan
Asylum, in Philadelphia. A black piece of crape, on top
of which was fastened a bit of immaculate white ribbon,
fluttered from the bell on the door of the asylum on that
day to inform the passer-by that this marvelous woman
had gone to receive her reward.

The obsequies of Sister Gonzaga took place on the
morning of Tuesday, October 12th. On the evening before

this event countless numbers took a last farewell of the devoted Sister. Hundreds of women and men kissed her dead face as she lay in her coffin. They kissed her hands, which held the Rosary, and about which was twined the broad, purple ribbon of her office as Superioress. Some of the women shed tears, but the men seemed even more deeply affected.

On the morning of the funeral the body lay in state. It was attired in the habit of the order, with a black gown and the white headdress. Clasped in her hand was a crucifix and Rosary and a small roll of paper, on which was written the vows that the deceased took when entering upon her work.

The casket was heavily trimmed in silver, and upon the lid was a plate containing this inscription: "Sister Mary Gonzaga, died October 8, 1897, aged 85 years." Near the top of the lid was a large silver cross, with a figure of the crucifixion. Upon the head of Sister Gonzaga there reposed a golden-leaved crown, that was presented to her when she had been 50 years a Sister of Charity.

There was a profusion of floral offerings tastefully arranged about the head of the casket. In a prominent place was a cross and crown from the "Children of Mary," a society composed of former inmates of St. Joseph's Orphan Asylum.

The body lay in the community room, beneath the altar. Half a hundred Sisters of Charity were seated along the side of the room. The entire apartment was draped in black. By 10 o'clock, when the doors were closed, several thousand persons had passed around the casket. At length the hearse drew up before the asylum, and eight students from St. Vincent's Seminary carried the coffin out to the street. A long procession quickly formed and slowly the march to St. Mary's Church was begun, the route being down Spruce to Fourth and up Fourth. Arriving at the church the eight theologians again acted as pall-bearers, and the casket was carried up the aisle and placed in front of the altar.

Among the mourners were the Board of Managers of the institution, Sisters of Charity from various houses of the order in this and nearby cities, Sisters of other orders, the Children of Mary, composed of those who were formerly inmates of St. Joseph's Orphan Asylum, numbers of them now mothers of families, and the orphans at present at the home. In addition to these a large congregation was present, which crowded the church.

Solemn Requiem Mass celebrated by Very Rev. J. A. Hartnett, C. M., of St. Vincent's Seminary, Germantown, who celebrated his first Mass at St. Joseph's Asylum chapel. Rev. E. O. Hiltermann, rector of Holy Trinity, was deacon; Rev. Edward Quinn, C. M., of Baltimore, subdeacon, and Rev. John J. Duffy, master of ceremonies. Mr. Johon F. Walsh, a seminarian, was thurifer. Bishop Prendergast, who occupied a seat on the Gospel side of the altar, was attended by Rev. James O'Reilly, of Downingtown, and Rev. T. B. McCormick, C. M., of St. Vincent de Paul's.

The sermon was delivered by Rev. John Scully, S. J., rector of St. Joseph's, who spoke in substance as follows:

"St. Paul tells us in his first letter to the Corinthians that the wisdom of this world is foolishness with God, and in order that God may show to us that this is so the same Apostle tells us that the base, the lowly of this world and the contemptible hath God chosen and the things that are not in order to confound the things that are. How true in all ages have been these in-spired words of the Apostle! How true to-day. This foolishness, this wisdom of the world, so foolish in the eyes of God, differs in degree and kind in different ages. In our age it shows itself in the attempt to divide human philanthropy and brotherly love from religion. Take the intellect and culture of this great city in which we live, and what does it lay down as law, except it be that mankind must practice altruism, as they call it, brotherly love, the civic virtue by which alone society among men can be made possible, yet not one word about the essential basis which even the modern pagan sees is necessary. When talking about our rights they say nothing of the rights of God, and when talking of our obligations to one another they say noth-ing of our obligations to God, without which nothing can rest on a solid basis.

"The wisdom of the world is foolishness. The lowly are chosen by God to confound the worldly wise. In the days of old God raised David from the shepherd of a flock to be the ruler of His people. Christ chose the poor fishermen to be His Apos-tles. He called St. Vincent de Paul from the lowly occupation of a shepherd to be a wonder-worker, a marvel, a propagator of charity, not only in his own days, but up to the present time. How many millions of dollars are spent in the spirit of modern philanthropy? For education, in order to raise men up as they think, to give men a chance in life. Because it is divided from religion it falls. The late Mr. Vaux said on what was perhaps his last official visit to the penitentiary: 'When I first came here I found the children of the poor and the ignorant. Now I find my own schoolmates.' Thus are spent millions in charity, or rather in almsgiving, for it is not worthy to be called charity. What is the result. It puffs up one with pride and another with envy.

"The reason why the thing is done differently is the motive under the acts of thousands and tens of thousands who have given up their lives to works of charity. Have you ever heard of a soldier wishing to become a member of a church to which a trained nurse belonged? How different when the motive is that of Jesus Christ. It is the experience of thousands who beg to be allowed to die in that religion of the devoted Sisters who attended them, and it was this that caused a bishop to receive a petition from a remote part of the diocese for a priest to be sent there and a church built. He replied that not only was he ignorant that so many Catholics were there, but that there was even one Catholic. The answer was, 'There are no Catholics here yet, but we are men who were attended by the Sisters and we want to be of the religion of the Sisters.' The base, ignoble and contemptible things of this world has God chosen for His work.

"What is more foolish in the eyes of the world; what is more despised and held in contempt by the intellectual and the cultured than poverty? Yet the Sisters are bound by vows of poverty to be as poor as Christ, to live a life of dependence, depending on one another for their very food and raiment. What more foolish in the eyes of the world than that! As the wise man has said, they are a parable of reproach, looked on with derision. What is more foolish, more base, more spiritless, more contemptible than to find women, ladies, willingly binding themselves, not by impulse, but by vocation, not as a mere whim, but perpetually to live by rule, doing that to which no man ever yet got accustomed, to purify their acts to make them meritorious in the sight of God? And obedience! The world hates and loathes obedience, yet our Divine Lord was obedient even unto death, the death of the cross.

"What is the result of all the so-called charity and philanthropy? Nothing lasting. Search the hearts of thousands of men, women and children who have been benefited by the Sisters and you will find there the love of God.

"Such was the life of the devoted woman who spent 70 years doing good. Many philanthropists have monuments raised to them and are looked upon as public benefactors and honored as such. Take him or her who was greatest among them, or all of them together, what are all compared with a life such as hers, spent in the care of the poor, sick and needy? One long life doing good. A life not only an imitation of Jesus Christ in its acts, but what is more necessary and more difficult, a life in imitation of His motives. The world looks in reproach upon such a life. How many times has she been sneered at on the street in her poor dress and strange bonnet! How often has the world looked with contempt on her that served the Lord so faithfully. How He loved that soul that did as He did and for the same reason. All I have said could be said of almost any other Sister of Charity, but of her, who lived for 70 years in religion, how much could be said those only can know who lived with her and knew her and loved her the more they knew her. Of how few can this be said—to have combined in one and the same person the power of execution, the power of government, and at the same time the spirit of kindness and of great-heartedness which does not make commands ever necessary. Without emotion, without anger. No one ever saw that kindly face ruffled. This is rare in the world—yes, even rare in the religious life. To speak of her life and to realize that thousands and tens of thousands of orphans have had her care, many becoming mothers of families and bringing up their children influenced by her example. To realize her hard work in the military hospital, to think of the thousands and tens of thousands dealt with directly by her or indirectly through her as superioress. What a world of well doing! Seventy years in religion; 85 years spent in the serving of Christ. What a wonderful crown is won by her whose dead body is lying here! Seventy years a member of the community whose very name is held even by the enemies of her faith as a synonym of all that is good in humanity—something which raises humanity and brings it close to God.

"Now the reign of sorrow and desolation has passed away. She has gone forth from the scene of her labor to her rest. She has gone into the sight of Jesus Christ, whom in life she made her Friend. Not to meet the severe face of a Judge, but the smiling countenance of a dear friend. Who would recall her? Not those who loved her most, who lived with her in community; not those who were the recipients of her bounty. What so glorious as a death such as hers after 70 years in God's service. Says St. Hilary, 'Shall I fear to die after I have served my Lord for 70 years?' So died she, because she knew the good Master she served.

"As theologians tell us, God makes known to His saints the needs of those whom they have left behind. 'Thou who knowest the needs of thy children be their advocate and pattern now as ever in life. Be unto us a mother and pray for us that we may go forth as thou hast from this valley of affliction and tears to the sunshine of God the Father, to live forever with His Son, our Lord, Jesus Christ."

The absolution of the body was performed by Bishop Prendergast, assisted by the officers of the Mass. The music was the Gregorian chant, with the introit, offertory, communion and "Benedictus" in harmony. This was rendered by the students of St. Vincent's Seminary, Germantown. From among them were chosen the pallbearers also. The prominent part taken in the services by he Congregation of the Mission was due to the fact that St. Vincent de Paul, its founder, was also founder of the Sisters of Charity.

Eleanor C. Donnelly, the gifted Philadelphia poetess, has written the following verses in memory of Sister Gonzaga and inscribed them to Sister Mary Joseph and her community, with affectionate sympathy:

> Thrice in the rounding of one little year,
>> Saint Mary's hallowed temple hath revealed
> An honored priest reposing on his bier,
>> His pallid lips in icy silence sealed.
>
> Thrice, have regretful tears bedewed the urn
>> Where sacerdotal ashes were enshrined;
> Youth, age and ripen'd manhood, each in turn,
>> Unto Saint Mary's funeral vaults consigned.[2]

---

(2). Rev. Hugh J. McManus, December, 1896; Rev. Eugene J. Bardet,

And now, before the fading flow'rs have strown
    Their last, sweet, withered petals round the place;
Or early snows lie white upon the stone
    That shuts from sight each well-remembered face—

Before the shades of the anointed Dead
    Have melted from Saint Mary's aisles away,
We hear once more the mourner's solemn tread—
    Another saint is here in death, to-day!

Dear Sister Gonzaga! good mother, friend
    Of Christ's own little ones—His precious poor!
From Life's beginning to its blessed end
    Thy words were Wisdom's, and thy works were pure.

In tender youth, betrothed to thy Lord;
    For three-score years and ten His faithful spouse,
He was thine aim—thy solace—thy reward—
    Bound to His Sacred Heart by deathless vows!

Toiler of yore with Kenrick, Neumann, Wood,
    One of our Faith's first local pioneers!
So long hath been thy service, and so good,
    Thou needest not our prayers or pitying tears!

For death is gain to thee, tho' loss to all
    Thou leavest here. Thy prayers must plead for them.
The orphans' tears that sparkle on thy pall
    Shall prove on high thy brightest diadem.

March, 1897; Right Rev. Mgr. Toner, September, 1897.

The dear old heart that loved them now is stilled,
    The dear old voice they loved is heard no more;
She waits afar with ardent yearning filled
    To bid them welcome to the eternal shore!

Prate not of sculptur'd immortality—
    Her children's virtues shall her heart content
If all who look upon their lives shall see
    In each their Mother's lasting monument.

The old-time friends may leave us, one by one,
    The ancient landmarks swiftly fade away—
The good that Sister Gonzaga hath done
    Shall live when brass and marble both decay!

Then lay her gently down, in peace and trust,
    Where angel-memories shall guard her bed;
Her soul is with her God; her virgin dust
    Sleeps sweetly with Saint Mary's sainted dead!
October 12, 1897.   ELEANOR C. DONNELLY.

Sister Gonzaga has a countenance of great benignity and firmness. A high forehead, a kindly mouth and eyes which even age has not been able to dim. She is a model of graciousness and good breeding. The effects of a good education are still visible, and the results of a well-balanced and well-trained mind are seen in a remarkably accurate and strong memory. The story of her life is well worth the telling, serving as it does as a model and incentive for those who would be successful in their chosen vocation.

CHAPTER XVI.

THE FALL OF RICHMOND.

———◆◆◆———

Preparing for the close of the war. Sisters of Charity in the West enlisted in the military prison at Altoona. Smallpox cases removed to an island in the Mississippi. Leaders of the Southern Confederacy realize that their cause is lost. Scenes of wild excitement in Richmond. Blessings for the Sisters

———◆◆◆———

General Grant, who had been laying siege to Vicksburg, had captured that stronghold on the Fourth of July, 1863. Then came the surrender of Fort Hudson and the battles of Chickamauga, Lookout Mountain and Missionary Ridge.

Grant in 1864 was made Lieutenant-General and placed in command of all the armies of the United States. Early in May he led the Army of the Potomac across the Rapidan toward Richmond. For six weeks he tried to get between Lee's army and Richmond without success. In this fruitless effort he fought the battles of the Wilderness, North Anna, Bethesda Church and Cold Harbor, losing 40,000 men. Then he moved his whole army south of the James and laid siege to Petersburg.

The burning of Chambersburg by the Confederates and the valor of General Sheridan in the Shenandoah Valley, with Admiral Farragut's achievements at sea, completed the notable events of 1864.

In the fall of 1864 Sherman began his march to the sea, which was unique in modern warfare, and was com-

pletely successful. The last campaign began in the spring
of 1865. On April 1, 1865, Petersburg was evacuated, the
Union Army entered Richmond on the 2d. On the 9th of
April came the surrender of Lee to Grant at Appomattox, which was the practical end of the war. Long before
this the Sisters of Charity felt that their work was drawing
to a close. In the meantime, however, their services were
being utilized in the West. Colonel Ware, who was then
in command of the prisons of that section, applied to the
Bishop of Alton, Ill., for the sisters of Charity to attend
the prisoners at Alton. Accordingly, Bishop Yonker applied to the Sister servant of St. Philomena's School, St.
Louis. One of the Sisters was at that time in St. Louis at
the Gratiot State Prison Hospital. She received a dispatch
from Father Burlando to go to Alton and take with her
three Sisters. They started early the next morning, March
15, 1864, and reached Alton in twenty-four hours. There
they were met by Father Harty, who conducted them
to the residence of a gentleman, a member of the City
Council.

Colonel Ware soon called to see them and accompanied them to the prison, which had been formerly
called the Illinois State Penitentiary. It had been vacated
before the war for a more commodious and healthy locality. Before reaching the main entrance the Sisters had
to ascend a very rugged road, well protected by guards.
Here a residence would have been provided for them, but
they did not think it safe or prudent to accept it. They
passed through the yard, which was crowded with prisoners, numbering four thousand Confederates and one
thousand Federals, the latter being confined there for desertion and through follies committed in camp. The two
parties were separated, except in the hospital. The poor

sick were so delighted to see the Sisters that they could scarcely contain themselves.

It is said that the men died in this hospital at the rate of from six to ten a day. The place was too small for the number of inmates, who were all more or less afflicted with diseases. Some were wounded, others a prey to despondency, typhoid fever and the smallpox; consequently the atmosphere of the prison was very foul. Fortunately the smallpox cases were removed to an island in the Mississippi as soon as discovered. The Sisters made arrangements with Colonel Ware to visit the sick twice a day. As there were no accommodations for the Sisters to remain in the prison they returned to the residence of Councilman Wise, who had so kindly received them in the morning. He could not accommodate them, but procured lodgings for them in the house of his sister, where they remained for nearly six weeks. On their return to the prison the next day the Sisters found written orders from the Government. They also met there the attending physicians, who appeared glad to see them and said that they hoped soon to see an improvement in the condition of the sufferers, who had been heretofore much neglected. The Sisters were informed that four of the patients had died during the previous night. A place was allotted to them to prepare drinks and nourishment for the sick. It was an old workshop, and the floors were in such a condition that the Sisters were continually in danger of falling through. The attendants, who were prisoners, were exceedingly kind and obliging, so much so that they would even anticipate the wishes of the Sisters.

Two weeks had scarcely elapsed before the sick began to improve. The doctors acknowledged a change for the better, saying that there were fewer deaths, and that

MULVANEY'S "SHERIDAN'S RIDE."

despondency had nearly disappeared. A look of com-
miseration or a word of encouragement soon made these
poor victims feel that they were cared for at least by the
lowly children of St. Vincent. The Sisters visited the Federal Guards Hospital and the smallpox island hospital
at the request of Colonel Ware. They visited the Federal
Guards Hospital once a day and the smallpox island
hospital once a week, but even that consoled the poor
patients, as the Sisters provided them with delicacies and
nourishment they mostly craved.

On the 1st of May the Sisters took possession of a
house belonging to St. Joseph's Emmitsburg, that had
been previously occupied as a school, but was then vacated. They were now one mile distant from the prison,
and an ambulance was sent daily to convey them to and
fro.

On July 1 they were notified that their services were
no longer required at the prison. They could do nothing
until the superiors were acquainted with their situation.
Meanwhile the citizens were anxious to have them remain in Alton and convert their house into a hospital.
They soon received a letter from the venerated Mother
Ann Simeon, giving permission to open a civil hospital for the citizens of Alton. One of the Sisters was sent
to St. Joseph's Hospital, Alton, to wait on the sick and
wounded soldiers from the battle of Winchester. There
was one man in the ward who was nicknamed "Blue
Beard," from his ferocious manners and large mustache.
He would never ask for anything nor take anything offered to him. One day when he was being urged to take
some nourishment he replied:

"Sister, I do not wish for anything that you have.

There is only one thing, and that I do not think you can procure for me."

The Sister inquired what it was and assured him that if it were in her power she would get it for him. He then replied:

"Sister, I should like to have a lily. I think it would do me so much good."

The wish was a strange one, nevertheless she at once determined to gratify him, which the kindness of a friend enabled her to do. This little act of kindness was not without effect, and from that time the man had a high regard for the Sisters.

A poor family who had been banished from their home took shelter in the city. Their misery was so great that three of the number died from starvation, but as soon as their distress was made known to the parish priest he procured immediate relief for them. The mother and grandmother died, but the other members of the family were brought to the hospital quite sick, with the exception of two little children, who were taken to the asylum. It was a pitiful sight to witness the poor dying man entrusting his orphan children to the good pastor.

At the termination of the war, in 1865, the prisoners received their discharge. It was sad to see the streets of the city lined with the ragged and distressed looking men. The sick were brought to St. Joseph's Hospital, which was soon filled. The Sisters gave the soldiers the very best attention and consideration, and within a few months the majority of the men were enabled to return to their homes and families.

The little band of Sisters who had been laboring in

Frederick City, Md., from 1862 to 1864 certainly did their share in caring for helpless humanity. They were kept actively employed in Frederick City during the summer and autumn of 1862. They found then that their work was not nearly done. The winter set in with heavy rains and deep snow, to which they were constantly exposed. The poor patients had likewise much to suffer from the badly constructed buildings. The wind, rain and snow penetrated through the crevices, leaving the poor men in a most uncomfortable condition. This was called to the attention of the chief surgeon, who immediately gave orders for the dilapidated barracks to be repaired as much as possible.

Some of the soldiers were quite amusing with their grateful intentions. A Sister was asked one day whether she ever wore any other color but gray or black, "for," he continued, "I wish to present Sister Agnes with a new dress; she has been so truly good to me."

The soldiers seemed to have the greatest confidence in the Sisters, whose advice they preferred before that of the physicians. General Hunter had now received command of the Shenandoah Valley. He visited the hospital and issued an order that all the prisoners should be placed by themselves in separate barracks entirely apart from the Union men. Soon after the United States surgeon in charge of the hospital inspected all the barracks and found one filled with Confederates and with no Sister to take charge of them. The sufferings of these poor men touched him so much that he immediately went to the Sister servant and requested her to send a Sister from a ward of the Union soldiers to take care of the Confederates. The patience of these poor sufferers was the admiration of all. A worthy clergyman once remarked that in his visits to the hospital he was always edified by their resignation. He said he had never heard the least murmur escape their lips, and commenting upon this he remarked: "I think the intensity of their pain, both mentally and physically, might, if offered in unison, expiate the sins of their whole life."

About this time the leaders of the Southern Confederacy began to realize that the clouds were gathering about them and that their cause was hanging in the balance, if indeed it was not already destined to failure. They resolved to concentrate their hospital facilities in and around the city of Richmond, Va. The Sisters who had been doing work upon the various battlefields in the South were summoned to the Southern capital. The Sisters had served at Harper's Ferry, Manassas, Antietam, Fredericksburg and White House, Va. They were given a chaplain and had the privilege of Mass four times a week.

The Sisters who were located in Richmond at this time began to feel "in their bones" that the fall of the city was imminent. They were right. The long expected event occurred in April, 1865. Jefferson Davis, the President of the Southern Confederacy, was at worship in an Episcopal church when he was handed a telegram telling him that Richmond must be evacuated. He presented a calm exterior, but bad news is hard to conceal, and the exact situation was soon noised about the city. The wildest excitement prevailed. Men, women and children rushed hither and thither, knowing not what to do or where to go. Finally their frenzy assumed a decisive shape and a general evacuation of the city began. The Sisters, who constituted the calmest portion of the population, looked on the scene with mild amazement.

The City Councils met and with the general interests of the people in view determined to destroy all the liquor in Richmond. This work was begun at midnight and before the first gray streaks of dawn revealed the terror-stricken city to the public gaze the streets and gutters were running with veritable lakes of whisky, wine and beer. Many of the soldiers and some of the residents balked the good intentions of the Councils by drinking the liquor, and then scenes of drunken revelry were added to the general confusion. Thieves broke loose, houses were robbed, public buildings were fired and bridges leading from the city were destroyed.

Notwithstanding the foresight of the authorities on the coming defeat, its arrival was most appalling. Medical stores, commissary departments and other houses were thrown open. The city was troubled from the blowing up of the gunboats in the river. The Sisters were preparing to go to Mass early in the morning when suddenly a terrific explosion stunned, as it were, the power of thought. The noise of the breaking of windows in the hospitals and neighboring buildings added greatly to the alarm. The Sisters soon learned that the Confederates had blown up their supplies of powder which were very near the hospital buildings; then followed an explosion of all the Government buildings.

After the surrender a Federal officer rode up to the door of the Sisters' house and told them they were perfectly safe, their property would be respected and that he would send a special guard to protect their house. No resistance was shown to the Union troops. The city was placed under military rule and General G. F. Shepley made Governor. One thousand prisoners were found in the city and five thousand sick and wounded were in the hospitals. The prisoners were set free and the Sisters with joy hailed the peace that was once again to dawn on a blood-washed land. They remained in Richmond until the sick and wounded were able to quit the hospitals and then returned home to Emmitsburg, followed by the gratitude and blessings of the men of both armies.

The soldiers who were in the Washington hospitals also returned to their homes impressed with the kindest feelings toward the Sisters. The officers and doctors all concurred in expressing unlimited confidence in them. Printed placards were hung in all the wards, reading: "All articles for the use of the soldiers here are to be placed in the care of the Sisters of Charity, as also papers, books and clothing."

Early in the summer of 1865 the Sisters took their departure and the hospital was permanently closed. Another hospital in Washington began its operations in March, 1865, and closed in October of the same year. The Sisters were placed in charge, and, since their customs and calling were known, did not experience as much annoyance as in the beginning of the war.

The house was well filled with the sick and wounded. During the month of July the Jesuit Fathers were giving a jubilee at their church in the city of Washington and many of the convalescents attended.

The officers of the hospital expressed much gratitude for all that had been done by the Sisters. The first surgeon was at a loss to know how to put his satisfaction into words, saying that the Sisters of Charity had marvelously lessened the cares of the physicians and surgeons in all of the hospitals in which they served.

This concludes the story of the work done by the Sisters of Charity of Emmitsburg from the beginning to the close of the war. While they were at work, however, the Sisters belonging to branches of the order and to other orders were not idle, as will be seen by the chapters that follow.

CHAPTER XVII.

SISTERS OF CHARITY OF NAZARETH.

Bishop Spalding sends a letter to General Anderson tendering the services of the Sisters. The offer accepted and the volunteers assigned to work in the hospitals in and around Louisville. "Oh, Sister, put your head down by me and don't leave me." The martyrdom of Sister Mary Lucy. Tender-hearted soldiers keep a vigil around the coffin with blazing torches made of pine knots.

The main body of the Sisters of Charity were not alone in their devotion to the sick and wounded soldiers. During the trying days between 1861 and 1865 no body  of men or women did more for suffering humanity than the patient, zealous Sisters of Charity of Nazareth, then, as now, of Bardstown, Kentucky. A score of Sisters in that community offered themselves and their services without pay and without hope of earthly reward of any character. It was in the spring of 1861, the opening year of the civil war, that bishop Martin John Spalding sent a formal communication to General Robert Anderson, of Fort Sumter fame, then in command of the Department of Kentucky, tendering the services of the Sisters of Charity of Nazareth to nurse the sick and wounded soldiers. Their services were willingly accepted, and the understanding was that the Sisters were to work in the hospitals in and around Louisville.

Three large manufacturing establishments in the

city of Louisville had been placed at the service of the Government and were being used as hospitals at that time. The rooms were long, and lines of cots extended along each side. The hospitals were divided into sections and each section was placed under the watchful charge of a Sister of Charity. The system that characterized the three establishments was such that no sufferer was neglected or without a nurse. This was in striking contrast with the disorder and lack of system that had prevailed prior to the advent of the Sisters. There were twenty-three Sisters in the three hospitals, in charge of an army surgeon, and they worked faithfully from their entrance into the hospitals until the close of the war, without a cent of compensation.

There had been one battle and several severe skirmishes in Kentucky about that time, and when the Sisters arrived at the hospitals the scene was enough to bring tears into the eyes of the most hardened. A great many Confederates had been captured and were being held as prisoners of war. Within the walls of the hospitals hundreds of Union men and Confederates lay groaning in a common agony. Those that were not mortally wounded and that had not submitted to the amputation of a leg or an arm were raving in the worst forms of fever or had contracted erysipelas, pneumonia and kindred ailments. About it all there was a heroism that was touching, and as the Sisters passed from cot to cot many a soldier suffering with a shattered limb or bullet-pierced body lifted his wan face and gave forth a smile of welcome and of recognition.

The Sisters soothed the restless patients, bathed the fevered brows and moistened the parched lips "with a touch impartially tender." The attitude of the men themselves was not without interest. Many of them had never seen a Sister before; the majority of them looked upon the Sisters with distrust and suspicion. The change that came in a short while came as actual knowledge comes when it dissipates prejudice and misrepresentation. They could not help but be impressed with the quiet demeanor and the self-sacrifice of the Sisters, and unreasoning dislike and bigotry soon gave way to natural respect and esteem.

But the beauty of the Sisters' lives, their habit of thinking of all but themselves, had its effect upon many a hardened sinner. Five hundred men died in "hospital number one," and of that number only one passed away seemingly indifferent to his future.

An incident told by one of the surviving Sisters carries a moral with it. One of the soldiers in the hospital, a Catholic, refused to do anything for the benefit of his soul. His end seemed to be approaching and he was transferred to some other place, where he could be reasoned into submission and repentance. A man who occupied a cot near that of the unrepentant Catholic had heard the Sisters pleading with him. He listened with a thoughtful manner, and when the hard hearted man had been removed, called a Sister to his side. He begged to be further instructed in the Catholic faith. His request was complied with, he was baptized, confessed, received Holy Communion and finally died a most holy and edifying death.

The parish priests of Louisville and several of the Jesuit Fathers paid regular visits to the hospitals. Each priest came on an average of three times a day, but there was not a moment during the day or night when the priest was not within easy call. The Sisters by their forethought and intelligence made the work of the clergy comparatively easy. A man who desired to be baptized was prepared by the Sisters and ready when the priest arrived. Those to whom it was necessary to administer the last rites of the Church were gradually brought to realize the importance of these rites by these same Sisters. So it was from day to day, from week to week, from month to month. The Sisters were unflagging in their devotion to the men in their charge. They nursed, they prayed, they consoled, in fact, as more than one grateful soldier exclaimed, proved themselves little short of earthly angels.

A pathetic scene took place one day in "hospital number two." A young soldier, a Catholic and a Scotchman, lay on his death-bed, far from home and family and country, but surrounded by all the loving devotion of the Sisters. He knew that his end was at hand and had been prepared by all of the sacred rites of the Church for his journey into the great unknown. He was slowly expiring from a fatal wound and was unable to move.

In a feeble voice he asked the Sister to hand him a package of letters that he had read over and over again, and which he always kept in view. They were given him and he read them over once again and for the last time. After that he selected several from the package and placing them close to his heart said slowly, but distinctly: "Sister, leave them here until I am dead. That will not be long. Then send them to my father and mother in Scotland. Tell them that I thought of them until the last. Get the money that is coming to me. Give some of it for Masses for an offering for my soul and forward the remainder to my parents. Now I am ready to die. Goodbye." With a faint smile he closed his eyes and in a short time the spirit had fled from his youthful body. The instructions were carried out to the letter, as were the last wishes of all the dying soldiers whenever it was possible and practicable. One of the most important tasks of the Sisters was to write to the near relatives of the deceased, giving accounts of their last moments and delivering entrusted messages from the dying.

On more than one occasion the Sisters supplied the place of a mother to the wounded and the dying. Many a pathetic death-bed scene is still fresh in the memory of the now venerable Sisters who have survived those trying times. They were able to repress their emotions in most cases, but there were times when nature asserted itself, and the tears of compassion flowed freely. This was especially the case when drummer boys and buglers—mere children—were brought into the hospitals. In such cases all the tenderness of the Sisters' gentle natures went out in abundance to the wounded "lambs," as they delighted to call the young ones. One day three blue-eyed, fair-haired lads in soldier attire were brought into "hospital number one." They were ill of typhoid pneumonia and they were in an advanced stage, too. They were placed on cots side by side and there they lay for days, uncomplaining and innocent, giving expression to the quaintest thoughts in the most childish way. They were like brothers, although they were not, and all three were of about the same height and age. The gratitude they expressed to the Sisters was more by their manner than anything they said.

One afternoon one of the three looked up at the Sister who was nursing him, and with a wistful look in his blue eyes exclaimed: "Oh, you are such a good lady; just like my mother to me." In spite of the care that was lavished on them the three little heroes died, as so many heroes have died—unknown, unhonored and unsung. In the same room another lad of twelve or thirteen, whose life was fast ebbing away, cried out: "Oh, Sister, put your head right down by me and don't leave me." The request was complied with, and the little fellow clasped the Sister about the neck and never let go his hold until grim death relaxed it soon afterward. Who could look on such scenes unmoved! Many boys died thus. Death seemed to pluck the choicest and freshest of the earth to make its bouquets during those four fearful years. The Sisters' care of their "lambs" after death was as tender and reverential as it had been in life. Their eyes were closed with a prayer, their silken locks parted and their little hands folded as if in supplication to the Divine mercy. Who can doubt but what the blessings of heaven were showered upon these innocent, heroic souls?

The Sisters were "always on duty," and sometimes the duty was more severe than at others. After great battles, such as Shiloh, the hospitals were hardly able to accommodate the hundreds that were brought there. When the orderlies had performed the first essential service for the newcomer he would be taken in charge by the Sisters. Refreshing draughts and nourishing food were intermingled with the remedies that would be administered from time to time. The ladies of Louisville were frequent visitors at the hospitals, and they brought many delicacies for the sick and the wounded. At length near the close of the war the Sisters were recalled to their home from the Louisville hospitals. The recall came none too soon for the survivors, as they stood much in need of rest and change of air. For nearly three years they had been confined in the close wards of the three hospitals, and this not unnaturally had its effect upon their health. Many of them overestimated their strength and their powers of

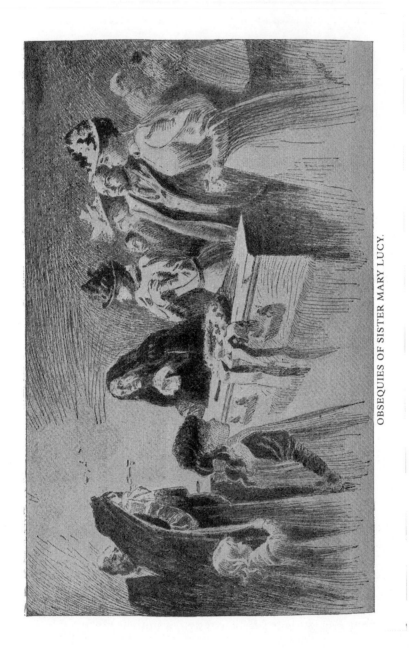

OBSEQUIES OF SISTER MARY LUCY.

endurance. Some died in the hospitals, soon after, at a premature age.

The actual number of Catholic Sisters who laid down their lives during the civil war, that their fellow creatures might live, will probably never be known, but there is no question that hundreds did so. Their names are not cut upon any earthly monuments, but they are surely emblazoned in letters of gold in the great book of the Recording Angel. The Sisters of Charity of Nazareth, as Mother Carrol could have testified, furnished their full quota of fair martyrs. Many instances have been lost in the long number of years that have elapsed since the closing of the war, but several well-authenticated cases still linger freshly in the minds of those that were witnesses of the great struggle. One of these is particularly pathetic. Sister Mary Lucy, one of the sweetest young members of the Order, richly endowed by nature, was the music teacher in St. Mary's Academy, at Paducah. When the exigencies of war compelled the temporary abandonment of this institution, Sister Mary Lucy volunteered as one of the hospital nurses. She was assigned to some of the severest typhoid cases, and the manner in which she nursed these patients won for her the unqualified praise of the hospital doctors and attendants.

The post of honor in this instance proved to be the post of danger. Sister Mary Lucy contracted the fever from one of her patients who was convalescent. This was in the latter part of December, during the first year of the war. Despite the best medical attention she rapidly grew worse, until December 29, when she expired as calmly and heroically as she had lived. Her death cast a gloom over the entire hospital, and the soldiers of both armies were filled with admiration and awe at the martyrdom of this gentle soul. They determined that she should be honored in death as she had been in life, and that her final obsequies should be of a character befitting her great merits.

Several files of soldiers marched with muffled drums and noiseless tread from the Central Hospital to the Ohio River, bearing in the midst of them the remains. There the coffin was placed in a gunboat in waiting, which had been especially designated for this service. Then the boat slowly steamed away, bearing its honored burden under a flag of truce to Uniontown, Ky. On landing, the remains were borne to St. Vincent's Academy, some miles distant, where the Sisters own a considerable tract of land and where they have a last resting place for their dead. Father Powers, at that time pastor of the Catholic Church at Paducah, said the Solemn Mass of Requiem and accompanied the body to the grave and recited over it the last offices of the Church, of which the deceased had been such an exemplary member. A guard of devoted soldiers watched by the coffin day and night from the time it left the Central Hospital until the earth covered it from mortal view. At night the tender-hearted warriors kept their vigil around the coffin with blazing torches made of pine knots. Sister Mary Lucy was born in the vicinity of the spot where she was buried. She received her education at St. Vincent's Academy, became a Daughter of Charity and died in the performance of her duty. This is the short but brilliant life history of one heroic woman.

A letter dated Louisville, February 1, 1862, written by one of the army surgeons to Mother Francis Gardiner, contained the following announcement: "I regret very much to have to inform you of the death of Sister Catherine at the General Hospital in this city. She, as well as the other Sisters at the hospital, has been untiring and most efficient in nursing the sick soldiers. The military authorities are under the greatest obligations to the Sisters of your Order."

Still another conspicuous loss was soon to be felt in the death of Sister Appollonia, the directress of "No. 1 Hospital." She served long and faithfully in this post and won warm commendation from stern soldiers, who, whatever else their faults, were never guilty of flattery. She was a woman of great executive ability, and was instrumental in causing order to come out of chaos in the hospital over which she presided. Her zeal was great. Not content to direct affairs, she also nursed individual cases. It was while engaged in this work that she contracted typhoid fever, from which she soon after died. She had endeared herself to the soldiers by her kind and motherly treatment of them, and her death caused universal regret.

The manner in which the Sisters were treated by the soldiers had in it a blending of the humorous and the sublime. Those of the Sisters that live to tell the tale say that nothing was wanting in the courtesy with which they were invariably considered by the men of both armies. On Sundays they were given especial consideration. They were escorted to Mass by a military guard of honor, and received the military salute in passing to and fro in the neighborhood of the hospital and the camps. Some of the invalid soldiers imagined that every Sister carried a charm about her, and was thus protected from the contagious diseases that caused such sad havoc among the men. But the supposed charms were not always successful in preventing the Sisters from wearing the martyr's crown in death. The only charms they carried, as the soldiers soon discovered, were blameless lives, absolute devotion to duty and entire self-forgetfulness.

There was one modest institution near the three large hospitals in Louisville where a great amount of good was done in an unostentatious manner. This was St. Joseph's Infirmary, conducted by the sisters of Charity of Nazareth. This was generally filled in war times with wounded officers and other invalids connected with both armies. The good done there, though not quite as conspicuous as elsewhere, was lasting, and bore fruit in after years.

CHAPTER XVIII.

MORE ABOUT NAZARETH.

Bardstown occupied successively by the Union and the Confederate troops. Six Sisters start for Lexington under a flag of truce. A courteous letter from Brigadier General Wood. Ex-Secretary of State Guthrie applies to President Lincoln for protection to the Nazareth Convent. A brief sketch of a famous school and some of its distinguished graduates.

Bardstown, three miles distant from Nazareth Academy, in Nelson County, Ky., was occupied successively by the Union and the Confederate armies. Some hos-tile engagements had taken place in the vicinity of the town and in the neighboring counties, and as a result the place was kept in a state of feverish anxiety. The victorious and the defeated were attended with the usual result, killed and wounded men and sickness and suffering on all sides. Here again the peaceful aid of the Sisters came at an opportune time. Fully aware of the great need there was for experienced nurses, the Mother in charge of Nazareth sent a devoted band of Sisters to the Baptist Female College in Bardstown, which had been temporarily fitted up for hospital uses. On their arrival they found that they had to care for a large number of disabled Confederate soldiers. They quickly began their humane work and carried it to a successful completion. The Confederates were on the march, and their wounds had to be bound up quickly or not at all. When they had withdrawn from the town, taking with them their convalescents, the Union forces came in. Their sick and wounded were also nursed by another band of the same Sisters at St. Joseph's College, which was conducted by the Jesuit fathers, but which, of course, at that time was not in educational use. Thus in the midst of civil strife, with the bullets flying thick and fast, did the Sisters work under one flag—a flag that was respected by Northerner and Southerner alike—the flag of humanity.

Some of the episodes connected with the work of the Sisters was of an exciting and dramatic nature. Late one night in September, 1862, twelve Confederate soldiers in their gloomy gray uniforms marched into Nazareth, after a wearisome journey from Lexington, Ky. They were received, as all visitors are, with kindness and hospitality. They came to ask the Sisters to nurse their sick and wounded comrades. The request was granted at once.

"How many Sisters can you spare for the work?"

"Six now and more later, if necessary," was the prompt reply.

"When will they be ready to return with us?"

"This very night, and at once," was the incisive reply.

Such promptness was as surprising as it was pleasing to the couriers. That very night six Sisters, without anything beyond the familiar garb which they wore, their usual Rosaries and a few books of devotion, started on their mission, ready, if need be, to offer up their lives in what they believed to be the service of God.. They proceeded on their long journey under the protection of a flag of truce. Resting in a farmhouse one night and in

Frankfort, the capital of the State, the next, they finally
reached Lexington in safety. In a few hours they were
installed in one of the large halls in that city, which had
been fitted up for hospital purposes, and without any
preliminaries they began at once to minister to the sufferers who were collected there. Later in the same year
another band of Sisters of Nazareth nursed the Union
soldiers in one of the colleges in another quarter of the
city. As far as can be ascertained this was Transylvania
University.

Events that took place about that time proved that
the Sisters believed no material sacrifices were too great
when made in the cause of suffering humanity. In the
spring of 1862 General Smith, who was then in command of the Union troops, nearly seven thousand strong,
in Paducah, Southern Kentucky, asked the Nazareth
Sisters to come to the assistance of the many sick and
wounded soldiers scattered about that city. He had been
advised to make the request by Dr. Hewit, who had the
general superintendence of all the hospitals in that section of the country. Dr. Hewit was a man of great executive ability, who stood in the very forefront of his profession. He had great faith in the ability of the Sisters as
nurses. He was a convert to the Catholic Church, and a
brother of the saintly superior of the Paulist Fathers of
New York city. As no communication could be had with
the Mother of the house at Nazareth at this time, owing
to the disturbed condition of affairs, the request caused
the Sisters some perplexity. Only for a time, though. A
conclusion was soon reached. Sister Martha Drury at
that time was at the head of St. Mary's Academy, probably the leading educational institution in Paducah. She
resolved to close the schools and go with all of her Sisters

to the relief of the soldiers. They went first to the Marine Hospital and then moved to the Court House, which was known as the Central Hospital. Their experiences in this place were similar to those of the Sisters who were engaged in the hospitals at Louisville.

Their greatest difficulty was experienced in caring for those soldiers who were afflicted with contagious diseases. Typhoid and similar fevers also held sway in their most virulent form. The havoc that war had made in the human frame was painfully evident in this particular hospital. After the close of the war the Sisters returned to their academy, which exists in the town to-day in a flourishing condition. It will ever remain as a monument to that brave little band of Sisters who gave up their peaceful pursuits to minister to the afflicted, and it will ever be pointed out as the house from which Sister Mary Lucy, the gentle music teacher, went forth to meet her martyrdom—a martyrdom as blessed in the sight of heaven as any ever undergone by the saints of old.

The gentleness and devotion with which the Sisters nursed all of the wounded soldiers, no matter what the color of their uniform and regardless of rank, was not unappreciated by either "the boys in blue" or "the boys in gray." Throughout the whole of the war, with but few exceptions, their institutions, mother houses and places of learning were exempt from the usual ravages of internecine strife. This is especially true of the Sisters of Charity of Nazareth. Being in close proximity to the contending armies and their camps, great apprehensions were felt at one time for the safety of Nazareth. This, too, in spite of the fact that the daughters and other relatives of the general officers of both sides were still pupils in the school. At intervals during the war some of the generals called at Nazareth for the purpose of visiting their children. On these occasions they were always hospitably entertained. Although the Sisters felt comparatively safe, they desired some official assurance of that fact. As is usual in such cases, over-timid persons, generally friends of the pupils, now and then sounded alarms. The following letter, received by the Mother Superior from General Wood, the original of which is still in possession of the Sisters, reassured the community that it need not fear an intrusion of the military into the sacred precincts. General Wood was in command of the Union troops:

"Headquarters U.S. Forces,
"Bardstown, KY., January 20, 1862.

"To the Lady Superior and Sisters of the Convent of Nazareth: I have just had the pleasure to receive by the hands of your messenger the very polite and complimentary note of the Right Rev. Bishop Spalding, and I hasten to a apprise you that it is my earnest desire and intention to afford you perfect protection and the enjoyment of all your rights both as an institution and as ladies individually. It is my earnest wish and intention to secure you and your ancient institution (which as educated so many of the fair daughters of my own native State, Kentucky), from all molestation and intrusion, and to this end I pray you will not hesitate to make known to me any grievances you may have on account of any misconduct on the part of any officer or soldier under my command. I assure you it will be equally my duty and my pleasure to attend to any request you may have to make. I beg you to dismiss all apprehensions on account of the presence of the soldiery in your sacred neighborhood, and to continue your peaceful and beneficent vocations as if the clangor of arms did not resound in our midst.

"I have the honor to be, ladies, your very obedient servant, Th. J. Wood

"Brigadier General Commanding.

"Will you do me the favor to send the accompanying note to Bishop Spalding?"

Later on Nazareth must again have been in dread of military trespass, for one of its patrons, Hon. James Guthrie, of Louisville, Secretary of State under a previous administration, applied to President Lincoln for protection for the institution. The President graciously issued the necessary orders, saying that the violation of such orders by any of the commanders would invoke his serious displeasure.

General Smith, Doctors Hewit, Fry, Kay, Austin, and the officers of the Union army surrounded the Sisters with every mark of respect and esteem, and they in turn devoted all their energies to ameliorating the condition of the suffering soldiers.

In addition to the labors of the Sisters of Charity of Nazareth already mentioned, they did very effective work in the neighborhood of Owensboro and Calhoun, Ky. At the last-named place the sick and wounded soldiers were quartered in the two Protestant churches of the town. The Sisters entered these places and attended the sufferers there with the same diligence and patience that characterized their work in every other locality. When Sisters had to be removed on account of their own illness, their places were promptly supplied by other sisters. Reinforcements were on hand to fill every gap in the ranks. As before mentioned, the Sisters of Nazareth neither required nor received compensation of any sort. The hundreds of brave souls that have passed away since the war have no doubt ere this received their reward in a better world. Dr. Foster, who was engaged in the Louisville hospitals while the Sisters were there, wrote eulogistic articles about them in the Louisville papers at that time, but unfortunately these papers were not preserved.

The famous convent school from which these Sisters came forth to do their great work is worthy of more than passing notice. The organization known as the "Sisters of Charity of Nazareth" was founded by Right Rev. Benedict Joseph Flaget, D. D., who was consecrated the first Bishop of Bardstown (now the Diocese of Louisville) in 1810. Henry Clay, who knew this good man well, pronounced him "the best representative of royalty off the throne." The Bishop with Rev. John B. David, built the little log cabin near Bardstown which was to be the birthplace of the new order. It was a success from the start. This was largely due to the piety and administrative capacity of the mothers in charge. They were sketched in an article in the "Catholic World" a few years ago. The first of these was Catherine Spalding, a member of the eminent Kentucky family of that name. She held the position of Superior for more than a quarter of a century, and by her great intellect and modesty won the affection and admiration of all with whom she came in contact. On her death, in 1858, she was attended by another distinguished member of her family, Right Rev. Martin J. Spalding. After her came Mother Francis Gardiner, who proved a worthy successor to a worthy Superior.

The last of this notable trio was Mother Columbo Carroll, in the world Margaret Carroll. For thirty-five years she was directress of studies and teacher of the first and second classes. In 1862, when the civil war was beginning to rage fiercely, she was elected Superioress, and for ten years held that position with credit to herself and the convent school.

While Mother Columbo took no active part in caring for wounded soldiers, she was nevertheless the presiding genius of the establishment at that time, and directed the movements of the Sisters with extraordinary tact and good judgment. She held many interviews with persons in power, and thus warded off many annoyances and troubles. The occasion of Mother Columbo's golden jubilee was celebrated with great fervor by the community on February 22, 1877. A drama, written by Sister Seraphia, entitled "Religion's Tribute to Our Mother on Her Golden Jubilee," was performed by the pupils, and was one of the most successful features of an elaborate programme. One of the touching incidents of the celebration was a poem inspired by the venerable Sister Martha, one of the original five that started at "Old Nazareth," and addressed to Mother Columbo. Mother columbo was one of the first pupils under the care of Sister Martha. The following lines from this graceful offering are worthy of a place here:

> There are many to-day, dear mother,
>   Who are crowning your head with gold,
> And writing fine things of the record
>   Your fifty long years have told.
> And, I too, should come with the others,
>   My offering before you to cast;
> But I am old, and my thoughts, dear mother,
>   Somehow will fain run on the past.
> On the days when our Naz'reth, dear Naz'reth,
>   Was not like what Naz'reth is now;
> When we lived like ravens and sparrows,

Our dear Lord only knew how.

Then we spun, and we wove, and we labored

Like men in the fields, and our fare

Was scanty enough, and our garments

Were coarse, and our feet often bare.

In the following year Mother Columbo's earthly career closed, but the force of her example still lives in the hearts of those who were fortunate enough to be her pupils and associates. Mothers Catherine, Francis and Columbo made a truly wonderful trio. They helped to give Nazareth the reputation it enjoys to-day, and while the school exists their memory will endure. The Sisters of Charity of Nazareth are particularly known in Kentucky, and they are to be found wherever suffering humanity calls.

The ancient house at Nazareth is the mother from which have sprung forty-seven branch houses in various parts of the country—schools, orphan asylums and hospitals. Perhaps the most conspicuous of the latter is the "Mary and Elizabeth Hospital," in Louisville, founded by William Shakespeare Cardwell as a memorial to his wife and a tribute to the Sisters who educated her. The mother house is located a few miles south of Bardstown, which is forty miles from Louisville. The buildings are extensive and imposing. There is a presbytery, a convent and academy, a chapel and the commencement hall. In the old-fashioned hall are full-length portraits of Bishops Flaget and David and Father Chambige. The library contains five thousand volumes, and in the corner is an excellent bust of the late Archbishop Spalding. Mother Helena is the present Superior, and in the administration of her office she has clung to the best traditions of the past.

I am sure I will be pardoned for digressing sufficiently from the main subject of this volume to mention
a few of the distinguished patrons and graduates of this
institution. The patrons included Henry Clay, who sent
his daughter, granddaughter and great-granddaughter
there; Judge Benjamin Winchester, John J. Crittenden,
Judge John Rowan, Zachary Taylor, Jefferson Davis,
James Guthrie, George D. Prentice and Charles Wick-
liffe. The graduates include Sarah Knox Taylor, daughter of President Zachary Taylor; Madame Henrietta
Spalding, now Superior of the Sacred Heart Convent,
in Chicago; the first wife of Jefferson Davis; Mary Eli-
za, daughter of James Breckinridge, of Kentucky; Mary
Gwendoline Caldwell, the original benefactress of the
Washington University; the wife of United States Senator Vance, of North Carolina; the four nieces of Jefferson
Davis, all converts; Mary Anderson, whose professional
career is as much a matter of pride to the good Sisters
as her private virtues, and Miss Taney, the author of the
State poem, "The Pioneer Women of Kentucky," written
for the World's Fair. Such is the institution that furnished
so many nurses for the camps and the hospitals.

CHAPTER XIX

SISTERS OF MT. ST. VINCENT.

A joint request from the Mayor of Cincinnati and the Archbishop of the Diocese promptly answered. Appalling sights witnessed by the Sisters. Young men seated on their own coffins prepare for execution. General Rosecrans and his kindness to the Sisters. The Governor of Indiana calls for nurses. Labors in Kentucky.

The work done by the Sisters of Charity of Mount St. Vincent during the war was of a high order. The first of the Sisters to enter the service as nurses were Sisters Anthony and Sophia. Both were sent to Camp Dennison, Cincinnati, O., on the 1st of May, 1861. On the evening before that date a peculiar holy calm was upon the beautiful convent, which is located on a hill top, just within the limits  of Cincinnati. The structure, surrounded by cedar trees and well-cultivated grounds, had in it the appearance of nobility, religion, peace and charity. The golden rays of the setting sun glanced, then darkened as the Sisters were enjoying their evening walk. A messenger suddenly called for the Superior. The Mother leaves her religious family to attend to business. Only a few minutes elapse when she returns to inform her Sisters that his honor, the Mayor of Cincinnati, and the Most Rev. Archbishop Purcell earnestly request the Sisters of Charity to attend the sick troops who are stationed at Camp Dennison. There were no commands; all willingly volunteered to nurse the sick soldiers. Preparations were quickly made, and on May 1, 1861, five members of the community were named for the camp. Sisters Sophia and Anthony were sent in advance, and Sisters Bernardine, Alphonse and Magdalen followed. Camp Dennison was situated about fifteen miles from Cincinnati, on the Little Miami Railroad. This location was advantageous for many reasons—easy of access, with ample space and abundance of water, level and suitable for military purposes. Mother Josephine, the presiding Superior, accompanied the Sisters to this new home. Their duties consisted principally in attending the soldiers who were suffering from measles, which had broken out in the ranks in the very worst form. After these soldiers had recovered health the Sisters returned to the Mother Superior House at Cedar Grove, Cincinnati.

After the return from Camp Dennison a hasty call was received from the Mayor of Cumberland to attend the sick and wounded of that place. Sister Anthony was among the number, and an amusing incident is related to the Sisters' leave-taking. As the good-byes were being said the train moved off, carrying only Sister Anthony. She arrived in Columbus some hours in advance of the others, who boarded the next train. Arriving at the station in Columbus she received a telegram from the Most Rev. Archbishop of Cincinnati to return immediately to St. John's Hospital to prepare for the sick and wounded soldiers who were there, being brought from different places. The Sisters named for Cumberland were Sisters Sophia, Ambrosia, Etienne, Agnes, Jane, Mary, Gabriella. They were kindly received by a Catholic family. Dr. McMahon, the attending physician, was kind and attentive.

The weather was cold, the accommodations poor and

the hospitals, of which there were twelve, were some distance from each other. There were crowded into these hospitals at one time 2200 poor soldiers, suffering from typhoid fever, pneumonia, erysipelas, etc. The duties were very trying, but a murmur never escaped from the lips of one Sister of Charity. Almighty God and His glory being their only aim, all seemed easy. "Sad and numerous were the scenes we witnessed in these hospitals," says one of the Sisters, "yet none presents itself more vividly to my mind to-day than the suffering of the boy soldiers longing for home and mother. How often were those endearing words, 'Mother,' 'Home,' mentioned!"

Sister Jane says: "I had in my ward a droll boy named Billy. Now, our Billy had watched the Sisters for some time and addressed me thus: 'Lady, what is that I hear the boys call you? Sister! Ah, that is a beautiful name. Well, Sister, will you give me your Bible? I would like to know something of your religion." Billy received the little Bible, or rather a small catechism, of which he made good use. He was soon baptized, made his first holy communion, and his zeal did not end here. "Often have I seen him on a platform explaining the words of his catechism to his comrades, many of whom became fervent children of the Church. Many hundreds of like instances could be cited, but I trust they are written in the Book of Life."

Sister Agnes spent about three months in Cumberland nursing the sick soldiers. She then returned to St. John's Hospital, Cincinnati, to nurse the soldiers who were being sent from Richmond and Nashville to the city. "It was here I witnessed the most appalling sights," she says; "men wanting arms or legs, and sometimes wanting both arms and legs—pale, haggard faces, worn from long marching and fasting. Many, I think, died of broken hearts. Faces and voices haunt me yet, calling for home and dear ones whom they were destined never again to behold on earth. The streets of this now flourishing city were then the scenes of extreme suffering and misery. Frequently fine young men, seated on their own coffins, passed through on their way to execution on some neighboring hillside."

About the 16th of February the Sisters received a hasty call from Cumberland. Mother Josephine and Rev. Father Collins were to accompany them to the scene of their duties. They reached Wheeling about 5 P. M. the next day, and received hospitality from the Visitation Nuns. The next morning, in the face of a blinding storm of sleet and snow, the Sisters started for Cumberland, where they were met at the station by Dr. McMahon, the surgeon of the post. They walked in procession through the streets, and were the objects of much curiosity. That evening they secured some rooms, but slept on the floor. The next morning they were assigned some apartments in the house of a Southern gentleman, Dr. Healy, whose sympathy with the South compelled him to leave home and family. The accommodations here were little better than at the hotel. The bunks were made of rough boards, covered with straw ticks, and the pillows were of the same material.

Pages would not suffice to relate all the good done in Cumberland. Often during the stillness of night one might have gazed on a Sister as she stood at the cot of a dying soldier, heard her whisper words of consolation and religion in his ears, saw her close gently his dying eyes. Thus they passed long, weary nights.

Early in March, 1863, the Sisters of Mount St. Vincent, who had already done valiant service in other localities, were invited to go to Nashville to nurse the sick and wounded of that place. Those named were Sisters Anthony, Constantina, Louise, Benedicta and Gabriella. They left Cincinnati March 19, 1863, and were accompanied by Rev. Father Tracy. There were four hospitals at this place, fairly well adapted for their purpose. Sister Constantina, who took charge of the first one, proved to be an angel of mercy to the poor invalids. The building was formerly an old cotton mill, located on an eminence known as College Hill. The Sisters were quartered in a small house opposite to this place, and during their stay were treated with the greatest consideration. Many of the wounded were sent to this place after the battle of Stone River. Most of the patients were young, and they suffered intense agony.

At one time measles became quite epidemic among the soldiers, from which many of them died. It was during the mission at this place that General Rosecrans, with his body-guard, made daily visits to the sick. He was wont to say in his kind, jovial way: "Come, come, boys, you are foxing; these Sisters are too good to you," then laugh heartily at his remarks. He was very kind to all the Sisters. The next important call to duty was at New Creek. The Sisters of Charity named for this colony were Sister Sophia, in charge, assisted by Sisters Ann, Cecelia, Beatrice, Stainlaus, Etienne, Laurence and Benedicta. The chaplain was Rev. Father Corcoran.

From the diary of one of the above-named sisters the following is extracted: "We left Cedar Grove Academy June 9, 1862, for New Creek. Arriving at our destination, we were assigned a tent, erected for our accommodation by order of Dr. McMahon. This gentleman, however,

BATTLE OF WILSON'S CREEK.

soon procured better quarters for us with a family named Dinges. Here we performed our duties of nursing the sick and wounded with energy and zeal During our stay at New Creek we were treated with great kindness and respect, particularly by Colonel Miller, who, although a Protestant, proved a sincere friend of priest and Sisters.

"It is not surprising that our peculiar dress was a source of amusement to many persons who had never before seen a religious. We were frequently asked why we dressed so differently from other ladies. We are happy to relate that our care and kindness removed many prejudices against our religion. We remained at New Creek about three months; then the army moved to Culpepper Court House. We followed in ambulances and nursed the sick soldiers in pitched tents on the camp grounds. Some of the soldiers had typhoid fever, of which disease many of them died. When the Confederates were victorious at Harper's Ferry we retreated to Washington, whence we returned to the Mother House, Cincinnati."

Gallipolis was the next assignment. The Sisters named for the field of charity were Sisters Louis, Ambrosia, Euphrasia, Basilia, Gonzaga, Laurence, Constantina and Seraphine. About eight months after their return from Cumberland they were ordered to this location to attend the soldiers from Winchester and Lynchburg. The wounded did not reach the hospitals until fourteen days after the battle. The misery and suffering presented was most frightful. The attending physician was Dr. Stone, and the chaplain was Rev. Father Callenberg. Sister Gonzaga, a very holy person, who has since gone to her reward, took quite and interest in little Toby, a little darky, who was conspicuous about the camp, and who endeavored, whenever an opportunity occurred, of instructing him in the knowledge and love of God. When she thought she had instructed him sufficiently and an examination would not be out of place, she called him to her and said: "Toby, who made you?"

"Dun no, Sister," he answered.

She then said to him: "Well, Toby, who made the trees, the grass, the flowers and all these beautiful things which we see around us?"

The little fellow looked at her for awhile and said: "Dun no; dey was all hyar when I comed."

The soldiers in Gallipolis acted as gentlemen in their intercourse with the Sisters. The sight of a Sister was sufficient to check the east levity. Men who had been taught to look on Catholics as dangerous people learned to love and respect the faith which taught even women to sacrifice their lives for the comfort or relief of the soldiers.

The Governor of Indiana made application to the Most Rev. Archbishop of Cincinnati for the Sisters to care for and nurse his troops in Richmond, Ky. Sisters Anthony and Sophia were among the first ones sent. They traveled in ambulances from Cincinnati. The following are extracts from the diaries of these religious:

"Much, very much, might be said of our work at Richmond, but God alone could tell the story. En route from here (Cincinnati) we witnessed sights the most appalling; the grounds were covered with wounded, dying and dead bodies. Some of the dead bodies were only partially covered, hands and feet protruding. The weather being very hot added not a little to the hardships of the scene of action.

"Arriving in Richmond, we began work immediately. The hospital had been an academy, affording wards larger and better than many other locations during the war. Shortly after attending to those suffering from the most severe wounds, a Sister discovered a poor soldier crouched in a corner. For hours he had lain under the burning rays of the sun, suffering severely from a wound received in his shoulder. The flesh surrounding the wound was dreadfully mangled, and owing to neglect was swarming with vermin. Pale and haggard he looked. I shall never forget him. We washed and dressed his wounds and administered the necessary cordials, and when we placed him in a clean cot the reader may imagine his joy.

"Another ward in this hospital accommodated more than one hundred men. Seventeen were lying on the floor, each of whom had lost one or more limbs. 'What shall we do with these poor men?' was the constant query.

"The first death that occurred was of a man who had been shot through the lung. He had been exposed to the heat of the sun, and had eaten no food for hours. Everything was done for him, but his moments on earth were few. He received the last sacraments and died a beautiful death. His last words were: 'Thanks to the Sisters.' This death and its attending circumstances were the cause of many conversions. One pious Episcopalian asked the Sisters for books on the subject of religion, saying that 'a religion which teaches gentle ladies such devoted self-sacrifice for suffering humanity must be divine.'

"No page in history can record such noble deeds of courage and devotion as that illuminating the life and labors of these Sisters during their stay at Richmond.

Particularly noble was our much esteemed Sister Anthony.([1])

"History can point to annals of devotion and self-sacrifice of noble women, but no annals are so rich in noble work and silent charity as that of our loved Sister. Hundreds of men scattered over the States will always remember and revere her. She seemed happy when engaged in alleviating the sufferings of others, particularly of the soldiers."

The following anecdote from the diary of a Sister illustrates the influence that the religious possessed with these soldier boys:

"It is midnight. The moon sends her welcome light to cheer my watching hours. There is stillness all around, although many soldiers are suffering. But listen! I hear moans. A poor soldier is dying; must away to his cot. Yes, he was dying. I prayed, then spoke: 'Now, my young friend, you are going home.' 'Home!' said the boy; 'what do you mean, Sister?' 'Why, would you not like to go to heaven?'" 'Sister, are you going there when you die?" I assured the boy that I sincerely hoped to go there. 'Well,' said he, 'so do I.' I called the chaplain, had the soldier baptized and ere the morning dawned this beautiful soul was in heaven."

---

(1). In order to preserve the continuity of the narrative as much as possible the most important work done by Sister Anthony and other Mother Seton Sisters has been outlined in Chapter VII.

CHAPTER XX.

THE SISTERS OF MERCY.

An application from the Secretary of War to the Superior of the order.
Nine Sisters depart for the Government Hospital at Beaufort,
N. C. A dinner of pork and beans and mouldy bread. The
steward who expected the Sisters to poison some of the patients.
Complimented by Jefferson Davis. A convent confiscated by
General Slocum. Secular ladies who had "other engagements"
when the smallpox appeared.

None of the Sisters who gave up their time and talents
to the cause of suffering humanity did better work than
the Sisters of Mercy. Their most conspicuous service was

on Southern battlefields, although, like their colleagues in
this merciful work, they were
subject to the call of duty no
matter whence it came. On the
19th of June, 1862, Vicar General Starrs, of New York, applied for a sufficient corps of
nurses to take charge of a mili-
tary hospital in North Carolina. The proposition was laid
before the Sisters of St. Catherine's Convent of Mercy,
in New York City, and the invitation promptly and cheerfully accepted.

Nine Sisters were selected for the mission. They in-
cluded Sisters Mary Augustine MacKenna, M. Elizabeth
Callanan, M. Paul Lennon, M. Gertrude Ledwith, M.
Paula Harris, M. Veronica Dimond and M. Agatha Mac-

Carthy. The Mother Superior and Mother Alphonsus decided to go with the party. The chaplain was Rev. Father Bruhl, a native of Hungary, sixty years of age. He had a long, flowing grey beard, and while he was not possessed of an adequate knowledge of English, he was equipped with a valuable experience of hospital work incident to warfare. This was derived from long and laborious service in the French army during the war which resulted in the taking of Algiers.

The Sisters bade adieu to their convent friends on the 15th of July, and boarded the Government boat Catawaba, which was to take them to the scene of their future labors at Beaufort, N. C. The Sisters were under the care of General Foster, who showed them every consideration.

It happened that 500 horses, destined for cavalry service, were to be passengers on the vessel, and as the tedious and somewhat distressing process of getting them into the hold only commenced after the Sisters boarded the boat the Catawaba could not leave the dock until the afternoon of July 16.

The structure which was known as the "hospital" is thus admirably described by Mother Mary Carroll: "It was a large building that had formerly been a summer hotel. It was so near the shore that at high tide the waves rolled in and out under the timber props on which it was erected. It was a frame building, containing 500 rooms. The Sisters arrived in the midst of a heavy rain storm. As they passed from the wharf to the building, in single file, all dressed in black, the patients, looking out of the windows, took them for nine lone widows, seeking the dead bodies of their husbands!

"The place contained no furniture except a few miserable bedsteads, and was in a most desolate condition. There was only one broom and very few utensils. The broom, in possession of Chloe, a saucy little negress, was seldom available. Along the shore were wrecks of pianos, tables, chairs, glass, etc. There were no candles or lamps, and every one was compelled to retire before night."

Truly, a forsaken habitation for women, the most of whom had been brought up in homes of comfort and refinement. The house was extremely dirty, and the Sisters got very little rest the first night. The next day a transformation took place. The new-comers, with what assistance they could obtain from the natives, began the work of housecleaning. "Bob" Sproul, a young negro, who was presented with a red shirt, was installed as water carrier. He was so delighted with the conspicuous but useful garment that he wore it outside of his Sunday coat and proclaimed himself "the best-dressed man in North Carolina."

The first dinner of the Sisters was a "sumptuous repast" of pork and beans and mouldy bread, to which was added coffee sweetened with molasses. Eight rooms were assigned to the nurses. These rooms were located on the second story, and opened out on a piazza overlooking the sound. In spite of the great consideration shown the Sisters, they were compelled to undergo many privations. Two of the Sisters, whose names are not recorded, died from the effects of these hardships, and several were dangerously ill.

Nearly all the patients differed from the Sisters in religious belief, and their coming caused several humorous as well as pathetic incidents. Many of the soldiers had never met "a real, live" Sister before. Their minds had been installed with false notions, and it was some days before they appreciated the Sisters in their real character and at their true worth. After the work in the locality was finished, the steward of the hospital confessed that he often sat up until 1 o'clock in the morning watching the Sisters, fully expecting them to poison the patients, or do some other terrible thing, they being "confessed emissaries of the Pope."

The dress of the Sisters scared some of the others. "Great heavens!" shrieked one patient to the nurse that bent over him, "are you a man or a woman? But your hand is a woman's hand; its touch is soft, and your voice is gentle. What are you?"

"Only a poor servant of the Great Master, come from afar to serve you," said the Sister.

"Sister," moaned another, I'm dying. I want to be what you are; help me."

"What the Sister believes, I believe," cried another, who had probably never known any religion. "Sister, tell me what to answer when the priest comes to baptize me."

When the patients finally recovered sufficiently to leave the hospital they would offer little keepsakes to the Sisters—a button, a shred of blue or gray, a pebble—with a fervent "God bless you, Sister. I'll never forget you. Pray for me."

The Sisters became part of the patients' lives. They did more than nurse them. They cheered them in their hours of despondency, and wrote letters for them to the anxious ones at home. Some of the Sisters, by reason of ill health, were compelled to return to New York. Their places were promptly filled with recruits from the Mother House.

The perfect discipline among the Sisters, the spirit of humility and self-sacrifice that prevailed generally, was exhibited when the Mother Superior in charge was succeeded by Mother M. Augustine MacKenna. Mother Augustine was one of the women who had previously prepared food for the soldiers. The patients and others were surprised to learn, after the change, that she was not only a person of great executive ability, but that she was also a woman of the utmost refinement, and one of the most intellectual members of the Sisterhood.

In October, 1862, it was found that Beaufort was too much exposed for the patients, and they were removed to Newberne. The residence of Governor Stanley was placed at the disposal of the Sisters. It was transformed into a handsome convent, the parlor being used as a chapel. After the raids at Goldsboro all of the wards were crowded with sick and wounded. Americans, Germans, Irish and Creoles, all came in the same ambulances, with their clothing matted to the skin from ghastly wounds. They were all treated alike by the nurses, who were working in the cause of humanity.

Some time after the war Jefferson Davis, ex-President of the late Confederacy, addressing a number of the Sisters, said: "Will you allow me, ladies, to speak a moment with you? I am proud to see you once more. I can never forget your kindness to the sick and wounded in our darkest days, and I know not how to testify my gratitude and respect for every member of your noble order."

Mr. Davis met Mother Mary Teresa Austen Carroll in 1887, and he reiterated his expressions of thankfulness toward the sisters who had performed what he called a great work. Many other dignitaries and soldiers on both the Union and Confederate sides testified to the good services rendered by the Sisters of Mercy. Their labors, however, did not end with the war, for after that cruel period they busied themselves in establishing homes for widows and asylums for the orphans.

The Sisters of Mercy also worked with unremitting zeal during the war at Mississippi Springs, Oxford, Jackson and Shelby Springs. The Southern Sisters, after devoting months to the service of the sick and wounded soldiers in these localities, returned home to Vicksburg only to find that General Slocum had confiscated their convent for a headquarters. Mather Michael O'Connor, S. J., formerly Bishop of Pittsburg, was a personal friend of Secretary of the War Stanton, and he at once interested himself in the cause of the Sisters. After a brief correspondence their property was restored to them.

In February, 1862, the Mayor of Cincinnati applied to the Archbishop of the same city for a sufficient number of Sisters to nurse the sick and wounded soldiers of the Ohio regiments, The application was sent to Mother Teresa, who not only complied with it, but headed the delegation of Sisters that went to the front. Grant and Johnson had met at Shiloh and the battle of Pittsburg Landing was the result. The Sisters went down the river on the Superior, preparing bandages and other hospital necessaries on the way.

There was plenty of work to do when they landed, and it was entered upon with zeal. A number of secular ladies also arrived upon the scene and insisted upon aiding in the work. The Sisters cheerfully accepted their assistance. In a few days small-pox broke out among the patients and the secular ladies suddenly remembered that they had important engagements elsewhere. They deserted the temporary hospitals with more haste than dignity, leaving the Sisters in undisputed possession. Mother Teresa was especially devoted during the small-pox epidemic, joining the other Sisters in personally dressing the wounds of the patients suffering from this loathsome disease.

The Sisters of Mercy also worked zealously in St. Louis. They visited almost daily the hospitals on the Fair Grounds in that city, where an average of from 1000 to 2000 sick and wounded men were being cared for. Many other visitations were made to private hospitals and private dwellings, where the necessities of the occasion happened to place the disabled soldiers. Particular attention was paid to the patients in the McDowell College, used as a hospital for sick prisoners of war. The Sisters sent large hampers to this institution filled with clothing and with delicacies in the way of food and drink.

Some of the poor sufferers were stone-blind, but as soon as they discovered that the Sisters of Mercy were among them they would stretch out their hands, crying, "Welcome, Sisters. If you had never given us anything we would still rejoice to have you amongst us with your consoling words."

Three of the prisoners of war in the McDowell Hospital were condemned to be shot as a measure of "retaliation"—one of the cruel customs of the war. The sentence of death had been passed with all due military solemnity, and the carrying out thereof was inevitable. Knowing this to be the case the Sisters visited the condemned men in their cells and urged them to make suitable preparations for death. The unfortunate men received the Sisters with cordiality, but they were furious at the decree which condemned them to death, and absolutely refused to consider any suggestions which would cause them to forgive their enemies. While the Sisters were pleading with the men an armed guard stood at the door and two other sentinels paced up and down the corridor with a regularity and grimness that filled the scene with awe.

Finally perseverance conquered. The doomed men relented, and a clergyman accompanied them to the scaffold. They were blindfolded when making fervent acts of contrition, and while engaged in this pious devotion were launched into eternity.

One of the duties that devolved upon the Sisters during the war, as well as thereafter, was the care of the widows and orphans of the soldiers. There was one pathetic case in the McDowell Institution. It concerned two little girls, daughters of Southern prisoners. Their mother and married sister had died in the prison, and their father was among the missing. The little ones were seriously ill when they were brought to the attention of the Sisters. They were in such a sad plight that their clothes had to be changed in the yard, and the cast-off garments buried. Baptism was administered to them, and their physical needs given immediate attention. The younger child, about 8 years of age, died a few days later. The other recovered and was instructed in the ways necessary for a life of virtue and usefulness. At the close of the war she was claimed by her father. He had searched the city in a vain endeavor to find his offspring, and when he had all but abandoned hope located her in the "House of Mercy," conducted by the Sisters. On being given positive pledges that the child would be properly cared for the Sisters restored her to the anxious father.

Mary Mulholland, who became known as Mother Francis of the Sisters of Mercy, did wonderfully effective work during the war. She was born in Armagh, Ireland, in 1808, but came to this country when a mere child. Her one desire was to become a member of one of those devoted Sisterhoods that give their lives to the service of the Creator. In spite of the opposition of her parents this object was finally achieved. The opportunity came when Bishop Quarter engaged a colony of Sisters of Mercy for Chicago in 1843. The journey to the Western city was by stage and boat. A terrific storm arose while the party was crossing Lake Michigan. A high wave swept over the deck of the vessel, carrying men, women and children into the angry waters.

Mary Mulholland was one of those that went overboard, and when a brave man—a Mr. Ogden, who afterwards became the first Mayor of Chicago—attempted to save her she cried: "Leave me to my fate; save the others." He did save others, but he saved her, too, for a future of usefulness and good works. The future Mother of the Order received the white veil from the Bishop in April, 1847, and was professed by dispensation December 28, 1848. Her business accomplishments made her a valuable member of the community.

Speaking of her experience in the Civil War Mother Carrol says([1]): When the Civil War broke out Mother

---

(1). Annals of the Sisters of Mercy.

Francis organized among the Sisters a band of volunteer nurses to minister to the sick and wounded on Southern battlefields. She accompanied them to Missouri, and set them to work. In Chicago she looked after the soldiers, whether sick or prisoners. A sister who shared with her the fatigues of these great works writes: "Many soldiers crying out in agony on their hard beds blessed her as she passed her holy hands over their burning brows. The absent fathers and mothers for whom they called could not come, but this gentle, humble, self-sacrificing soul supplied their places. A Southern lad of 18 cried like a child when she laid her hand on his clammy brow. 'Oh, God,' he murmured, 'I thought you were my mother.' She prepared him for death, and he died in her arms.

Mother Francis was a power in the prisons and hospitals when the most influential gentlemen and committees were refused admission. There were so many sympathizers with Confederates in Chicago that a general uprising between Federals with Secessionists was often feared. Whenever or wherever the Sisters of Mercy appeared the sick and wounded soldiers, whether in blue or gray uniform, were abundantly supplied with everything necessary for their comfort. Once when Secretary Stanton refused to supply more rations during the current month the case was laid before the President, who wrote:

"To all whom it may concern:—On application of the Sisters of Mercy in Chicago of the Military Hospital in Washington furnish such provisions as they desire to purchase and charge the same to the War Department.

ABRAHAM LINCOLN."

After the war Mother Francis continued her useful work in many convents of her order, dying peacefully on December 8, 1888.([2])

---

(2). Many of the facts in the foregoing chapter have been gleaned from the annals of the Sisters of Mercy, which have been ably edited by Mother Mary Carroll.

CHAPTER XXI.

THE NORTH CAROLINA HOSPITALS.

Solicitude of the Sisters for the patients under their care. Friendships formed that were only parted by death. Interesting reminiscences of Mother M. Augustine MacKenna concerning the Government Hospital at Beaufort, N. C. A victim of camp fever and how he was relieved by the nurses.

There were many incidents of interest in the hospitals at Beaufort and Newberne, N.C., told by Mother M. Augustine MacKenna to her niece, Sister Dolores,  and other members of the community of the Sisters of Mercy. Some of these were incorporated in a neat little book called the "Milestone," issued last year to commemorate the golden jubilee or 50th anniversary of the Sisters of Mercy in New York City. The principal points are embodied in the paragraphs that follow.([1])

Beaufort is a village on a little peninsula that runs out into Bogue Sound. It is directly opposite to Fort Macon, which is built on an island in these shallow waters. Before the war Beaufort was a place of fashionable resort for sea bathing, and its principal hotel, though a frame building, contained five hundred rooms and was elabo-

---

(1). The author desires to express his thanks to General James R. O'Beirne, of New York city, who aided him very materially in obtaining the material in question.

rately furnished; but having been sacked in the spring of 1862 everything of value was destroyed. It was therefore in a sadly denuded condition when it was utilized as a hospital and made the temporary resting place of two hundred disabled men, just two months previous to the coming of the Sisters.

Only the common army rations had been provided for these sufferers, and their situation was painful in the extreme. A complete dearth of utensils in every department marked the early management of the hospital. There was no modern means of washing clothes, it had to be done with a few small, old-fashioned tubs, and the untrained hands of some escaped field slaves.

No artificial light of any kind, not even a candle, could be procured at that time in Beaufort, and there was no proper food or refreshing drink for the patients. The Sisters sent an urgent requisition to the United States Sanitary Commission, and very soon the hospital was amply provided with all necessaries and many comforts in the line of dressing-gowns, towels, sponges, castile soap, "Aunt Klyne's cologne," etc.

Even in the midst of such suffering many amusing incidents frequently occurred, as for instance when a Sister undertook the task of getting the kitchen cleaned. This establishment had been until now under the control of a certain functionary called the kitchen steward. He was a native of Maine, of short, stout build; never wore shoes (on account of the heat, he said), but always wore an immense straw hat in the house and out of it, and constantly sat in a wheelbarrow at the kitchen door with a huge bunch of keys dangling from the belt of his ticking apron. He was a woodcutter in his native forests before he was drafted into the army; he could neither read nor write, and his name was Kit Condon. The negroes, and indeed his fellow-soldiers, called him "Mr. Kit!" It took a great amount of persuasion to induce "Mr. Kit" to relinquish his keys, the token of his dignified office, to the "North lady," as the Sister in charge was called, and he eyed the cleaning process from his wheelbarrow with evident disapproval.

"Mr. Trip," a soldier six feet high, was another important personage in the culinary department, and this with "Edward, the baker," who made his "cookies," buns, pies, etc., on the marble top of a ruined billiard table, completed the kitchen force.

The renovating that kitchen received was marvelous! Piles of greasy sand were swept into the ocean through a never-to-be-forgotten hole in the very midst of the kitchen floor. The house being built on "piles" or timber supports, this portion of it was directly above the water. After the debris of a meal had been thrown them through this opening the fishes could be seen by hundreds when the tide was in, and nothing could surpass their veracity, unless indeed it was their quarrelsomeness, for they seemed bent on annihilating one another.

One day much excitement was created by the arrival of an escaped slave. A tall young girl was seen running breathlessly across the sort of bridge or causeway that connected the hospital premises with the village of Beaufort. She was quickly followed by an elderly Southerner, and he was very close to her when she got the end of her perilous race.

The soldiers cheered her wildly, and called to her that she was safe with them, while they pointed their bayonets at her pursuer and swore in no measured terms that they would pitch him into the sea if he laid a finger on the girl.

However, some of the officers took up the case and brought both man and girl into the General's office, in order to come to an understanding. The man cried out, "She is my gal; she is my gal' she was born upon my place; she is mine." But the General would not listen to this claim, and told the man the girl was free from the moment she claimed the protection of the army.

She was all trembling and exhausted with fear, fatigue and excitement, and during the remainder of that day she had to be encouraged and consoled and petted like a baby, although she was 17. Her name was Ellen, and she had a sweeter face and softer manners than are usually found among colored persons.

Towards the end of October the tides became very high, and the water was driven under and around the hospital with greater impetuosity by the wind. On one occasion the water was profane enough to invade the "Hall" where a good old Unitarian minister held forth to his sparse congregation, and the "meeting" had to be discontinued. The next tide was still more daring, for it swept clear through the kitchen and dining room, leaving in both a debris of dead crabs and little fish, not to mention seaweed of every variety. All this rendered the place very uninhabitable, and General Foster, with his usual thoughtfulness, authorized the Sisters to move to New Berne and to take possession of Stanley House, the officers and doctors receiving orders at the same time to remove the patients thither as soon as possible.

The two Sisters sent to inspect the prospects in New

AN ARMY EXPRESS OFFICE.

Berne had a delightful sail in an open boat through the sound, past Fort Macon and past the sea-green islands on to Moorhead city, which "city" consisted of twelve houses and a few "shanties." On arriving at New Berne the Sisters were agreeably surprised at the aspect of the "Stanley" House, so-called because it had originally been the home of Governor Stanley, of North Carolina.

A handsome lawn or courtyard lay in front of the house. Beautiful large cedars grew within this enclosure, and as their berries were now ripening flocks of mock-ingbirds were rejoicing in their branches and filling the air with their own inimitable harmony. In a corner stood a grand old "Pride of India," the first tree of the kind the Sisters had ever seen; climbing roses clustered around the windows, and numbers of little songsters made their abode in the foliage.

The house was fine and in perfect repair, having been used as General Burnside's headquarters. It had not been ransacked or rifled as most of the other houses had been. Of the two large handsome parlors one was set aside for a chapel, and a beautiful one it became soon afterwards.

In the last week of October the hospital at Beaufort was vacated, and the sick soldiers were much more com-fortably settled in their winder quarters. The "hospital" was distinct from the "Stanley residence" and consisted of three houses and several newly-erected pavilions; a nice shady path and a large garden separated these from the Sisters' domicile.

In December, 1862, General Foster, with a large de-tachment of the men under his charge made an attack on the town of Goldsboro, North Carolina, and almost ru-ined it. An immense number of soldiers were wounded, and, as the doctors' stores had not arrived, the surgeons had no old linen or lint with which to bind up the wounds of the poor sufferers. For this reason they presented a most fearful spectacle. Some had their heads and faces wrapped in coarse cloth, and were so besmeared with blood that the sight was a painful one.

Others, indeed the greater number, had either one or both feet in a terrible condition, the feet having been pierced with balls. There were broken legs, broken arms and one unhappy victim had both hands shot off, and the condition of these agonizing wounds was something terrible.

The first task of the Sisters was to feed the wretched sufferers, who had had but little care bestowed upon them. After that the difficult and distressing duty of cleansing their wounds was undertaken and was left entirely to the Sisters.

One very large man named Sherman, an Englishman, had his mouth and chin so shattered that the doctors decided that his mouth had better not be touched, as he must certainly die. However, the Sisters with soft sponges and warm water began to loosen the horrible rags with which the poor man's face and head were covered. He, poor fellow, had heard enough of the doctors' opinion to render him hopeless, and when he found that efforts were being made to relieve him he tried to evince his gratitude by signs. When the wraps were removed blood began to flow from his mouth, and a Sister took out with her finger several loosened teeth, and thus greatly facilitated his breathing. The utmost possible care was taken of this patient, and the satisfaction of seeing him perfectly restored to health, though disfigured in a dreadful manner, was in itself a great reward. The dumb gratitude he displayed when he came to say "good-bye" as he was leaving the hospital was very pathetic.

Another interesting case was that of David Brant, a ruddy-faced lad about 18 years of age. He was suffering in some way that could not at first be discovered. It was noticed that he kept moving his feet in a distressing sort of way. These members were uncovered, when, to the surprise of the Sister attending him, it was found that he had still his boots on and that they seemed ready to burst. Some of the soldiers at hand came with knives and cut them off, piece by piece, with great difficulty, and then, alas! it was found that veins of the boy's legs had burst open, and his boots were filled with clotted blood. The doctors were sent for, and had great trouble in stanching the blood, and in tying up the arteries. It need hardly be added that the poor lad died the next day in great agony. He was the victim of a forced march in which the men were made to run for several miles without stopping. The Sisters wrote to his father the least painful account possible of the poor son's death, and received a most grateful reply, the bereaved gentleman adding that but for them he would never have known the real truth of the sad event.

"Hiram" was a victim of camp-fever; unfortunately for him he had been kept in camp too long after he took sick, and the fly-blister had been applied to the back of his neck. Some of his comrades took it off, but applied no dressing of any kind, so that the coarse blue flannel collar of his shirt grew into the raw sore, and his hair also festered into it. It was his cries that first attracted the attention of a Sister, for he was brought into the hospital in this condition.

She found a soldier trying to relieve him by applying a coarse wet towel in cold water to his neck, and this caused the screams of the sufferer. A soft sponge, warm water and castile soap came into requisition here, and when the hair was cut so as to free it from the sore, and the gathers of the shirt loosened from the collar, the poor boy began to feel a little relief. As he lay with his face buried in the pillow he did not see who was attending him.

"Who is doing that?"

"A Sister of Mercy," was the reply.

"No," said he, "no one but my mother could do it."

By degrees the sore was nicely dressed with soft old linen and cold water —the only dressing allowed by the doctors—and then Hiram stole a glance at his new friend and nurse.

"What are you, at all?" was the first question.

The Sister tried to make him understand what a Sister of Mercy does, or tries to do for those who suffer, and he sank back in his pillow, saying,

"I don't care what you are; you are a mother to me."

He was only 16, full of bright intelligence and wit, but after suffering dreadfully for six weeks from the fatal fever he died in the arms of his father, who had been apprised by the Sisters of poor Hiram's condition , and had come from Boston to remain with him.

Many such sad incidents might be related, but no doubt such are the records of every hospital. The Sisters continued their services until May, 1863, when General Foster, under whose protection they had been able to effect much good, was ordered to Tallahassee, Florida, where there was no need of a military hospital. The necessity for the Sisters was now not so great in North Carolina—most of the poor men having been released from their sufferings, many by death and others by recovery—so preparations were commenced for returning to New York.

The Sisters felt very much for the poor negro girls who had attached themselves to them so affectionately, and who in their simple ignorance thought that the "North ladies" could do anything and everything. Some very amusing incidents took place in connection with our "contrabands." One night a Sister, having forgotten something in the kitchen, went for it at a later hour than usual. All the negro girls and women who worked for the hospital—scrubbing, washing, ironing, etc.—slept in the rooms over the kitchen; and Sister, hearing peals of laughter, did not think it beneath her dignity to act the part of a listener under these "colored" circumstances.

She therefore went noiselessly up the stairs, and to her great amusement, heard herself perfectly imitated by one of the girls. This Sister had for many months been giving the general instructions to the women and girls; now she heard the very tones of her voice and the manner of her delivery most perfectly reproduced; another genius undertook to represent another Sister, and so on until every Sister was portrayed, to the great delight of the company, the members of which never dreamed of the amused listener on the kitchen stairs.

The solicitude of the Sisters for the welfare of their patients frequently caused warm friendships that continued long after the close of the war. Sister Mary Gertrude

and Mother Mary Augustine were two of the Sisters attached to the hospitals in Beaufort and Newberne. One
of those cases that came under their care was that of
Charles Edward Hickling, of the Forth-fifth Regiment,
Massachusetts Volunteers. The bravery and manliness of
this young soldier won the hearts of all.

Illness contracted in the service finally caused his
death in 1867. He bore all his suffering with great fortitude. During his illness the Sisters visited him at his
home, and after his death sent consoling letters to the
bereaved family.

These letters show the tender sympathy and generous interest of the Sisters towards the soldiers to such an
extent that the writer feels justified in giving brief extracts
from what were intended to be personal missives.

Sister Mary Gertrude, under date of January 3, 1868,
wrote to the parents: "How can I express to you in adequate terms the very great grief and affectionate sympathy I feel toward you in your great affliction. May God
be your comfort and your refuge in this trying hour, for
in sufferings such as these no creature can give you consolation. We must look higher. He who sent the cross can
alone give the power to sustain its weight. Do not give
way to despondency, my very dear friends. The dear boy
has only gone before you for a time—we are all hasten-
ing towards our turn. In a very little time we, too, shall
have passed the eternal gates, there to meet all we have
loved and lost, and with them praise the tender mercy of
the good God to us whilst in our exile * * * I have
been, and am still with you, in thought and spirit, going
through the least detail of all the trying circumstances of
this sad bereavement."

Mother Augustine, who was the Superior of the Sisters at Newberne Hospital, writing to a devoted friend—Miss Susan Messinger—said on January 4, 1868:

"So our brave soldier boy is gone, his long and trying march has brought him to the goal, and in his young enthusiasm he has gone to join the numerous band of those who were his companions on the field and in the fight, in danger and in privations, exposure and fatigue, but not in the long years of patient and heroic endurance which requires more of a martyr's fortitude than a soldier's courage. Dear Charles! He is the last of our soldier boys—the last link that bound us to the Boston Regiment, the brave Massachusetts Volunteers, whose heroism we shall never forget. ★ ★ ★ Eternity! Dear Charles knows its wonders now. Let us pray that we may so live, so use our powers here that our eternity may be with those who have fought their way through the trials and sorrows of life to its unending peace."

CHAPTER XXII.

LABORS IN THE WEST.

The Sisters of Mercy attended the sick and wounded in the "Irish
Brigade," the command organized by Colonel Mulligan, whose
life was sacrificed in the Union cause. Sisters leave Chicago for
Lexington, Mo. One brave, religious Sister who wanted to finish
her office before being shot. General Fremont and his staff call
upon the Sisters. Taking charge of the hospital department of
the steamship Empress.

Soon after the beginning of the war the "Irish Brigade" was organized in Chicago by Colonel Mulligan,
whose life was sacrificed in the Union cause towards
the close of the war. He was
a devout Catholic, and warm
friend of the Sisters of Mercy.
As his command were nearly
all Catholics he determined
to secure the services of the
Sisters in behalf of his sick
and wounded, and, before
his departure from Chicago,
called on Reverend Mother
Francis, from whom he ob-
tained the promise that the
suffering among his soldiers should be cared for by her
children. This is the mother of whom a brief sketch is
given in a previous chapter. The regiment left Chicago
in the summer of 1861, and was finally stationed at Lexington, Missouri. On September 3, six Sisters of Mercy,
escorted by Reverend Mother Francis and her assistant,
left Chicago under the care of Lieutenant Shanley. The

COLONEL MULLIGAN.

Superiors were to return when the Sisters were settled in Lexington.

The hospital was to be in charge of Sister M. Alphonsus Butler, assisted by her companions. To those who had never been within sight or sound of "war's alarms," this appeared to be an undertaking of no small hazard. The Sisters believed they were risking their lives. "Yes," said one, "I was full convinced I should never see Chicago again."

They went by St. Louis to Jefferson City, from which point they were to proceed to Lexington. During their stay in Jefferson they were the guests of Mr. and Mrs. Mosely, who were ardent sympathizers with the Southern cause. Nothing could exceed their attention and kindness to the Sisters, to whom they showed every mark of respect. When Mr. and Mrs. Mosely withdrew to St. Louis they left their beautiful home at the disposal of their valued guests.

It was rumored that Confederate forces were stationed along the river banks, and that communication with Lexington would be speedily cut off. The Sisters, therefore, embarked on the first boat leaving Jefferson, the "Sioux City," which was to carry them to their destination. It was under the command of Lieutenant Shanley, who was conducting a detachment of troops to Lexington. Several ladies were on board, among whom was Mrs. Mulligan, who with her infant daughter was going to join her husband. As the steamer proceeded up the river the rumors of "danger ahead" became more and more alarming. At length, at the earnest request of some of the ladies, Lieutenant Shanley gave orders to return to Jefferson. On reaching that city the officer in command directed that the ladies who were not willing to undertake the voyage should be put ashore, and that the "Sioux City" should resume her voyage to Lexington.

The second attempt, however, proved that the alarm of the ladies was not unfounded. Danger was constantly apprehended. It was given out as certain that the Confederates were stationed at Glasgow, a small town on the Missouri. When the boat came within a few rods of it the Confederates were seen rushing from the woods on both sides of the river. Sister M. Alphonsus, who was saying her office on deck, saw the men on the right bank uncovering a cannon and preparing to fire. She hurriedly entered the state room saying:

"Here they are!"

"Who?" asked a Sister.

"The Confederates," she replied.

While they were still speaking they heard the whizzing and rattling of bullets outside. The head of the boat was immediately turned, but the firing from both sides of the river continued for some minutes. Had the assailants waited till the boat had come within range of the cannon nothing could have saved her. Their impetuosity defeated their attempt. As it was, the escape of the boat was considered miraculous. The Sisters afterwards met a gentleman who had been among the Confederates at Glasgow on that occasion. He told them that the Southerners never could account for the escape of the "Sioux City." There were five hundred infantry on the right bank and one thousand cavalry on the left. No one on board was wounded, but the craft was very much damaged. The pilot-house was completely riddled, as the

Confederates had aimed particularly at the helmsman. The Southerners afterwards declared they did not know there were women on board when they fired on the boat, above all, the Sisters, for they were especially courteous to all who wore the religious habit. During the danger the other ladies were placed by the officers in the part of the boat which was least exposed. The Sisters stood in readiness to wait on the wounded, but blessed God that there were none such this time. When all peril was over one of the Sisters caused much amusement by saying "I continued to say my office all through the firing, so that I might have it finished before being shot."

During the return voyage much apprehension was felt, because the Confederates were supposed to be in ambush at different points. About ten miles below Glasgow the boat stuck in a sand-bar, and the efforts of the men to release her were more terrifying than the Southern bullets. This was the last attempt made to reach Lexington. Meanwhile Colonel Mulligan's brigade of two thousand men was surrounded by Price's men, supposed to number twenty thousand. For three days the brigade made a gallant resistance. Their supply of water had been cut off for forty-eight hours, when they surrendered to General Price, September 20, 1861. The General proved himself a generous enemy, and his conduct won the esteem and gratitude of his distinguished prisoner. The two men became sincere friends before they parted.

The Sisters continued to occupy the Mosely residence. They experienced the greatest kindness and respect from the colored people left in charge of it. To the simple souls they were a great curiosity.

The old housekeeper wanted all her friends to come

to see the Sisters, and the numbers responded to her ardent invitations. These guests were puzzled to account for the want of resemblance between persons related to each other, as they thought, in the first degree. "You say this lady is your sister," said one, "but she doesn't look like you at all, nor this one, either." It took some time to make them understand that the relationship was not in blood, but in spirit and profession.

The Jefferson City Hospital for the sick and wounded was placed under the care of the Sisters. This charge they readily undertook at the request of the authorities, as their original project of going to Lexington had proved impracticable. They found the poor soldiers in wretched condition. The hospital, a very recently established institution, had not yet sufficient furniture. Convalescing soldiers, who were the only nurses, could not be expected to bestow on the sick the tender care they required. No woman of a religious order had ever before been seen in Jefferson, and such of the soldiers as had heard of them had heard little that was construed to their advantage. The Sisters, therefore, on taking charge of the hospital met with a very cold reception. They showed neither surprise nor annoyance at this, and very soon the coldness and prejudice disappeared, being followed by appreciation and gratitude.

On entering the hospital they found a poor soldier in a woefully neglected condition, lying on a blanket laid on the floor. One of the Sisters requested the nurse to allow her to have a little water. When she received it she knelt beside the poor sufferer and bathed his face and hands, The nurse, a rather stern person, stood by during the process.

"May I ask, madam," said he when she finished, "is that man a relative of yours?"

"No, sir," she replied, "I never saw him before; we are here to take care of the sick, and we attend every patient as we would our nearest and dearest relative."

In a short time the Sisters, by their self-devotion, had gained the good will of the inmates and officers; and the hospital began to wear a better appearance. It took a good while, however, for the citizens and soldiers to become so accustomed to the Sisters as always to recognize them as such. One morning, as they were going procession-ally to Mass they met a new detachment of soldiers, who stepped aside to allow them the sidewalk. They kept a respectful silence until the Sisters had passed, when one turning to another inquired, "Who's dead?"

When General Fremont and his staff came to Jeffer-son they at once visited the sick soldiers. Desiring to have an interview with the Sisters the General was shown to their apartment just as they had assembled for their fru-gal meal. When he knocked the door was opened, and, to their great astonishment, he and his staff, in brilliant uniform, stood before them. The interview was a very pleasant one. General Fremont was on all occasions most courteous to them, and granted everything they asked. Eloquently did they represent to him the wants of the poor soldiers, for whom he promised to provide, and his promises were religiously kept. This officer was noted for his kindness to his soldiers, especially the sick.

The Sisters also received several visits from Colonel Mulligan and his brave little wife, an old pupil of theirs. When she heard of her husband's capture, although she had but just recovered from a severe illness, she made her

way across the country to Lexington, to comfort him by
her presence. Soon after he was paroled, and they journeyed homeward together, stopping at Jefferson on their
way. Mrs. Mulligan gave the Sisters a glowing account of
her husband's exploits, and moved them to tears by her
description of his sufferings. She was proud of him for
he was a genuinely brave man. To rare merit he added
rare modesty, and were it not for the animated recital of
his devoted wife the Sisters would have heard but little of
his thrilling adventures in Lexington.

It is in order to state here that on the 20th of December, 1861, Mr. Arnold, rising in his seat in the House of
Representatives, at Washington, introduced a joint resolution giving the thanks of Congress to Colonel James A.
Mulligan and the officers and men under his command
for the heroic defense of Lexington, Missouri, which was
read a first and second time. The joint resolution was as
follows:

Resolved by the Senate and House of Representatives that
the thanks of Congress be extended to Colonel James A. Mulligan and the gallant officers and soldiers under his command,
who bravely stood by him against a greatly superior force in
his heroic defense of Lexington, Missouri.

Resolved, That the Twenty-third Regiment of Illinois Volunteers—the Irish Brigade—in testimony of their gallantry on
that occasion are authorized to bear on their colors the word
"Lexington."

Resolved, That the Secretary of War be requested to com-
municate these resolutions to Colonel Mulligan and his officers and soldiers.

The joint resolution was ordered to be engrossed
and read a third time and, being engrossed, it was ac-

cordingly read a third time and passed.([1])

Rev. William Walsh, of Jefferson City, was a sincere friend of the Sisters during their abode in the hospital, and they remember him with lively gratitude. On New Year's Day, 1862, they made their renewal of vows in the church. They also derived much comfort and support from the many kind and encouraging letters they received from their superior, Rev. Mother Francis. The warmest sympathies of this noble-hearted woman were aroused for her children, working in a cause so dear and sacred. She visited them during the fall, and frequently sent them contributions, provisions and delicacies for their sick soldiers. These soon became so numerous that two more Sisters and several elderly women and young girls were sent to their aid.. An additional hospital was required, and a building formerly used as a seminary was devoted to that purpose. The assistants of the Sisters wore a uniform of gray, and as all went to Mass every morning, when hospital duties permitted, the procession of the black and gray-robed maidens looked rather solemn.

Except in case of Catholics the ministrations of the Sisters were confined to the bodily ills of the sick. They rarely touched on religious subjects, save when the patient desired it. On one occasion they found a dying man whom they believed to be a Catholic. The Sisters who attended him asked him to what church he belonged. He looked cautiously around the ward and whispered:

"I am ashamed to tell."

---

(1). From the Congressional Globe containing the debates and proceedings of the second session of the Thirty-seventh Congress, page 158, Vol. 1.

"But," said she, "you should not belong to a church of which you are ashamed."

The poor man then acknowledged that he was a Catholic, though, through human respect, he had concealed it until then. The Sister spoke words of advice and encouragement to the poor man—a brave soldier of earth, an indifferent soldier of Christ—and had the consolation of inducing him to receive the sacraments. His death took place soon after, and his fellow-soldiers, having arrayed him in his uniform, placed upon his bosom the crucifix which the Sister had given him. This act of reverence in men who seldom gave religion a thought surprised and pleased the Sisters not a little.

They remained in charge of the Jefferson City Hospital until April, 1862, when, the army having been ordered to another division, their services were no longer required. They, therefore, made preparations to return to Chicago. The night before the day appointed for their departure they were much surprised by receiving a serenade from the military band. The next morning Father Walsh said Mass in the hospital. The Sisters then bade "good-bye" to the few soldiers who remained, and the poor fellows were very much affected at the parting.

When the Sisters reached St. Louis they were waited on by Mr. Yateman, Sanitary Commissioner, who requested them to take charge of the hospital department of the steamboat "Empress," then about to start for the battlefield of Shiloh, in order to transfer the wounded to places where they could receive proper care. Many of the sick and wounded were on the battlefield, sheltered only by tents, and deprived of almost every comfort. When the necessary permission from home was obtained the

Sisters went aboard the "Empress," bound for Pittsburg Landing, which they reached on Palm Sunday. They had been anxious to reach it that day, hoping to be in time for Mass; but they were surprised and disappointed to find that, instead of being a town or village, Pittsburg Landing consisted of only one house, a log cabin, in which there was no prospect of hearing Mass. They went ashore at once to visit the sick and wounded of both armies, who were in separate tents, and distributed to the poor men some refreshments, which were most gratefully received. Next day the "Empress," laden with sick and wounded, started for Keokuk, Iowa. There were over three hundred sufferers aboard, and the Sisters were occupied from early morning till midnight waiting on them and endeavoring to soothe their depressed spirits. The "Empress" reached Keokuk on Holy Saturday, April 16, 1862. The removal of the sick to the hospital began at once and occupied two days, during which time the Sisters were engaged in doing everything possible to ease the pains of their patients.

On Easter Sunday they had the happiness of hearing Mass and receiving the sacraments. The Sisters of Notre Dame, who were present at Mass, awaited the Sisters of Mercy at the church doors, and, knowing they were fasting, invited them to come to their convent to breakfast. Much as the Sisters appreciated their kindness, they were obliged to decline, as they had to return as quickly as possible to their sick on the hospital boat. In the evening the Visitation Nuns sent a message to invite the Sisters of Mercy to dine at their convent. This invitation was accepted, as the sick and wounded had had their wounds dressed, and were made as comfortable as possible. At the Visitation Convent they received much kindness, and had the happiness of being present at benediction. At Mound City the Holy Cross Sisters, under Mother Angela Gillespie, showed much kindness to the Sisters of Mercy.

Next day the "Empress" returned to Pittsburg Landing for another cargo of the sick, who were conveyed to St. Louis. The boat made many voyages of this kind. The Sisters strove to get delicacies of all sorts for the sick wherever they landed, and in distributing these there were scenes at once amusing and touching. The men would gather around the Sisters like big children, holding out their piece of bread and begging for "just one little bit of jam." The Sisters, not having the heart to refuse anyone, would give away all they had, trusting to kind Providence to send them more. The "Empress" also made a voyage to Louisville, where the Sisters placed under proper care the last cargo of the sick and wounded from the terrible battle of Shiloh. The end of May, 1862, concluded five weeks' service on the hospital boat. To this day the Sisters of Mercy express gratitude for the kindness and almost reverential courtesy they experienced during their stay with the invalid soldiers. Accustomed to a life of seclusion and tranquillity, they did not venture on this undertaking without nerving themselves to encounter much that might be repugnant to their nature and profession. But none of their gloomy anticipations were realized. They always felt that they owed a special tribute to the brave men of both armies for the deference and courtesy they invariably received from Confederate and Federal alike. The soldiers under their care showed them a child-like docility and respect, and never was a word uttered in their presence by a warrior of either side that could offend the most delicate ear. "If," writes one of the survivors of the nursing band, "the man who knows how to treat a woman with respect is himself worthy of respect, then all honor to the soldiers of the war, North and South."

CHAPTER XXIII.

THE STANTON HOSPITAL.

———◆———

The authorities in Washington invite the Sisters of Mercy to take
charge of both the institutions at the capital and the Western
Pennsylvania Hospital, in Pittsburg. Death of the Superior of
the Stanton Hospital. Buried with military honors. President
Lincoln commends the Sisters for their self-sacrificing labors. A
warm tribute from Father Canevin. How the Civil war helped to
wipe out religious bigotry.

———◆———

In the autumn of 1862 application was made by the
authorities in Washington to the Mother Superior of the
Sisters of Mercy for nurses to take charge of the wounded

soldiers in the Stanton Hospital in Washington City. Accordingly, four Sisters from
the mother house in Pittsburg were appointed for the
work. They hastily prepared
and departed for the scene of
duty, arriving in Washington
the day before Thanksgiving.
Finding that the Stanton, a
long row of one-story frame buildings, was not quite
ready for occupancy, the Sisters remained for a few
days with the Sisters of mercy, who were in charge of
the Douglas Hospital then in operation in Washington.
These Sisters were members of the Baltimore Community, founded some years previously from the house at
Pittsburg. In a short time the next hospital was opened,
and the Sisters repaired thither, and began their work

by caring for one hundred and thirty wounded soldiers, who had just been carried in from an engagement. On December 8 four more Sisters arrived from Pittsburg, making in all eight, which number constituted the staff of Sisters engaged in the Stanton Hospital. Some of these did not remain until the close of the war, but were relieved as circumstances required by Sisters from home. These changes were not made without necessity, as the health of several of the original volunteers was hopelessly shattered by the severe duties entailed upon them. To the bodily fatigue incident to the care of so many patients was added much mental anxiety, caused by the responsibility attending the charge of grave cases. The successful issue in many severe surgical operations depended almost entirely on the vigilance of the nurse.

Too much praise cannot be given to the officials of the Stanton Hospital for their careful supervision and attention to the patients, and the unvarying kindness and confidence reposed in the Sisters. The surgeon is in charge, Dr. John A. Liddell, and his assistant, Dr. Philip Davis, deserve special mention. Abundant supplies of everything needful for the sick were most liberally provided. As far as possible no want of the patients was left ungratified.

This was a source of great satisfaction to the Sisters, and lightened their cares considerably. What has been said of the work of Sisters in other hospitals might be repeated here. Their labors were arduous and unceasing. After every battle numbers of wounded were brought in, and received unwearied attention day and night. As a rule the soldiers appreciated the work of the Sisters, and regarded them as their best friends. Often patients, when convinced that the hope of recovery was gone, confided their last wishes to the Sisters. They were frequently called upon to send messages to the loved ones far away, and write letters to absent friends. These and similar acts of kindness, with words of comfort and encouragement, made the day more than full "pressed down and running over" with meritorious acts. The Sisters frequently had the consolation of witnessing happy deathbed scenes, often of persons who, under less favorable surroundings might not have enjoyed this great blessing. Entire freedom of conscience was secured to all, each patient being at liberty to summon to his side the spiritual adviser of his choice. The Catholics were attended by the Jesuit Fathers, among whom Revs. Father Wagit, Brady and Roccofort were untiring in their efforts to console the sick and fortify the dying with the consolations of religion. The Sisters remained at the Stanton until the close of the war, when, their services being no longer required, they returned to Pittsburg, where they resumed their usual avocations.

The Western Pennsylvania Hospital in Pittsburg was used by the Government for a military hospital at this time, principally for Pennsylvania soldiers. Such men as were able to bear the fatigue of transportation from Washington or other places were sent to this institution in order to make room at the Stanton for cases direct from the field of battle. The Sisters of Mercy were invited to give their services, a request with which they cheerfully complied, early in 1863. In this institution the Sisters experienced the same courtesy from the officers as was extended to them elsewhere. Every arrangement compatible with existing circumstances was made to lighten their duties. In both these hospitals a chapel was fitted up and Mass was celebrated daily, which such convalescent patients as desired were at liberty to attend. The Sisters continued their work in the Pennsylvania Hospital until May, 1865. In Washington and Pittsburg the members of the Sanitary Commission gave very efficient aid towards alleviating the conditions of the patients by providing delicacies and reading matter. After each visit supplies were left in the hands of the Sisters to be distributed at their discretion.

The Douglas Hospital in Washington had been erected out of three large dwellings in the then fashionable part of the Capital City. It was so named from the fact that the most important of these three houses had been the residence of the famous Senator of that name.

Sister M. Collette O'Connor was in charge of this institution, and was revered by all who became acquainted with her. She died at the hospital, July 16, 1864, and her remains were escorted to Baltimore and buried with military honors.

One day President Lincoln visited the Stanton Hospital in Washington. Those who were fortunate to be present on this remarkable occasion received impressions that should remain ever fresh in their minds. None of the Sisters had ever met the Chief Executive, but when a tall, angular man with just the suggestion of a stoop about the shoulders sauntered up the path leading to the main entrance of the hospital they intuitively knew that it was President Lincoln. The homely, wrinkled face, with its careworn appearance, and the patient, almost pathetic eyes appealed at once to the tender sensibilities of the Sisters. They knew little, and were without leisure to inquire, about the merits of either the Northern or Southern side of the bloody controversy then raging at its height, but

GRANT, SHERMAN AND SHERIDAN.

they had a keen appreciation of human suffering and human sympathy, and their hearts went out at once to this plain man who so uncomplainingly carried the woes of the nation upon his shoulders.

The President went from cot to cot shaking hands with the poor patients and addressing them in the jocular manner he frequently employed to conceal the anguish caused by the sight of so much suffering. On occasions of this character the very simplicity and naturalness of the President only served to bring his greatness into brighter relief. The Sisters had a good opportunity of observing the man who had been called from his modest home in Illinois to become ruler of the Republic at the most serious crisis in its history. They saw in him a person who with a single stroke of the pen was destined to liberate nearly four millions of slaves. They saw a man who was daily performing the most painful duties under the most trying circumstances, but who did each act "with malice toward none; with charity for all." They saw in him the one distinctively grand figure of the war. They realized with others that amid the clash and roar and smoke of battle; amid the perplexities and contentions of legislative halls, and the difficulties and differences of Cabinets, there arose pre-eminent above all the peaceful, pathetic, powerful personality of Abraham Lincoln.

Mr. Lincoln remained at the hospital for some time. With the trained eye of a man of affairs he observed the cleanliness of the place, and did not fail to notice all that the Sisters were doing for the comfort and relief of the patients. When he departed he cordially shook hands with each of the Sisters, and congratulated them on the work they were performing in the cause of humanity.

Rev. J. F. Regis Canevin, rector of St. Paul's Cathedral, Pittsburg, has paid a high tribute to the work of the Sisters of Mercy in the late war. [1] A passing reference is made to some of the events already detailed in this chapter, but it is such an able presentation of the case that it deserves reproduction in these pages. Father Canevin said in part:

"The Sisters went forth from their peaceful convent homes to serve their God and country in the Stanton Military Hospital at Washington and in the Western Pennsylvania Hospital at Pittsburg. The military physicians regarded them as valuable assistants, and oftentimes the nuns had the entire charge of the patients, administering of medicines and arranging bandages with deft and skillful hands.

The Sisters had four hundred and fifty wounded men under their care in the Stanton Hospital at one time, and after the second battle of Fredericksburg, December 13, 1862, a number of Confederate wounded were laid side by side with those whom they had wounded.

"'It was a beautiful sight,' said one if the Sisters, "to see how tenderly the convalescent Union soldiers helped to nurse back the health of those whom they had so fiercely fought a short time before. Those who are first in war are also first in peace.'

"'The bravest are the tenderest,'

"'The loving are the daring.'

"Southern sympathizers in Washington sent large supplies of provisions and delicacies for their Confeder-

---

(1). In an address delivered in Pittsburg about seven years ago.

ate friends. 'We took all they sent,' said a veteran Sister, 'but we saw that the boys in blue fared as well as their foes.' This was holy simplicity. At the time the Sisters were engaged in their work of mercy in the hospitals and on the battlefields of the North some of their companions who had left their side a few years before were under the shot and shell which were hurled from land and water when Grant besieged Vicksburg, and fear and famine stalked the confederate camp and city. The Sisters followed the ill-fated army through all the hard fortunes of the struggle; nursed the sick, stanched the blood, bound up the wounds of those who fell on the battlefield, and spoke words of consolation and hope to the dying.

"We can read in military annals how the dying soldier fancied a mother or a sister to be supporting his head as the black-robed nun bade him confide in the Saviour of Calvary, and poured refreshing drops on his lips parched and quivering in the throes of death. It was loyalty to the Divine Master that caused these women to serve on both sides of the line.

"After the war the Vicksburg Community returned to their convent and found their latest golden opportunity in the South in the great yellow fever scourge of 1878, which spread sorrow and gloom over the land, until even hope was almost paralyzed. Yes, when fear had dissolved all the ties which hold society together; when succor could not be bought with gold; when the strongest natural affections yielded to the love of life, then a band of Sisters of Mercy, led by the same fearless heroines from Pittsburg who fifteen years before had seen duty on the battlefield, were to be found bending over the plague-stricken couch, praying, ever encouraging and holding up to the last before the expiring patient the image of the Cross.

"When the brave men of both armies had fought out the nation's quarrel, and when the roar of cannon died away and the smoke of battle was lifted from the land, the bright sun of peace shone upon a people more united than they had ever been before. Religious bigotry and sectarian hatred had received a deadly stroke. There was more Christianity amid the rough scenes of war than there had been in preceding years of peace. The best blood of the Roman Catholic and of the Protestant co-patriot had reddened the same stream and mingled on many a well-fought field; side by side they met the charge; side by side they repelled th shock; side by side they fell.. In the same pit their bodies were deposited. The dew fell from Heaven upon their union in the grave.

"Misfortune had taught them to know and respect and trust and love each other. Those who survived learned to despise the cowards and hypocrites and bigots who at home, in ignorance or malice, had armed man against his brother, and in the name of religion kept us in perpetual conflict. The soldier descendant of the New England Puritan, and of the Papist hating Orangeman, discovered that his Catholic comrade was a brave, generous-hearted man, and a consistent Christian; that the Roman Catholic Church was not the sworn enemy of free institutions; that the Sisters of that Church were kind, earnest, hard-working, useful and devoted women in the service of that Christ whose doctrine is that we should love one another. And thus the Sisters of Mercy returned from war to find the good they and other religious women had done had won the grateful recognition of the whole country. Thoughtful men learned from their deeds that even a Covenanter need not fear to offend the Creator in acknowledging that there rested a holy influence in hearts consecrated to God."

CHAPTER XXIV.

SISTERS OF ST. JOSEPH.

The Surgeon General applies for nurses to care for the sick soldiers in Camp Curtin, Harrisburg. Bishop Wood gives a ready assent. Their valuable Services at the State capital. An official letter of thanks from Governor Curtin. Down the James River in the Commodore to bring the wounded from the battlefield of Yorktown. A poor soldier abandoned in an isolated tent. Rescued from death itself. A grateful patient.

In January, 1862, Dr. Henry H. Smith, Surgeon General of the State of Pennsylvania, applied to Rev. Mother St. John at the Mt. St. Joseph Convent, Chest-

JEFFERSON DAVIS.

nut Hill, Philadelphia, "for Sisters to serve as nurses of the sick soldiers in camp Curtin, Harrisburg, saying he had had experience of the Sisters' efficiency in nursing while he attended at St. Joseph's Hospital in Philadelphia, and they felt they would be able to do good work at the State Capital.

Bishop Wood, to whom the Doctor had spoken of the matter, gave ready assent, and writing on the 22d of the same month, the Doctor speaks of the arrangements for the Sisters' journey as having been effected, and adds: "The Doctor hopes the Sisters will not disappoint him. Whilst best by applicants, every female nurse has been refused, Dr. Smith being unwilling to trust any but his old friends, the Sisters of St. Joseph. There is a large field of usefulness, but it is to be properly cultivated only by those whose

sense of duty will induce them to sacrifice personal comfort. The living is rough, the pay poor, and nothing but
the sentiments of religion can render the nurses contented."

On January 23 three Sisters under the direction of
Mother Monica Pue, went to Harrisburg, and on the
following day the Surgeon-General took them to Camp
Curtin Hospital, which he placed under their charge. At
the camp there were then about three thousand militia.
The hospital was merely a temporary frame building,
roughly put together, and to make the apartments at all
habitable blankets and other such improvised tapestry
had to be hung over the boards. The Sisters arrived at
the hospital towards evening. They found that three ma-
trons had been in charge, and with them a number of
the soldiers acting as nurses. The reception accorded the
Sisters was not at all cordial. One man had been given
the charge of seeing to the Sisters' wants, and coming to
them he asked what they wished to have for supper, saying: "I know that the discipline of the Church is bread
and water, but I do not know what you ladies may want
to have." The Sisters replied that anything would do,
and were shortly afterwards summoned to the table the
nurses had just left in a most uninviting condition. The
viands were left untasted, and the Sisters began to see
what work was before them, and to arrange matters accordingly.

It was not long before the sick soldiers as well as those
employed in the hospital began to feel the beneficial effects of the Sisters' care, and their efficiency in hospital
administration; and respectful attentions and military
salutes of the men became almost oppressive. Bishop
Wood paid several visits to the Sisters at the camp, and

also to the Church Hospital, Harrisburg, where three Sisters, under charge of Sr. Mary John, afterward the Rev. Mother of the Community, took charge of the sick, who, among the arriving militia, were unable to proceed as far as the camp.

Finding themselves always addressed by the physicians as "Sisters of Charity" or "Mercy," the Sisters drew the Surgeon-General's attention to the misnomer, but he replied that the name accorded with their work, and it would be no use in trying to explain to the doctors about the different orders. Hence in all newspaper reports and in various accounts of their work given at the time the Sisters were always mentioned as Sisters of Charity or Mercy, which they took as another sign that their patron, St. Joseph, desired them to labor as he had done, in silence and obscurity, unknown and unnoticed by the world.

On the 2d of February the Surgeon-General, after visiting the hospitals, wrote to Mother St. John: "I have found all the Sisters perfectly well, with no complaints after their trial of the inconveniences and exposure attendant on military life. Already each hospital shows the blessing attendant on their presence. Everything is now neat, orderly and comfortable. Sr. P. is 'Captain of the Ward' in the camp hospital, and has a drummer boy to attend her. Sr. C. in the kitchen is also in authority, and has a sentry at the kitchen door. ⋆ ⋆ ⋆ Sr. M. is 'the Major,' and commands the surgeons, keeping them in good humor by her kind acts. All seem happy and contented, and the Governor and others speak frequently of the good move made in bringing them there. ⋆ ⋆ ⋆ At the Church Hospital Sister C. shines in the refectory, and everything is in excellent order."

On the 18th of the same month the doctor called for more Sisters, adding, however, "Matters are so unsettled by the recent victories I am at a loss whether to send for extra help. There are rumors of closing the camp or rather of giving it up to the U. S."

What Dr. Smith had anticipated came to pass; the soldiers at Camp Curtin were called to the front, and the Sisters left the Church Hospital March 27, and Camp Curtin April 8, '62. It was indeed touching to see the difference between the reception the men had given the Sisters on their coming and the feeling of sorrow that marked their parting with them. Many of the men sobbed aloud, and the Sisters themselves were deeply moved at the thought of how many, who were starting off in health and strength, would ere long meet a sad and painful death.

On the 14th of April, by order of Governor Curtin, the following letter was sent by Dr. Smith to Madam St. John, Superior of the Sisters of St. Joseph:

"Madam:—During a period of several weeks, amidst the confusion of a constantly changing camp, and amidst an epidemic of measles, with typhoid fever, etc., six of "The Sisters of St. Joseph,' sacrificing all personal comfort, ministered faithfully and truly to the comfort and welfare of the sick. Neatness, order and efficient ministration immediately followed their arrival in the camp.

"Highly appreciating their valuable services and Christian devotion to the relief of human suffering, the State authorities desire to express to them and your order high appreciation of the self-sacrificing spirit which they exhibited among the sick soldiers, both at Camp Curtin and the Church Hospital in Harrisburg.

"By order of

"A. G. CURTIN, Governor of Pennsylvania."

Dr. Smith himself wrote:—"It affords me pleasure to transmit the accompanying order, acknowledging the valuable services of the Sisters recently engaged at Harrisburg. * * * In the event of a fight at Yorktown I shall go there with a party on a steamboat and stop at Fortress Monroe. If some hardy Sisters will volunteer for duty with me I will perhaps be able to take them. The notice will not be more than six hours. * * * I will share the exposure with them, and will do all that is possible to make them comfortable, bringing them back with the wounded, unless you allow them to stay. Your Order is, I believe, the only one that is doing duty with the army. I think they can do much good, under my care. Sr. —— will be especially useful in cooking for the wounded in the boat I shall take at the Fortress."

On the 18th the orders came, and, under the escort of Captain Bankson, U. S. A., three Sisters went to Baltimore and thence to Fortress Monroe. On the 26th the Doctor sent a request for six more Sisters, promising plenty of occupation.

In a letter dated April 27, 1862, Archbishop Wood, after naming the Sisters detailed "for attendance on the wounded and sick soldiers under the direction of Dr. Henry Smith, Surgeon-General of the Pennsylvania Volunteers," adds "We commend them to the kind care and protection of the Surgeon-General, and to the attention of all persons, ecclesiastical and civil, with whom they may be in any way associated, holding it as a special and personal favor bestowed on ourselves."

On April 21, writing from Fortress Monroe, the Doctor informs Mother St. John that the Sisters on their arrival had been put at once on hospital duty, and were doing much needed work, especially in the preparation of sick diet, etc. He adds: "They are sure to be appreciated. ★ ★ ★ They come into friendly competition with a party of nurses under the direction of Miss Dix. They will win the good will and opinion of all."

The three Sisters first sent were again under the direction of Mother Monica Pue. The were kindly and eagerly welcomed by Dr. Smith, who, with the aid of a spy-glass, saw the boat approaching and hurried to meet them. There were then some sick and wounded on board the floating hospital, the "Whillden." Other Sisters went down later under charge of one of the hospital surgeons, who, poor man, was anything but pleased with being detailed to act as escort to five ladies. But all his fears, as he afterwards declared, were speedily dispelled when he found his office rather a sinecure, since the Sisters did not call on him for the thousand and one attentions it had been his fortune to have been called on to give while attending secular ladies.

At Fortress Monroe they went aboard the two floating hospitals, the "Whillden" and the "Commodore." On May 3 they had the great consolation of receiving the Sacraments from Rev. Father Dillon, of the Congregation of the Holy Cross, who drove up and down the Camp by Fortress Monroe, hearing the confessions of the soldiers. He said Mass on board the "Commodore" May 3 and 4.

On May 6, in company with the Surgeon-General and his assistants, three of the Sisters went down the James River in the "Commodore" to bring up the wounded from the battlefield of Yorktown. All night from 5 P. M. till 2 A. M. of next day the wounded were being carried to the vessel on stretchers. Harrowing, indeed, were the scenes that there met their eye, and sad it was to find how inadequate were their efforts to fully assuage the terrible sufferings of the victims. But all that could be done was done, and the supply of coffee and stimulants was thankfully received by those who for days had languished without any attentions. A company of Pennsylvania Volunteers, whom the Sisters met near the landing had not had any food for two, and some for three days, the steamer laden with provisions having been unaccountably delayed. On their way up the river the "Commodore" passed the vessel with the longed-for supply of food on its way down to the men.

Among the wounded were many of the Southern soldiers, who had been taken prisoners; and they seemed particularly grateful for the attentions of the religious. The wounded lay in rows along the decks of the steamers, and in the state rooms, so close together that it was almost impossible to pass along without treading on them.

On May 16 Dr. Smith wrote to Mother St. John: "The Sisters have given universal satisfaction, and have done much good. It will be acknowledged hereafter in proper form. In the meantime I should like to take six of them with me again, ending perhaps at Richmond." Six of the Sisters came up with the wounded on the "Commodore" to the port of Philadelphia, and stayed with them until they had all been removed to the different hospitals of the city. After a few days' rest they returned to receive the wounded from the battle fought near Richmond.

Meanwhile the camp at Harrisburg had been re-opened, and three Sisters were again called to attend the hospital. One of them relates that on her rounds about the place on their return she saw an isolated tent by the door of which lay a coffin. To her inquiries an officer replied that in the tent there was a man dying of camp fever. She inquired whether it was possible to save the man, and, on hearing that it was not known, declared her intention of going to see. The officer refused to allow her to go in, saying it would be suicide, as she could not go without contracting the fever. She, however, persisted, and entering the tent, beheld a man in apparently a state of collapse. For days, it would seem, he had received very little attention, and the filth of the bed and floor was in-describable. That day the poor patient had had nothing but a drink of water. The Sister at once prepared and gave him a bowl of stimulating broth. He became suf-ficiently strong to tell her he was from St. Paul's Parish, Philadelphia. The priest, Rev. Father Maher, of Harris-burg, was sent for. In the meantime, by dint of warnings and entreaties, the Sister got two of the male nurses to lift the man from the bed, to which parts of his body ad-hered. The floor was cleansed, the man washed, his sores attended to, and then the priest came, heard his confes-sion and gave him the last Sacraments, and immediately his recover seemed to set in. His gratitude was touching in the extreme. The Sisters had word sent to his wife in Philadelphia that she might be able to have him removed home, but before she came they themselves had been recalled from what to them was a blessed field of labor.

On June 9, 1862, Dr. Smith wrote to Mother St. John, saying: "The U. S. have agreed to take charge of all the State hospitals. * * * I have requested the Sisters at Harrisburg to return to you and hope I shall not have again to trouble you until the war is ended. The Sisters did great good, were very kind and useful. All will be acknowledged in due time." Several of the Sisters who attended the soldiers have already entered on their reward, and rest in the beautiful cemetery of Mt. St. Joseph, where on Decoration Day the Sisters and children love to pay special attention to the graves of those departed ones "of the Soldiers of Christ who went out to attend on the soldiers of war."

No words could adequately express the gratitude of the Sisters for the delicate and fatherly attentions they received from Surgeon-General Smith and his corps of assistants. Dr. Smith was truly "one of Nature's noblemen," with a soul free from every taint of prejudice, with a heart open to every phase of human suffering and a charity that never wearied in alleviating the horrors of war. [1]

---

(1). The fiftieth anniversary of the foundation in Philadelphia of the Sisters of St. Joseph was celebrated May 5, 1897, at the Mount St. Joseph's Novitiate, in Chestnut Hill. About ninety priests from Philadelphia and adjacent dioceses were present, and the venerable Monsignor Cantwell, who, with Bishop O'Hara, of Scranton, was the only one then living who extended the hand of welcome to the three Sisters who came from St. Louis fifty years previous, was among the guests. There were present also about two hundred visiting Sisters from the various Catholic institutions in the city and several from Rochester, N.Y., and Flushing, L. I. Archbishop Ryan made a brief address of congratulation to the pupils and the community. He said that forty-five years ago he knew the Sisters of the St. Louis Community, and that he had watched their astounding growth with much interest. He paid a glowing tribute to the beneficence and charity of the community, and prayed that God would cause them to prosper in the future as He had done in the past.

CHAPTER XXV.

SISTERS OF THE HOLY CROSS.

The heroic life and labors of Mother Angela. A cousin of the late James
   G. Blaine. She gives up her school at South Bend, Ind., to serve
   through the war. A historic meeting between Mother Angela and
   General Grant. Rev. L. A. Lambert, the chaplain at Mound City.
   Sixty Sisters of the Holy Cross on duty. Sister Angela, of the
   Visitation Community, and her love for the soldiers.

Mother Angela, of the Holy Cross Sisters, was one of
the most devoted nurses in any of the orders that served
during the civil war. She was a woman of high birth and

considerable refinement.
She came from a well-
known Pennsylvania Irish
family—the Gillespies. It
was from this family that
James Gillespie Blaine was
so named. She was a cous-
in of the illustrious man,
and was also related to the
Ewings and the Shermans.
Her parents migrated from
Pennsylvania to Illinois while she was quite young, and
her education was received at the Academy of the Visitation, in Washington, D. C. Mother Angela always had a
high regard for Blaine. She was intimately acquainted
with the details of his early life and his home at Browns-
ville, Pa. To those in whom she placed great confidence
she frequently gave touching incidents of the young
man's early career, and on more than one occasion she

repelled slanders which were no doubt implicitly be-lieved by the public at large. She became connected with the Holy Cross Sisters many years before the war. When the first gun was fired at Sumter Mother Angela was in charge of a flourishing school at South Bend. When the need for nurses became pressing this was given up, the scholars returned to their homes, and the Sister teach-ers volunteered their services to those in charge of the hospitals. Mother Angela was sent out by the Very Rev. Father Sourin, Superior General of the Congregation of the Holy Cross, whose head house was at Notre Dame, Indiana.

Mother Angela met many of the great generals of the war, and they all united in declaring her a woman of marvelous executive ability. Besides this she had many other accomplishments of a high order. Although she was the Mother in charge, she gave her personal atten-tion to many of the patients. On several historic occa-sions she waited upon Confederate and Union soldiers at the same time. "Johnny Reb," as he was facetiously called, and the "Yank" would like in cots side by side, with the peaceful face of Mother Angela between them. Often man lying helpless on their backs would get into heated disputes over the relative merits of the war, and but for their physical disability would have done each other violence. The Sisters alone possessed the power to quell these quarrels, and they did it with all the tact and diplomacy becoming their gentle natures.

The story of the first meeting between General Grant and Mother Angela comes from an eye-witness of that historic episode, and can be vouched for as strictly correct. Grant was just then beginning to develop the traits of a leader, which were to mark him later as the greatest captain of his time. His headquarters were in an old brick building that had formerly served as a bank in Cairo. Mother Angela came to this place to report for duty to General Grant. She was accompanied by the late Dr. Brinton, an honored physician of Philadelphia, and Rev. Louis A. Lambert, D. D., LL. D.([1])

Dr. Lambert, who was to act in the capacity of chaplain, escorted Mother Angela into Grant's presence. The great Captain was seated at a desk behind the iron bars, which had evidently been formerly used by the cashier of the bank. He was writing with the air of a man who was absorbed in his task and unconscious of his surroundings. An ordinary cheap pipe was in his mouth, and every now and then he mechanically blew forth a cloud of smoke. The characteristics of the man so well-known in later years were just as pronounced then. The people all around him were plainly agitated with the thought of the great war that was about to rage in all its fury. He sat at his work calm, silent, and with an imperturbability of countenance that was sphinx-like. Dr. Brinton, who had been one of the first to suggest the Sisters, introduced Mother Angela to Grant. The General came out from behind the iron grating with his head bare, and, taking Mother Angela's hand, gave it a hearty shake. The pipe he had been smoking was temporarily laid aside. There was a moment's silence, and then Grant, looking at his visitor with a pleasant smile, said:

---

(1). Father Lambert is one of the most notable priests in the United States. His ancestors on his mother's side came over with William Penn and eventually settled in Mt. Holly, N. J. Father Lambert had some very interesting experiences as an army chaplain. He is a writer of some note and has been a worker in Catholic journalism for many years. His best known work is probably his "Notes on Ingersoll," which had a tremendous sale.

"I am glad to have you with us, very glad."

There was a pause for a second, and then he added:

"If there is anything at all I can do for you I will be glad to do it. I thoroughly appreciate the value of your services, and I will give orders to see that you do not want for anything."

After a few more minutes of general conversation, in which Dr. Brinton and Father Lambert joined, Mother Angela and the Sisters started for their mission at Mound City. In later years General Grant frequently expressed profound admiration for Mother Angela, not only as a nurse, but as a woman of unusual ability.

The party had quite an experience in reaching their destination. The wagon which had been detailed as their conveyance broke down when they were half way thither, and there was some difficulty in patching it up sufficiently to finish the journey. But it was done, and the Sisters eventually reached Mound City, and began their work of mercy in the hospital located there. Sister Ferdinand was a fellow laborer with Mother Angela at this time. Father Lambert, the chaplain, attended the Post Hospital at Mound City and said Mass at 4 o'clock in the morning for the benefit of Mother Angela and her Sisters.

There was one incident that was kept quiet and which did not become generally known until after the war. Small-pox was raging at the time, and one of the brave Sisters was stricken down. She was hastily stowed away in a garret of the hospital building and a special guard placed over her. She recovered, and after that devoted herself to nursing others with even more zeal than she had shown before she was stricken down. Ordinarily

LEE, JACKSON AND BEAUREGARD.

small-pox cases were sent to the pest house, but in this instance the tenderness of the Sisters would not permit them to part with their afflicted colleague It was against the rules, to be sure, but who can blame the Sisters for this merciful breach of discipline? It is only proper to state that the case was so isolated that not even one of the twelve hundred patients was affected even in the remotest degree. One who was in the hospital at this time says that he is not certain but that the Surgeon General knew of the hidden case. The Very Rev. Father Corby, now Superior General of the Congregation of the Holy Cross at Notre Dame, was probably the most conspicuous chaplain during the war. He belonged to the same order with Mother Angela.

There were between 1200 and 1400 patients in the hospital, and all received the kindest care and attention. Mother Angela served through all the war, winning extraordinary distinction for tact, diplomacy and faithfulness.

The official communication written by Commander Davis after a battle on White River, June 17, 1862, indicates that Mother Angela was not unknown to the authorities.

Hon. Gideon Walls, Secretary of the Navy.

U. S. Flag Steamer Benton, Memphis, June 20, 1862.

Sir: —The number of men on board the hospital boat Red Rover is forty-one. The account given me yesterday was incorrect. I shall still wait for further knowledge before presenting a final report of the casualties attending the capture of the St. Charles forts. The Department will be gratified to learn that the patients are, most of them, doing well.   ★   ★   ★   Sister Angela, the Superior of the Sisters of the Holy Cross (some of whom are performing their offices of mercy at the Mound City Hospital), has kindly offered the services of the Sisters for the hospital boat of this squadron when needed. I have written to Commander Rennock to make arrangements for their coming.

I have the honor to be, very respectfully your obedient servant,

CHARLES H. DAVIS,
Flag Officer Commanding Western Flotilla.

The following reference to the Holy Cross Sisters from the pen of Father Corby is apropos:

"Sixty Sisters of the Holy Cross went out under Mother Angela. These Sisters volunteered their services to nurse the sick and the wounded soldiers, hundreds of whom, moved to sentiments of purest piety by the words and example of these angel nurses, begged to be baptized in articulo mortis—at the point of death. The labors and self-sacrifice of the Sisters during the war need no praise here. The praise is on the lips of every surviving soldier who experienced their kind and careful ministration. Many a soldier now looks down from on high with complacency on the worthy Sisters who were instrumental in saving the soul when life could not be saved. Nor was it alone from the Order of the Sisters of the Holy Cross that Sister nurses engaged in the care of the sick and wounded soldiers. Many other orders made costly sacrifices to save life and to save souls, notably the noble Order of the Sisters of Charity. To members of this order I am personally indebted. When prostrate with camp fever, insensible for nearly three days, my life was entrusted to their care. Like guardian angels these Daughters of St. Vincent watched every symptom of the fever, and by their skill and care I was soon able to return to my post of duty."[2]

There was another Sister Angela who was prominent during the civil war, but who was not so conspicuous as her illustrious namesake. She is thus referred to in a recent work:[3]

"Sister Angela became a member of the Community (Vis-

---

[2]. From Father Corby's "Memories of Chaplain Life."

[3]. A "Story of Courage," by Rose Hawthorne and George Parsons Lathrop

itation Sisters) about 1819. She was one of those characters who convey to the mind the image of a soul of spotless innocence. She celebrated her golden jubilee and lived for several years afterwards, retained to the last her full mental faculties and childlike simplicity. She was made Superioress of the foundation in Philadelphia. On the breaking up of the house there she was recalled to Georgetown. Then for twelve years at different times she served as Superioress of Georgetown Convent and governed with a gentle firmness and a lovely spirit of forebearance; enduring the many trials incidental to authority with the utmost patience.

"During the civil war her energy and wisdom shone forth especially. She was at that time most generous in trying to aid poor chaplains, and she showed a true zeal for souls in the advice she gave to soldiers who applied to her for help. Her charity was remembered, as the nuns of Georgetown had reason to realize not long ago, during the encampment of the Grand Army of the Republic, when one of the veterans called to see "Sister Angela," not knowing she had been dead several years. The veteran gave as his reason for desiring to see her that the angelic Superioress had converted him. Whenever worn out with marching and laden with dust, regiments halted in front of the Convent during the war, a liberal lunch was served to the weary soldiers, and objects of piety sent out to those who wanted them by Sister Angela."

CHAPTER XXVI.

NON-CATHOLIC TRIBUTES.

Comment of Mary A. Livermore upon the work of Mother Angela
at Mound city: "The world has known no nobler and more
heroic women than those found in the ranks of the Catholic
Sisterhoods." A famous scout gives his impressions of the
Sisters. Susan D. Messinger tells of the work of the Sisters at
New Berne, N. C.

No tributes that have been paid to the work of the Catholic Sisterhoods during the war have been more  cordial or more emphatic than those coming from non-Catholic sources. It is a significant fact that those most prejudiced against the Sisters have been persons who knew the least about them, while the warmest friends of the dark-robed messengers of charity and peace have been persons who came in contact with them and their labors for humanity.

Mary A. Livermore, whose personal services during the war were by no means inconsiderable, is one non-Catholic writer who does not hesitate to give the Catholic Sister full credit for what she did. Miss Livermore says the Mound City Hospital, in charge of the Sisters of the Holy Cross, was considered the best military hospital in the United States. She writes:[1]

---

(1). A woman's story of the war.

"There was one general hospital in Cairo, called by the people 'the Brick Hospital.' Here the Sisters of the Holy Cross were employed as nurses, one or more to each ward. Here were order, cleanliness and good nursing. The food was cooked in a kitchen outside of the hospital. Surgeons were detailed to every ward and visited their patients twice a day, and oftener if necessary. The apothecaries' room was supplied with an ample store of medicines and surgical appliances, and the store-rooms possessed an abundance of clothing and delicacies for the sick."

The work done at Mound City is thus graphically set forth: "Except in Mound City everything was in a chaotic condition compared with the complete arrangement afterwards. The hospital at Mound City occupied a block of brick store, built before the war to accommodate the prospective commerce of the war. They had not been occupied, and as the blockade of the Mississippi rendered it uncertain when they would be needed for their legitimate use, they were turned over to the medical department for hospital use. At the time of my visit the Mound City hospital was considered the best military hospital in the United States. This was due to the administrative talent of Dr. E. S. Franklin, of Dubuque, Ia., who, despite poverty of means and material, transformed the rough block of stores into a superb hospital, accommodating 1000 patients. Fifteen hundred had been crowded in it by dint of close packing.

"The most thorough system was maintained in every department. There was an exact time and place for everything. Every person was assigned to a particular work and held responsible for its performance. If anyone proved a shirk, incompetent or insubordinate, he was sent off in the next boat. A Shaker-like cleanliness and sweetness of atmosphere pervaded the various wards; the sheets and pillows were of immaculate whiteness and the patients who were convalescent were cheerful and contented. The Sisters of the Holy Cross were employed as nurses, and by their skill, quietness, gentleness and tenderness were invaluable in the sick wards. Every patient gave hearty testimony to the skill and kindness of the Sisters.

"Mother Angela was the Superior of the Sisters—a gifted lady of rare cultivation and executive ability with winning sweetness of manner. She was a member of the Ewing family and a cousin of Mr. and Mrs. General Sherman. The Sisters had nearly broken up their famous schools at South Bend to answer the demand for nurses. If I had ever felt prejudiced against these Sisters as nurses, my experience with them during the war would have dissipated it entirely. The world has known no nobler and more heroic women than those found in the ranks of the Catholic Sisterhoods."

Captain "Jack" Crawford, who became famous as a scout in the Union army, in the course of a lecture delivered after the war speaks of the Sisters as follows:

"On all God's green and beautiful earth there is no purer, no nobler, no more kind-hearted and self-sacrificing women than those who wear the sombre garb of Catholic Sisters. During the war I had many opportunities for observing their noble and heroic work, not only in the camp and hospital, but on the death-swept field of battle. Right in the fiery front of dreadful war, where bullets hissed in maddening glee, and shot and shell flew madly by with demoniac shrieks, where dead and mangled forms lay with pale, blood-flecked faces, yet wear the scowl of battle, I have seen the black-robed Sisters moving over the field, their solicitous faces wet with the tears of sympathy, administering to the wants of the wounded and whispering words of comfort into the ears soon to be deafened by the cold, implacable hand of death. Now kneeling on the blood-bespattered sod to moisten with water the bloodless lips on which the icy kiss of the death angel has left its pale imprint; now breathing words of hope of an immortality beyond the grave into the ear of some mangled hero, whose last shots in our glorious cause had been fired but a moment before; now holding the crucifix to receive the last kiss from somebody's darling boy, from whose breast the life blood was splashing and who had offered his life as a willing sacrifice on the altar of his country; now with tender touch and tear-dimmed eye binding gaping wounds, from which most women must have shrunk in horror; now scraping together a pillow of forest leaves, upon which some pain-racked head might rest until the spirit took its flight to other realms—brave, fearless of danger, trusting implicitly in the Master whose overshadowing eye was noting their every movement; standing as shielding, prayerful angels between the dying soldiers and the horrors of death. Their only recompense the sweet, soul-soothing consciousness that they were doing their duty; their only hope of reward that peace and eternal happiness which awaited them beyond the star=emblazoned battlements above. Oh! my friends, it was a noble work.

"How many a veteran of the war, who wore the Blue or the Gray, can yet recall the soothing touch of a Sister's hand as he lay upon the pain-tossed couch of a hospital! Can we ever forget their sympathetic eyes, their low, soft-spoken words of encouragement and cheer when the result of the struggle between life and death yet hung in the balance? Oh! how often have I followed the form of that goo Sister Valencia with my sunken eyes as she moved away from my cot to the cot of another sufferer and have breathed from the most sacred depths of my faintly beating heart the fervent prayer: 'God bless her! God bless her!'

"My friends, I am not a Catholic, but I stand ready at any and all times to defend these noble women, even with my life, for I owe that life to them."

Miss Susan D. Messinger, of Roxbury, Mass., writes the following eloquent letter to the author:

"It is with real pleasure I pay my tribute to that noble band of Sisters of Mercy, who did such a Christian work of love and helpfulness for our suffering soldier boys in New Berne, N. C. My brother, Captain (afterwards Colonel) Messinger, was on the staff of Major General John G. Foster, Eighteenth Army Corps, stationed at New Berne, N. C. After the taking of New Berne my brother was made Provost Marshal and given quarters near the general at the request of Mrs. Foster, my sister. Mrs. Messinger and I were sent to stay a few weeks, although in no official capacity. No woman could be in the army without finding much she could do to relieve and comfort, and especially through the home our little quarters became to all, from major generals to privates. We could not go home. We stayed until summer. I write all this personal matter to show how I was thrown into the companionship of these Catholic Sisters. Although my brother and myself were Unitarians we became close, congenial friends with these brave women, who had to seek constantly advice and help from my brother on account of his position as Provost Marshal.

"General Foster was a Catholic and brought to New Berne six Sisters from the Convent of Mercy, in New York, to take charge of a hospital in New Berne for special cases. He took for their convent a house which had been General Burnsides' headquarters, and which also, during the war of the Revolution, had been occupied by Washington, his room and writing table sacredly preserved. This house communicated by a plank walk with another house, or houses, used as hospitals, and only over that plank walk did those devoted women ever take any exercise or recreation. They literally gave themselves as nurses to the poor, wounded, maimed and sick soldiers brought to them day after day. And most beautifully did they fulfill the charge. Many a soldier will never forget their tender, unselfish care and devotion. I was witness myself to much of it, as I was privileged to go from ward to ward. Many a dying man blessed them as angels of mercy, almost looking upon them as sent from the other world.

"One dear young fellow, who was almost reverenced by doctors and nurses for his patience and fortitude (young George Brooks, brother to the late Bishop Philipps Brooks), looked up into the sweet face of Mother Augustine, as she bent over to minister or to soothe the dear boy, with: 'Mother, thank you, Mother,' and with such an ineffable smile of peace. We could never tell if in his delirium he thought it was his own mother, but the peace on the boy's face showed what his nurse had been to him. His sickness was short and death came just before the father reached New Berne.

"One dear young friend of mine, Sergeant Charles Hinkling, was sick under their care many weeks; finally brought home to linger and die; but he and his family were most deeply grateful to the kind Sisters for the tender care bestowed upon him in their hospital, especially by Sister Gertrude.

"Sister Mary Gertrude is now the Mother Superior of an in institution in California, after a life of hard work among the poor and suffering. I think she is perhaps the only one living of those dear women I knew in New Berne.

"It was through the winter of 1862-63 that the Sisters were in New Berne. The next year the headquarters were removed to Fortress Monroe and the Sisters returned to New York.

"Through these thirty years more—my brother and many,

many more who could have borne evidence to the faithful work of the Sisters of Mercy in New Berne—have answered the roll call to the Home above. But those days stand out in my memory as clearly as if yesterday, with all the pain, anxiety, hope, fear and faith, and no scenes are more real to me than those hours with those devoted women who were helping God's children so wisely, so gently, with no thought of reward or glory! God bless their memories to us all."

CHAPTER XXVII.

A LESSON IN CHARITY.

An incident of the war in which a gentle Sister of Charity and a stern military commander played the leading parts. "What do you do with your beggings?" The Red River campaign and its fatal results. The general in the hospital. "Did you get the ice and beef?" A grateful patient and his appreciation of the real worth of the Sisters.

"During the late war, and when General S. was in command of the department at New Orleans, the Sisters of Charity made frequent applications to him for assistance.([1]) Especially were they  desirous to obtain supplies at what was termed 'commissary prices;' that is, at a reduction or commutation of one-third the amount which the same provisions would cost at market rates. The principal demand was for ice, flour, beef and coffee, but mainly ice, a luxury which only the Union forces could enjoy at anything like a reasonable price. The hospitals were full of the sick and wounded of both the Federal and Confederate armies, and the benevolent institutions of the city were taxed to the utmost in their endeavors to aid the poor and the suffering, fir those were trying times, and war has many victims. Foremost among these Christian workers stood the various Christian Sisterhoods. These

---

(1).This interesting narrative was originally published in "The Philadelphia Times" and afterwards in Father Corby's "Memories of Chaplain life."

noble women were busy day and night, never seeming to know fatigue, and overcoming every obstacle that, in so many discouraging forms, obstructed the way of doing good—obstacles which would have completely disheartened less resolute women, or those not trained in the school of patience, faith, hope and charity, and where the first grand lesson learned is self-denial. Of money there was little, and food, fuel and medicine were scarce and dear; yet they never faltered, going on in the face of all difficulties, through poverty, war and unfriendly aspersions, never turning aside, never complaining, never despairing. No one will ever know the sublime courage of these lordly Sisters during the dark days of the Rebellion. Only in that hour when the Judge of all mankind shall summon before Him the living and the dead will they receive their true reward, the crown everlasting, and the benediction: 'Well done, good and faithful servant.'

"It was just a week previous to the Red River campaign, when all was hurry and activity throughout the Department of the Gulf, that General S., a stern, irascible old officer of the regular army, sat at his desk in his office on Julia street, curtly giving orders to subordinates, dispatching messengers hither and thither to every part of the city where troops were stationed, and stiffly receiving such of his command as had important business to transact.

"In the midst of this unusual hurry and preparation the door noiselessly opened, and a humble Sister of Charity entered the room. A handsome young lieutenant of the staff instantly arose and deferentially handed her a chair, for those sombre gray garments were respected, if not understood, even though he had no reverence for the religious faith which they represented.

"General S. looked up from his writing, angered by the intrusion of one whose 'fanaticism' he despised, and a frown of annoyance and displeasure gathered darkly on his brow.

"'Orderly!'

"The soldier on duty without the door, who had admitted the Sister, faced about, saluted and stood mute, awaiting the further command of his chief.

"'Did I not give orders that no one was to be admitted?'

"'Yes, sir; but—'

"'When I say no one, I mean no one,' thundered the General.

"The orderly bowed and returned to his post. He was too wise a soldier to enter into explanation with so irritable a superior. All this time the patient Sister sat calm and still, biding the moment when she might speak and meekly state the object of her mission. The General gave her the opportunity in the briefest manner possible, and sharply enough, too, in all conscience.

"'Well, madam?'

"She raised a pair of sad, dark eyes to his face, and the gaze was so pure, so saintly, so full of silent pleading, that the rough old soldier was touched in spite of himself. Around her fell the heavy muffling dress of her order, which, however coarse and ungraceful, had something strangely solemn and mournful about it. Her hands, small and fair, were clasped almost suppliantly, and half-hidden in the loose sleeves, as if afraid of their own trembling beauty; hands that had touched tender-

UNION LEADERS OF THE CIVIL WAR.

HOWARD   KEARNY   BURNSIDE   SCOTT   ROSECRANS   WALLACE   CUSTER
THOMAS   HANCOCK   McCLELLAN   HOOKER   BUTLER   LOGAN

ly, lovingly, so many death-damp foreheads; that had soothed so much pain; eyes that had met prayerfully so many dying glances; lips that had cheered to the mysterious land so many parting souls, and she was only a Sister of Charity—only one of that innumerable band whose good deeds shall live after them.

"'We have a household of sick and wounded whom we must care for in some way, and I came to ask of you the privilege, which I humbly beseech you will not deny us, of obtaining ice and beef at commissary prices.'

"'Always something,' snarled the General. 'Last week it was flour and ice; to-day it is ice and beef; to-morrow it will be coffee and ice, I suppose, and all for a lot of rascally rebels, who ought to be shot, instead of being nursed back to life and treason.'

"'General!'—the Sister was majestic now—'Rebel or Federal, I do not know; Protestant or Catholic, I do not ask. They are not soldiers when they come to us; they are simply suffering fellow-creatures. Rich or poor, of gentle or lowly blood, it is not our province to inquire. Ununiformed, unarmed, sick and helpless, we ask not on which side they fought. Our work begins after yours is done. Yours the carnage, ours the binding up of wounds. Yours the battle, ours the duty of caring for the mangled left behind on the field. Ice I want for the sick, the wounded, the dying. I plead for all, I beg for all, I pray for all God's poor suffering creatures, wherever I may find them.'

"'Yes, you can beg, I'll admit. What do you do with all your beggings? It is always more, more! never enough!'

"With this, the General resumed his writing, thereby giving the Sister to understand that she was dismissed.

For a moment her eyes fell, her lips trembled—it was a cruel taunt. Then the tremulous hands slowly lifted and folded tightly across her breast, as if to still some sudden heartache the unkind words called up. Very low, and sweet, and earnest was her reply:

"'What do we do with our beggings? Oh, that is a hard question to ask of one whose way of life leads ever among the poor, the sorrowing, the unfortunate, the most wretched of mankind. Not on me is it wasted. I stand here in my earthly all. What do we do with it? Ah! some day you may know.'

"She turned away and left him, sad of face, heavy of heart, and her dark eyes misty with unshed tears.

"'Stay!'

"The General's request was like a command. He could be stern; nay, almost rude, but he knew truth and worth when he saw it, and could be just. The Sister paused on the threshold, and for a minute nothing was heard but the rapid scratching of the General's pen.

"'There, madam, is your order on the Commissary for ice and beef at army terms, good for three months. I do it for the sake of the Union Soldiers who are, or may be, in your care. Don't come bothering me again. Good-morning!'

"On less than three weeks from that day the slaughter of the Red River campaign had been perfected, and there neared the city of New Orleans a steamer flying the ominous yellow flag, which even the rebel sharpshooters respected and allowed to pass down the river unmolested. Another, and still another, followed closely in her wake, and all the decks were covered with the wounded and dying whose bloody bandages and, in many instances, undressed wounds gave woeful evidence of the lack of surgeons, as well as the completeness of the rout. Among the desperately wounded was General S. He was borne from the steamer to the waiting ambulance, writing in anguish from the pain of his bleeding and shell-torn limb, and when they asked him where he wished to be taken he feebly moaned:

"'Anywhere, it matters not. Where I can die in peace.'

"So they took him to the Hotel Dieu, a noble and beautiful institution, in charge of the Sisters of Charity. The limb was amputated and then he was nursed for weeks through the agony of the surgical operation, the fever, the wild delirium; and for many weary days no one could tell whether life or death would be the victor. But who was the quiet, faithful nurse, ever at his bedside, ever ministering to his wants, ever watchful of his smallest needs? Why only 'one of the Sisters.'

"At last life triumphed, reason returned, and with it much of the old, abrupt manner. The General awoke to consciousness to see a face not altogether unknown bending over him, and to feel a pair of small, deft hands skillfully arranging a bandage, wet in ice-cold water, around his throbbing temples, where the mad pain and aching had for so long a time held sway. He was better now, though still very weak; but his mind was clear, and he could think calmly and connectedly of all that had taken place since the fatal battle—a battle which had so nearly cost him his life and left him at best but a maimed and mutilated remnant of his former self.

"Yet he was thankful it was no worse—that he had not been killed outright. In like degree he was grateful to those who nursed him so tenderly and tirelessly, especially the gray-robed woman, who had become almost angelic in his eyes; and it was like him to express his gratitude in his own peculiar way, without preface or circumlocution. Looking intently at the Sister, as if to get her features well fixed in his memory, he said:

"'Did you get the ice and beef?'

"The Sister started. The question was so direct and unexpected. Surely her patient must be getting—really himself!

"'Yes,' she replied simply, but with a kind glance of the soft, sad eyes, that spoke eloquently her thanks.

"'And your name is—'

"'Sister Francis.'

"'Well, then, Sister Francis, I am glad you got the things—glad I gave you the order. I think I know now what you do with your beggings. I comprehend something of your work, your charity, your religion, and I hope to be the better for the knowledge. I owe you a debt I can never repay, but you will endeavor to believe that I am deeply grateful for all your great goodness and ceaseless care.'

"'Nay; you owe me nothing; but to Him, whose cross I bear in whose lordly footsteps I try to follow, you owe a debt of gratitude unbounded. To His infinite mercy I commend you. It matters not for the body; it is that divine mystery, the soul, I would save. My work here is done. I leave you to the care of others. Adieu.'

"The door softly opened and closed, and he saw Sister Francis no more.

"Two months afterward she received a letter sent to the care of the Mother Superior, enclosing a check for a thousand dollars. At the same time the General took occasion to remark that he wished he were able to make it twice the amount, since he knew by experience 'What they did with their beggings.'"

APPENDIX.

———◆◆◆———

I.

AN INNOCENT VICTIM.

The frontispiece, entitled "an Innocent Victim," that adorns this volume is taken from a famous painting executed by S. Seymour Thomas, an artist who is rapidly rising to fame. Mr. Thomas was born in San Augustine, Tex., studied in New York at the Art Students' League, and from there went to Paris, where he is recognized as an artist of great power. This picture was exhibited at the World's Columbian Exposition, in Chicago, where it attracted great attention.

———◆◆◆———

II.

MEDALS FOR SISTERS.

The official gazette of the French Government recently published an order of the Minister of War granting medals to certain Catholic Sisters. A gold medal has been awarded to Sister Clare, of the Order of Sisters of St. Charles, for twenty-seven years' service in the wards of the military hospital at Toul, and for previous service at Nancy, during the whole of which time she had given constant evidence of her devotion to duty. Silver medals have been given to Sister Gabrielle for thirty-six years' work, during twenty-three of which she has been Superior; to Sister Adrienne for thirty-eight years' service, and to Sister Charlotte, for eleven years' service. These last three religious have been attached to the mixed hospital of Verdun, and, according to the official notice, have been remarkable for their zeal and their devoted care of the sick soldiers.

III.

HONORED BY THE QUEEN.

The Queen of England only a few months ago showed her appreciation of the work of the Sisters in time of war by bestowing the Royal Red Cross upon the venerable Mother Aloysius Doyle, of the Convent of Mercy, Gort, Ireland. The following correspondence deserves to be preserved:

Pall Mall, London. S. W.,
February 15, 1897

Madam:—The Queen having been pleased to bestow upon you the decoration of the Royal Red Cross, I have to inform you that in the case of such honors as this it is the custom of Her Majesty to personally bestow the decoration upon the recipient when such a course is convenient to all concerned, and I have, therefore, to request that you will be so good as to inform me whether it would be convenient to you to attend at Windsor some time within the next few weeks. Should any circumstances prevent your receiving the Royal Red Cross from the hands of Her Majesty it could be transmitted by post to your present address. I am, madam, your obedient servant,

GEORGE M. FARQUHARSON.

SISTER MARY ALOYSIUS.

St. Patrick's, Gort, County Galway.

Sir:—I received your letter of the 15th, intimating to me that Her Most Gracious Majesty the Queen is pleased to bestow on me the Order of the Royal Cross in recognition of the services of my Sisters in religion and my own in caring for the wounded soldiers at the Crimea during the war. My words cannot express my gratitude for the great honor which Her Majesty is pleased to confer on me. The favor is, if possible, enhanced by the permission to receive this public mark of favor at Her Majesty's own hands. The weight of seventy-six years and the infirmities of age will, I trust, dispense me from the journey to the palace. I will, therefore, with sentiments of deepest gratitude ask to be permitted to receive this mark of my Sovereign's favor in the less public and formal manner you have kindly indicated. I am, sir, faithfully yours in Jesus Christ,

SISTER M. ALOYSIUS.

February 17, 1897.

IV.

VETERANS OF THE CRIMEAN WAR.

In August, 1897, at the close of the ceremonies incident to the celebration of her Diamond Jubilee, the Queen of Great Britain conferred the decoration of the Royal Red Cross upon Army Nursing Sisters Mary Helen Ellis, Mary Stanislaus Jones, Mary Anastasia Kelly and Mary de Chantal Huddon, in recognition of their services in tending the sick and wounded at the seat of the war during the Crimean campaign of 1854-56. Their services were very much appreciated by Miss Nightingale, who, indeed, has ever since shown her interest in them in many ways.

The three Sisters first mentioned, together with another who has died since, were on their return from the East, asked to undertake the nursing at a hospital, just then being established in Great Ormond street, for incurable and dying female patients, and to this hospital they have been attached to the present time.

V.

POOR SISTER ST. CLAIRE.

Professor Edward Roth, the well-known Philadelphia educator, is authority for this episode of the Franco-German war. He quotes General Ambert, who fought as a private in the war, as follows:

"Oh, yes; one of them I shall never forget. Poor Sister St. Claire! I see her this moment, her big black veil trimmed with blue, as she makes her way through the blood-smeared straw of our crowded barn. The roaring of the cannon was awful, but she did not seem to mind it; she did not seem to mind even the terrible fire that was now raging through the last houses of the village, the flames near enough to cast an unearthly glimmer on the suffering faces of the wounded men. But, oh! how her sharp ear caught the slightest complaint! How she flew towards the faintest whisper!

"Everywhere at once—with each one of us at the same time! What iron strength God must have put into that little body! Your Eye had hardly caught glimpse of it when you felt already at your lips the cool refreshing drink that you had not the courage to ask for. You had hardly opened your dimmed eyes, heavy with pain and fever , when you were aware of a face bending over you, keen, indeed, and bright, though slightly poxmarked; but so resolute, calm, smiling and kindly that you instantly forgot your sufferings, forgot the Prussians with their bombs bursting around you, forgot even the conflagration that was drawing nearer and nearer and threatened soon to swallow up the barn in which our ambulances had taken shelter. Good Sister St. Claire, you are now with your God, the voluntary victim of your heart and your faith, but I have often wished since that you were once more among us, listening to the thanks and prayers of such of us as are still alive and never to forget you. But you did not hear even the tenth part of the blessings of those that died with your name on their lips as they sank to their eternal sleep tranquilly, resignedly, hopefully, thanks to your holy ministrations!

"It was the evening of August 16, 1870, the day of our bloodiest battle—Gravelotte. For hours and hours the wounded had been carried persistently and in great numbers to the rear. In a large barn near Rezonville those of us had been laid whose intense sufferings would not permit them to be removed further. Thrown hurriedly down wherever room could be found, the first arms you saw extending towards you, were those of that little dark-faced woman, her lips smiling, but her eyes glistening with tears. A few yards only from the field of battle, from the very thick of the fight; a few yards only from the muddy, blood-slipping ground where you had just sunk, fully expecting to be soon trampled to death like so many others, what heavenly comfort it was to meet such burning charity! How it at once relieved your physical sufferings, soothed off your mortification and drove away your deadening despair!

"Poor Sister St. Claire! All that evening and all that long night to get water for the fifty agonized voices calling for it every moment you had to cross a yard hissing with bullets, but every five minutes out you went with your two buckets and back you soon came as serene and undisturbed as if God Himself had made you invulnerable. And so the long night wore away.

"But next morning our army, after a fifteen hours' valiant struggle and after resting all night on the battlefield, had to fall back towards Metz, and the barn had to be immediately vacated. There was no time for using the regular ambulances, for the Prussians, though they could not take any of our positions the previous evening, being heavily reinforced were now steadily advancing. The wounded, picked up hastily and carried out without ceremony, were piled on trucks, tumbrils and every available vehicle.

"Oh, the cries! the pains! the sufferings! Still, dear Sister St. Claire, though for forty-eight hours you hadn't had a second for your own rest, you contrived to pass continually from one end of that wretched column to the other, with a little water for this one, a good word for that, a smile or friendly nod for a third, your little arms lifting out of danger a head that leaned over too far, or shifting into a more comfortable position the poor fellow whose leg had been cut off during the night and who

CONFEDERATE LEADERS OF THE CIVIL WAR.

BRAGG   SMITH   PEMBERTON   HAMPTON   EARLY   FITZ-HUGH LEE   PICKETT
    "JOE" JOHNSTON   A. S. JOHNSTON   LONGSTREET   STUART   GORDON

would probably be dead in an hour or two. Then you found a seat for yourself on the last wagon.

"Alas! you were not there half an hour when the bullet struck you—struck you as you were striving to keep a poor, wounded, helpless man from rolling out. A squadron of Uhlans suddenly cut us off from the army and made us all prisoners.

"Poor Sister! It was by the hands of our enemies that the grave was dug where you are now lying in the midst of those on whom you expended the treasures of your saintly soul. Of us that survive you there is probably not one in a thousand that will ever know the name of that little Sister of the Trinity—in religion Sister St. Claire—that bright vision of charity flashing continually before us during the long ride of agony in the barn near Rezonville.

"Your holy limbs are now resting in an unknown corner of Lorraine—no longer your dear France—but your blessed memory will live forever in the grateful hearts of those you have died for!"

VI.

LORD NAPIER'S TESTIMONY.

Lord Napier, who held a diplomatic position under Lord Stratford de Redcliffe, in Constantinople, during the Crimean War, gives the following testimony to the worth of the Sisters of Mercy:

"During the distress of the Crimean war the Ambassador called me in one morning and said: 'Go down to the port; you will find a ship there loaded with Jewish exiles, Russian subjects from the Crimea. It is your duty to disembark them. The Turks will give you a house in which they may be placed. I turn them over entirely to you.' I went down to the shore and received about 200 persons, the most miserable objects that could be witnessed, most of them old men, women and children, sunk in the lowest depths of indigence and despair. I placed them in the cold, ruinous lodging allocated to them by the Ottoman authorities. I went back to the Ambassador and said: 'Your Excellency, those people are cold and I have no fuel or blankets; they are hungry, and I have no food; they are very dirty, and I have no soap; their hair is in an undesirable condition and I have no combs. What am I to do with these people?' 'Do?' said the Ambassador; 'get a couple of Sisters of Mercy; they will put all to rights in a moment.' I went, saw the Mother Superior and explained the case. I asked for two Sisters. They were at once sent. They were ladies of refinement and intellect. I was a stranger and a Protestant, and I invoked their assistance for the benefit of Jews. Yet these two women made up their bundles and followed me through the rain without a look, a whisper or a sign of hesitation. From that moment my fugitives were saved. No one saw the labors of those Sisters for months but myself, and they never endeavored to make a single convert."

In his speeches in after times Lord Napier repeatedly referred to the singular zeal and devotedness constantly shown by the Sisters to the sick of every denomination. On one occasion, in Edinburgh, he remarked that the Sisters faithfully kept their promise not to interfere with the religion of non-Catholics, but, continued his Lordship, "they made at least one convert; they converted

me, if not to believe in the Catholic faith, at least to believe in the Sisters of Mercy."

The few months spent at Balaklava by the devoted
Sisters witnessed a repetition of the deeds of heroism
which had achieved such happy results at Scutari and
Koulali. The cholera and a malignant type of fever had
broken out in those days in the camp. By night as well
as by day the Sisters were called to help the patients, yet
their strength seemed never to fail in their work of charity. Besides the soldiers, there were sick civilians, Maltese,
Germans, Greeks, Italians, Americans and even negroes,
and they all endeavored to give some attention.

The medical orders reveal the constant nature of the
nursing required at their hands. At one time the doctor "requests that a Sister would sit up with his Dutch
patient in No. 9 ward to-night." Again, "Sisters to sit up
with the Maltese and the Arab." "Kind attendance on
Jones every night would be necessary until a notification
to the contrary be given." "Keep the stump moist; a little
champagne and water to be given during the night." "El-
liot is to be watched all night; powder every half hour;
wine in small dose if necessary." The very confidence
placed by the physicians in their careful treatment added
to their toil. As the deputy purveyor-in-chief reported
to the Government in December, 1855: "The medical
officer can safely consign his most critical case to their
hands; stimulants or opiates ordered every five minutes
will be faithfully administered, though the five minutes'
labor were repeated uninterruptedly for a week."

The heroism of the nuns, however, was now well
known in camp, and never did workers find more sympathetic subordinates than the Sisters had in their or-

derlies. The fact that they would never lodge complaints or have the orderlies punished only made the men more zealous in their service. One of the Sisters found it necessary to correct her orderly. "Perhaps, James," she said "you do not wish me to speak to you a little severely." He at once interrupted her: "Troth, Sister, I glory in your speaking to me. Sure the day I came to Balaklava I cried with you when I saw your face." One who had taken a glass too much was so mortified at being seen by the Rev. Mother—whom the soldiers call their commander-in-chief—that he sobbed like a child. Another in the same predicament hid himself that he might not be seen by the Sister. He had never hidden from the enemy; a medal with three clasps bore eloquent testimony to his bravery. "I don't like to say anything harsh," said the Sister. "Speak, ma'am," interrupted the delinquent; "the words out of your blessed mouth are like jewels falling over me."

One of the Sisters writes: "We have not a cross here with anyone. The medical officers all work beautifully with us. They quite rely on our obedience. Sir John Hall, the head medical officer of the army, is quite loud in his promise of the nuns. The hospital and its hunts are scattered over a hill. The respect of all for the Sisters is daily increasing. Don't be shocked to hear that I am so accustomed to the soldiers now and so sure of their respect and affection that I don't mind them more than the school children." The soldiers in the camp envied the good fortune of stratagem to have a few words with the nuns. "Please, sir," they would say to the chaplain, "do send a couple of us on an errand to the hospital to get a sight of the nuns."

As the time for the nuns' departure approached the

cordial manifestations of respect and kindly feeling were only more multiplied. "The grateful affection of the soldiers (a Sister writes) is most touching, often ludicrous. They swarm around us like flocks of chickens. A black-veiled nun, in the midst of red coats all eyes and ears for whatever she says to them, is an ordinary sight at Balaklava. Our doors were besieged by them to get some little keepsake; a book in which we write 'Given by a Sister of Mercy' is so valuable an article that a Protestant declared he would rather have such a gift than the Victoria Cross or Crimean medal."

The Sunday after the nuns' departure the men who went to the chapel sobbed and cried as though their hearts would break. When the priest turned to speak to them and asked their prayers for the safe passage of the nuns they could not control their emotion. "I was obliged to cut short my discourse," wrote the chaplain, "else I should have cried and sobbed with my poor men." This sympathy was shown by Protestants and Catholics alike, and from the commander-in-chief to the private soldier, from the first medical officers to the simple presser in the surgery, all was a chorus in praise of the "untiring, judicious and gentle nursing of the Sisters of Mercy."

Two Sisters of Mercy were summoned to their crowns from the hospitals of the East. One was English, a lay Sister from the convent at Liverpool. She fell a victim to the cholera which raged at Balaklava. The other was a choir Sister from Ireland, Sister M. Elizabeth Butler. Already rumors of peace had brought joy to the camp, when toward the close of February 7, 1855, she caught typhus attending the sick and in a few days joyfully bade farewell to the world. One of the surviving Sisters describes her funeral. The Eighty-ninth Regiment obtained the honor and privilege of bearing the coffin to the grave. One officer earnestly desired to be among the chosen, but thought he was not worthy, as he had not been at Holy Communion on that morning. The whole medical staff attended. The Sisters of Charity at the Sardinian camp sent five of their number to express sympathy and condolence. Eight chaplains attended to perform the last rites for the heroine of charity.

The place of interment was beside the departed lay Sister, on a rocky hill rising over the waters of the Black Sea. The funeral was a most impressive sight. The soldiers in double file, the multitudes of various nations, ranks and employments, the silence unbroken, save by the voice of tears, the groups, still as statuary that crowded the brocks above the grave, the moaning of the sullen waves beneath, all combined in a weird pageant never to be forgotten by the thousands that took part in it. The graves of these cherished Sisters were tended with loving attention. Marked by crosses and enclosed by a high iron railing set in cut stone, they are still quite visible from the Black Sea beneath. Many a pilgrim went thither to strew the graves with flowers; and to the present day many a vessel entering the Black Sea lowers its flag in memory of those heroines, who in the true spirit of charity devoted their lives to alleviate the suffering of their countrymen.

VII.

VERY REV. JAMES FRANCIS BURLANDO, C. M.

The Very Rev. James Francis Burlando, of the congregation of the Mission, who is mentioned several times in the text of this volume, was born on May 6, 1814, in the city of Genoa, Italy. Very early in life he became impressed with the desire of adopting the priesthood as his vocation, and on the 16th of February, 1837, his Archbishop, Cardinal Tadini, conferred on him the holy orders of sub-deacon and deacon.

Soon after this he sailed for the United States and enlisted for the American missions under Rev. John Odin, C. M., late Archbishop of New Orleans, who at that time was seeking recruits for the infant seminary at the Barrens, Missouri. Before Father Burlando could come here he was obliged to meet and overcome a very strong opposition on the part of his good father, who, although a fervent Christian, could not bear the idea of being separated from his first-born son.

The very day that Father Burlando was to be admitted to the novitiate he perceived his father at the Archiepiscopal Hall, waiting for an audience with Cardinal Tadini. Guessing at once the motive of such an interview, namely, that he might exercise his authority and command the young deacon, in virtue of holy obedience to remain with his father and family, which would prevent him from carrying out his holy desire, the young man sought to baffle the intention of his father by seeing the Archbishop first and securing his permission and blessing.

Accordingly he had recourse to the following stratagem: He borrowed from his friends the various articles of a clerical suit; from one a hat, from another a cassock differing from his own, from a third a cloak, and, to render the disguise more complete, he put on a pair of spectacles and wig. Thus equipped, he entered the house of the Cardinal, had a conversation with him, in which he received his approbation and blessing, and passed out again without being recognized by his father, who he left standing at the door watching closely every young seminarian who entered. Fearing he might be discovered, the young man quickened his pace, and repaired immediately to the venerable R. Bartholomew Gazzano,, then Superior of the Lazarists, who received him.

In the following June he left Genoa and repaired to Turin, where he was ordained priest on the 9th of July by the Most Rev. Aloysius Fransoni, Archbishop of that See. To mitigate in some measure the pain which his good father experienced on account of this separation, Father Burlando wrote him a pressing invitation to honor and gratify him by being present at his first Mass, on the 10th of July. Touched by his son's filial respect and affection, he at last relented and assisted with tearful devotion at the impressive ceremony.

A few weeks after Father Burlando went to the Mother House, in Paris, whence he set out for New-Orleans. Having landed safely on the American shore, he proceeded by steamboat to Missouri, and reached the Seminary of the Barrens towards the close of the same year. He filled many positions of trust and honor. The last and most important field of his apostolic labors was the Community of the Daughters of Charity, at the Central House of St. Joseph's near Emmitsburg, Md., whither he repaired in the spring of 1853, and where he remained for the space of twenty-three years.

"During all that time," says Father Gandolfo, his assistant, "I had more occasion than anyone else of observing his noble qualities of mind and heart. As a Superior he was always kind, discreet, obliging, generous, amiable and edifying in all that regarded the observance even of the least rule, beginning from rising at 4 o'clock in the morning at the first sound of the Benedicamus Domino. He was exceedingly charitable and ever ready to assist me at the first request in the performance of my duties, and this notwithstanding his frequent attacks of neuralgia and weakness of the digestive organs. I never saw him misspend a minute of his time. If he was not occupied in answering his numerous correspondents he was drawing plans of hospitals and other buildings, or attending to similar important affairs of the Community. He never retired to rest without having first read the many letters he daily received from every quarter of the United States. Although he frequently retired very late and slept but a few hours during the night, he was always ready for the hard labor of the next day."

It was largely due to the wise administration of this worthy director that the Community owed, and owes, its singular prosperity and development. It suffices to state that when he assumed the duties of his position there were only three hundred members distributed among thirty-six houses, and he lived to see the white Cornette on the brow of one thousand and forty-five Daughters of St. Vincent, having under their control ninety-seven establishments for the service of the poor, affording relief for almost every species of misfortune. Owing to his superior knowledge of architecture, he not only planned but personally supervised the erection of the greater number of these charitable institutions.

It would be impossible to enumerate the long and painful journeys he took, the multiplied dangers to which he exposed himself, and the many privations he endured for the particular welfare of the different establishments of the Sisters. How many sleepless nights he passed during our late civil war! There were Sisters in the North and Sisters in the South, but, by his constant vigilance, his consummate prudence, his repeated fatherly admonitions, and especially by his continual and fervent prayers, he had the consolation of seeing the entire Community free from all reproach and danger.

He has left many valuable volumes which prove his ability as a writer as well as a thinker. One of these is the "Ceremonial," which was entrusted to him by the Most Rev. Archbishop Kenrick, approved by the Provincial Council, and which is now largely used throughout the United States. In this valuable work all the details relative to the Mass and offices of the Church, the sacred vessels and other articles used are minutely described, so that solemnity, beauty and becoming uniformity may be maintained. He also compiled the life of Father De Andreis, the pioneer of the Lazarists in this country. To him we are also indebted for the publication of the beautiful life of "Sister Eugenie, Daughter of Charity."

A person remarked that he must be well and extensively known throughout the United States, as he was always traveling and had to register his name in the hotels. "Oh, no," he replied, "I give my name in as many different languages as I can. In this way I pass unnoticed, and get a little recreation at the expense of the poor recorder, who is often at a loss to spell the foreign name. He looks bewildered, repeats it several times, and casts an inquiring glance at me; meantime I pretend stupidity and leave him write whatever he likes. Then, you see, Francis Burlando is not known."

This devoted priest breathed his last on Sunday, February 16, 1873, at the close of a day well spent in the exercise of his sacred functions. The funeral service took place in the Central House of the Sisters of Charity, St. Joseph's, Emmitsburg, February 19, and the remains were interred in the little cemetery of the Sisters of Charity, besides the mortuary chapel, wherein repose the venerated remains of Saintly Mother Seton, foundress of the Sisters of Charity in the United States.

VIII.

MOTHER SETON.

Mother Elizabeth Ann Seton, the founder and first Superior of the Sisters of Charity in the United States, was one of the most remarkable women in the history of the Catholic Church in America. She was reared in the doctrines of the Protestant Episcopal Church and did not embrace the Catholic faith until after the death of her husband.

This distinguished woman, who was born in the city of New York on the 28th of August, 1774, was a younger daughter of Richard Bayley, an eminent physician of the metropolis. Her mother died when she was but three years of age, but her father watched over her with all the loving care of a good parent. As Miss Bayley advanced in years, nature and education combined in developing those admirable traits of character that were to make her so lovable and merciful in later life. All of her friends and relatives were members of the Protestant Episcopal Church, but the physician's daughter was more fervent in her religious duties than any of those with whom she was associated. From her earliest years she wore a small crucifix on her person, and was frequently heard to express regret and astonishment that the custom was not more general among the members of her church.

At the age of twenty Miss Bayley was married to William Seton, a prosperous and most estimable merchant, of New York city. It was a happy marriage, and husband and wife lived in mutual love and esteem. In 1800 Mr. Seton became embarrassed through a reaction in business, caused mainly by the consequences of the Revolutionary war. In this crisis Mrs. Seton was a helpmate in every sense of the word. She not only cheered her husband by her encouraging counsel, but rendered him practical aid in arranging his business affairs.

In the course of her married life Mrs. Seton became the mother of five children, Anna Maria, William, Richard, Catherine Josephine and Rebecca. She was a model mother, restraining, guiding and educating her offspring with a mingling of tact, tenderness and edifying example. She did not confine her goodness to her children, but was ever ready to assist the poor and suffering. One of her biographers says she was so zealous in this respect "that she and a relative who accompanied her were commonly called Protestant Sisters of Charity."

The death of Mrs. Seton's father in 1801 was a source of great sorrow to this devoted woman. Years had only served to cement the affectionate relations between father and daughter. During the last three or four years of his life Dr. Bayley was Health Officer at the Port of New York. He was naturally of a philanthropic disposition, and his official duties called him to a field that presented an unbounded field for Christian charity. It was while in the discharge of his duty among the immigrants that Dr. Bayley contracted the illness which carried him to his grave within a week's time.

Mrs. Seton had scarcely recovered from the shock of her father's death when her husband's health, which had never been robust, began to decline rapidly. A sea voyage and a sojourn in Italy were recommended. Mrs. Seton could not permit her husband to travel alone in his weak and exhausted state, and she accompanied him, along with her oldest child, a girl of eight. The other children were committed to the care of relatives in New York city. The child caught the whooping cough on the way over, and the anxious mother was constantly occupied in nursing the husband and daughter. Before landing the unfortunate trio were detained for many days at the lazaretto station in the harbor of Leghorn. After they landed the good wife was untiring in her attentions to her husband, but, in spite of her love and solicitude, he died on the 27th of December "among strangers and in a foreign land."

On the following 8th of April, with her tears still fresh upon the grave of her devoted husband, Mrs. Seton sailed for home. Prior to this voyage and during the fifty-six days that it occupied, Mrs. Seton began to take a deep interest in the doctrines and practices of the Catholic Church. She eagerly devoured all of the literature upon the subject that opportunity offered, and also learned much by frequent conversations with friends. Deep meditation finally strengthened her in the desire to become a Catholic. Her only fear was that a change in her religious faith might bring about a coldness and a severance of the friendship that existed between herself and her friends and relatives—particularly her pastor—Rev. J. H. Hobart, a man of singular talent and goodness, who afterwards became the Protestant Episcopal Bishop of New York.

Writing of the possibility of such an estrangement in her diary at this time, Mrs. Seton says with evident feeling: "If your dear friendship and esteem must be the price of my fidelity to what I believe to be the truth, I cannot doubt the mercy of God, who, by depriving me of one of my remaining dearest ties on earth, will certainly draw me nearer to him." She was not mistaken. When she returned home the coldness of many of her Protestant friends was a great trial to her warm and still bleeding heart. The storm of opposition added to her grief.

The fact that Mrs. Seton was in doubt upon the question of religion made her a subject of attack for the friends of all denominations. Writing of this, she says: "I had a most affectionate note from Mr. Hobart to-day, asking me how I could ever think of leaving the Church in which I was baptized. But, though whatever he says has the weight of my partiality for him, as well as the respect it seems to me I could scarcely have for anyone else, yet that question made me smile; for it is like saying that whatever a child is born and wherever its parents place it, there it will find the truth; and he does not hear the droll invitations made me every day since I am in my little new home and old friends come to see me.

"It has already happened that one of the most excellent women I ever knew, who is of the Church of Scotland, finding me unsettled about the great object of a true faith, said to me: 'Oh, do, dear soul, come and hear our J. Mason and I am sure you will join us.'

"A little after came one whom I loved, for the purest and most innocent of manners, of the Society of Quakers (to which I have always been attached), she coaxed me, too, with artless persuasion: 'Betsey, I tell thee, thee had better come with us.' And my faithful old friend of the Anabaptist meeting, Mrs. T——, says, with tears in her eyes: 'Oh! could you be regenerated; could you know our experiences and enjoy with us our heavenly banquet.' And my good old Mary, the Methodist, groans and contemplates, as she calls it, over my soul, so misled because I have got no convictions. But, oh, my Father and My God! all that will not do for me. Your word is truth, and without contradiction, whatever it is. One faith, one hope, one baptism, I look for, whatever it is, and I often think my sins, my miseries, hide the light. Yet I will cling and hold to my God to the last gasp, begging for that light, and never change until I find it."

Mrs. Seton's doubts were finally set at rest, and on Ash Wednesday, 1805, she was received into Catholicism in old St. Peter's Church, New York city. The embarrassed state of her husband's finances at the time of his death had involved her, and she opened a boarding house for some of the boys who attended a neighboring school. Some months later Miss Cecilia Seton, the youngest sister-in-law of Mrs. Seton, followed her into the Catholic Church. The one thought of Mrs. Seton was now to devote her life to the poor and to the Church. The opportunity came sooner than she anticipated. The co-operation of the Church authorities, and financial resources being forthcoming, a little Community was formed in St. Joseph's Valley, Emmitsburg. Vows were taken in accordance with the rules of the institute of the Sisters of Charity, of France, and in a few months ten Sisters were employed with the instruction of youth and the care of the sick. They were poor but happy. The first Christmas day, for instance, "they rejoiced to have some smoked herring for dinner. Rigid regulations were adopted for the government of the new order, and its growth was remarkable. Mother Seton had the satisfaction of receiving her eldest daughter into the Sisterhood. This child, as well as her youngest daughter, died soon after this. Her sons were prosperously launched in business enterprises.

Mother Seton died on the fourth of January, 1821, in the forth-seventh year of her age. Her bedside was surrounded by the dark-robed Sisters of Charity and her only surviving daughter, Josephine. Her end was happy and tranquil. Her career was one of great piety and usefulness. She has gone but her memory will live forever through the perpetration of the great order that she planted in the United States, and which has already grown to proportions far beyond the most sanguine expectation of its tender and affectionate founder.

IX.

"THE SISTER OF CHARITY."

This beautiful poem, descriptive of a Sister of Charity, written by Gerald Griffin, has taken its place among those precious bits of literature that never die. The author was born in Limerick, Ireland, in 1803, and began his literary career as a reporter for a London Daily. He wrote many novels, a tragedy and various poems. He died in Cork, in 1840. "The Sister of Charity" is as follows:

She was once a lady of honor and wealth,
Bright glowed on her features the roses of health,
Her vesture was blended of silk and of gold,
And her motion shook perfume from every fold;
Joy reveled around her—love shone at her side,
And gay was her smile as the glance of a bride;
And light was her step in the mirth-sounding hall
When she heard of the daughters of Vincent De Paul.

She felt in her spirit the summons of grace,
That called her to live for the suffering race;
And heedless of pleasure, of comfort, of home,
Rose quickly like Mary and answered, "I come."
She put from her person the trappings of pride,
And passed from her home with the joy of a bride;
Nor wept at the threshold as onward she moved,
For her heart was on fire in the cause it approved.

Lost ever to fashion—to vanity lost,
That beauty that once was the song and the toast.
No more in the ball room that figure we meet,
But gliding at dusk to the wretch's retreat.
Forgot in the hall is that high-sounding name,
For the Sister of Charity blushes at fame;
Forgot are the claims of her riches and birth,
For she barters for heaven the glory of earth.

Those feet that to music could gracefully move
Now bear her alone on the mission of love;
Those hands that once dangled the perfume and gem
Are tending the helpless or lifted for them;
That voice that once echoed the song of the vain
Now whispers relief to the bosom of pain;
And the hair that was shining with diamond and pearl
Is wet with the tears of a penitent girl.

Her down-bed a pallet—her trinkets a bead,
Her lustre—one taper that serves her to read;
Her sculpture—the crucifix nailed by her bed;
Her paintings one print of the crown-thorned head;
Her cushion—the pavement that wearies her knees;
Her music—the Psalm or the sigh of disease;

The delicate body lives mortified there,
And the feast is forsaken for fasting and prayer.

Yet not to the service of heart and mind,
Are the cares of that heaven-minded virgin confined.
Like Him whom she loves, to the mansions of grief
She hastes with the tidings of joy and relief.
She strengthens the weary—she comforts the weak,
And soft is her voice in the ear of the sick;
Where want and affliction on mortals attend
The Sister of Charity there is a friend.

Unshrinking where pestilence scatters his breath,
Like an angel she moves mid the vapor of death,
Where rings the loud musket and flashes the sword
Unfearing she walks, for she follows the Lord.
How sweetly she bends o'er each plague-tainted face
With looks that are lighted with holiest grace;
How kindly she dresses each suffering limb,
For she sees in the wounded the image of Him.

Behold her, ye worldly! Behold her, ye vain!
Who shrink from the pathway of virtue and pain;
Who yield up to pleasure your nights and your days,
Forgetful of service, forgetful of praise;
Yet lazy philosophers—self-seeking men—
Ye fireside philanthropists, great at the pen,
How stands in the balance your eloquence weighed,
With the life and the deeds of that high-born maid?

X.

SISTERS OF CHARITY.

(In Mr. Southey's "Sir Thomas More" the following account of the Beguines of Belgium and the Sisters of Charity of France is reprinted from the London Medical Gazette, Vol. I.)

A few summers ago I passed through Flanders on my way to Germany, and at the hospital at Bruges saw some of the Beguines, and heard the physician, with whom I was intimate, speak in strong terms of their services. He said "There are no such nurses." I saw them in the wards attending on the sick, and in the chapel of the hospital on their knees washing the floor. They were obviously a superior class of women, and the contrast was striking between these menial offices and the respectability of their dress and appearance; but the Beguinage of Ghent is one of their principal establishments, and, spending a Sunday there, I went in the evening to vespers. It was twilight when I entered the chapel. It was dimly lighted by two or three tall tapers before the altar and a few candles at the remotest end of the building, in the orchestra, but the body of the chapel was in deep gloom, filled from end to end with several hundreds of these nuns seated in rows, in their dark dresses and white cowls, silent and motionless, excepting now and then one of them started up, and, stretching out her arms in the attitude of the crucifixion, stood in that posture many minutes, then sank and disappeared among the crowd. The gloom of the chapel, the long line of these unearthly-looking figures, like so many corpses propped up in their grave clothes—the dead silence of the building, once only interrupted by a few voices in the distant orchestra chanting vespers, was one of the most striking sights I ever beheld. To some readers, the occasional attitude of the nuns may seem an absurd expression of fanaticism, but they are anything but fanatics. Whoever is accustomed to the manners of Continental nations knows that they employ a grimace in everything. I much doubt whether, apart from the internal emotion of piety, the external expression of it is graceful in anyone, save only a little child in his night-

FARRAGUT IN THE RIGGING.

shirt, on his knees, saying his evening prayer.

The Beguinage, or residence of the Beguines at Ghent, is a little town of itself, adjoining the city, and inclosed from it. The transition from the crowded streets of Ghent to the silence and solitude of the Beguinage is very striking. The houses in which the Beguines reside are contiguous, each having its small garden, and on the door the name, not of the resident, but of the protecting saint of the house; these houses are ranged into streets. There is also the large church, which we visited, and a burial ground, in which there are no monuments. There are upwards of six hundred of these nuns in the Beguinage of Ghent, and about six thousand in Brabant and Flanders. They receive sick persons into the Beguinage, and not only nurse, but support them, until they are recovered; they also go out to nurse the sick. They are bound by no vow excepting to be chaste and obedient while they remain in the order; they have the power of quitting it and returning again into the world whenever they please, but this, it is said, they seldom or never do. They are most of them women, unmarried, or widows past the middle of life. In 1244 a synod at Fritzlau decided that no Beguine should be younger than 40 years of age. They generally dine together in the refectory; their apartments are barely yet comfortably furnished, and, like all the habitations of Flanders, remarkably clean. About their origin and name little is known by the Beguines themselves, or is to be found in books. For the following particulars I am chiefly indebted to the "Histoire des Ordres Monastiques" (tome viii):

Some attributed both their origin and name to St. Begghe, who lived in the seventh century; others to Lambert le Beague, who lived about the end of the twelfth century. This latter saint is said to have founded two Communities of them at Liege, one for women, in 1173, the other for men, in 1177. After his death they multiplied fast, and were introduced by St. Louis into Paris and other French cities. The plan flourished in France, and was adopted under other forms and names. In 1443 Nicholas Rollin, Chancellor to Philip the Good, Duke of burgundy, founded a hospital at Beaune and brought six Beguines from Malines to attend upon it, and the hospital became so famed for the care of its patients that the opulent people of the neighborhood, when sick, were often removed to it, preferring its attendance to what they received at home. In one part of the hospital there was a large square court, bordered with galleries leading to apartments suitable to such patients; when they quitted the hospital the donations which they left were added to its funds.

The Soeurs de la Charite, of France, are another order of religious nurses, but different from the Beguines in being bound by monastic vows. They originated in a charity sermon, perhaps the most useful and extensive in its influence that ever was preached. Vincent de Paul, a celebrated missionary, preaching at Chatillon, in 1617, recommended a poor sick family of the neighborhood to the care of his congregation. At the conclusion of the sermon a number of persons visited the sick family with bread, wine, meat and other comforts. This led to the formation of a committee of charitable women, under the direction of Vincent de Paul, who went about relieving the sick poor of the neighborhood, and met every month to give an account of their proceedings to their superior. Such was the origin of the celebrated order of the Soeurs de la Charite. Wherever this missionary went he attempted to form similar establishments. From the country they spread to cities, and first to Paris, where, in 1629, they were established in the parish of St. Savious.

And in 1625 a female devotee, named Le Gras, joined the order of the Soeurs de la Charite. She was married young to M. Le Gras, one of whose family had founded a hospital at Puy, but, becoming a widow in 1625, in the thirty-fourth year of her age, she made a vow of celibacy, and dedicated the rest of her life to the service of the poor. In her Vincent de Paul found a great accession. Under the direction she took many journeys, visiting and inspecting the establishments which he had founded. She was commonly accompanied by a few pious ladies. Many women of quality enrolled themselves in the order, but the superiors were assisted by inferior servants. The Hotel Dieu was the first hospital in Paris where they exercised their vocation. This they visited every day, supplying the patients with comforts above what the hospital afforded, and administering, besides, religious consolation. By degrees they spread into all the provinces of France, and at length the Queen of Poland requested Mademoiselle Le Gras, for though a widow that was her title, to send her a supply of Soeurs de la Charite, who were thus established in Varsovia, in 1652. At length, after a long life spent in the service of charity and religion, Mademoiselle Le Gras died on the 15th of March, 1660, nearly seventy years of age, and for a day and a half her body lay exposed to the gaze of the pious.

A country clergyman, who spent several years in various parts of France, gives an account of the present state of the order, which, together with what I have gathered from other sources, is in substance as follows:

It consists of women of all ranks, many of them of the higher orders. After a year's novitiate in the convent, they take a vow which binds them to the order for the rest of their lives. They have two objects, to attend the sick and to educate the poor; they are spread all over France, are the superior nurses at the hospitals, and are to be found in every town, and often even in villages. Go into the Paris hospitals at almost any hour of the day, and you will see one of these respectable-looking women, in her black gown and white hood, passing slowly from bed to bed, and stopping to inquire of some poor wretch what little comfort he is fancying will alleviate his sufferings. If a parochial curé wants assistance in the care of his flock he applies to the Order of Les Soeurs de la Charite. Two of them (for they generally go in couples), set out on their charitable mission; wherever they travel their dress protects them. "Even more enlightened persons than the common peasantry hail it as a happy omen when on a journey with a Soeur de la Charite happens to travel with them, and even instances are recorded in which their presence has saved travelers from the attacks of robbers." During the Revolution they were rarely molested. They were the only religious order permitted openly to wear their dress and pursue their vocation. Government gives a hundred francs a year to each Sister, besides her traveling expenses; and if the parish where they go cannot maintain them, they are supported out of the funds of the order. In old age they retire to their convents and spend the rest of their lives in educating the novitiates. Thus, like the vestal virgins of old, the first part of their life is spent learning their duties, the second in practicing them, and the last in teaching them.

XI.

"THE ANGELS OF BUENA VISTA."

(Written by John Greenleaf Whittier with reference to the work of the Sisters of Mercy at the battle of Buena Vista, during the Mexican war.)

Speak and tell us, our Ximena, looking northward far away,
O'er the camp of the invaders, o'er the Mexican army.
Who is losing? Who is winning? Are they far or come they near?
Look ahead, and tell us, Sister, whither rolls the storm we hear.

"Down the hills of Augostura still the storm of battle rolls;
Blood is flowing, men are dying; God have mercy on their souls!"
Who is losing? Who is winning?—"over hill and over plain,
I see but smoke of cannon, clouding through the mountain rain."

Holy Mother! keep our brothers! Look, Ximena, look once more.
"Still I see the fearful whirlwind rolling darkly as before,
Bearing on in strange confusion, friend and foeman, foot and horse,
Like some wild and troubled torrent sweeping down its mountain course."

Look forth once more, Ximena! "Oh! the smoke has rolled away;
And I see the Northern rifles gleaming down the ranks of gray.
Hark! that sudden blast of bugles! there the troop of Minon wheels,
There the Northern horses thunder, with the cannon at their heels.

"Jesu, pity! how it thickens! Now retreat and now advance!
Right against the blazing cannon showers Pueblo's charging lance!
Down they go, the brave young riders; horse and foot together fall;
Like a plowshare in the fallow through them ploughs the Northern ball."

Nearer came the storm and nearer, rolling fast and frightful on;
Speak, Ximena, speak and tell us who has lost and who has won?
"Alas, alas! I know not, friend and foe together fall,
O'er the dying rush the living; pray my Sisters for them all."

"Lo! the wind the smoke is lifting; Blessed Mother save my brain!
I can see the wounded crawling slowly out from heaps of slain.
Now they stagger, blind and bleeding; now they fall and strive to rise;

Hasten, Sisters, haste and save them, lest they die before our eyes.

"O my heart's love, O my dear one! lay thy poor head on my knee;
Dost thou know the lips that kiss thee? Cans't thou hear me? Cans't thou see?
Oh, my husband, brave and gentle! O my Bernal, look once more
On the blessed cross before thee! Mercy! Mercy! all is o'er!"

Dry thy tears, my poor Ximena; lay thy dear one down to rest;
Let his hands be meekly folded, lay the cross upon his breast;
Let his dirge be sung hereafter, and his funeral masses said;
To-day, thou poor bereaved one, the living ask thy aid.

Close beside her, faintly, faintly moaning, fair and young a soldier lay,
Torn with shot and pierced with lances, bleeding slow his life away;
But, as tenderly before him the lorn Ximena knelt,
She saw the Northern eagle shining on his pistol belt.

With a stifled cry of horror straight she turned away her head;
With a sad and bitter feeling look'd she back upon her dead;
But she heard the youth's low moaning, and his struggling breath of pain,
And she raised the cooling water to his parching lips again.

Whisper'd low the dying soldier, press'd her hand and faintly smiled.
Was that pitying face his mother's? Did she watch besides her child?
All his stronger words with meaning her woman's heart supplied;
With her kiss upon his forehead, "Mother!" murmur'd he and died.

"A bitter curse upon them, poor boy, who led thee forth,
From some gentle sad-eyed mother, weeping, lonely in the North!"
Spoke the mournful Mexic woman, as she laid him with her dead,
And turn'd to soothe the living, and bind the wounds which bled.

Look forth once more Ximena! like a cloud before the wind
Rolls the battle down the mountains leaving blood and death behind.
Oh! they plead in vain for mercy—in the dust the wounded strive;
Hide your faces, holy angels! O thou Christ of God forgive!

Sink, O night, among thy mountains! let the cool gray shadows fall;
Dying brothers, fighting demons, drop they curtain over all!
Through the thickening winter twilight, wide apart the battle rolled,
In its sheath the sabre rested and the cannon's mouth grew cold.

But the noble Mexic women still their holy task pursued,
Through that long dark night of sorrow worn and faint and lacking food;
Over weak and suffering brothers, with a tender care they hung,
And the dying foeman bless'd them in a strange and Northern tongue.

Not wholly lost, O Father, is this evil world of ours;
Upward, through its blood and ashes spring afresh the Eden flowers;
From its smoking hill of battle love and pity send their prayer,
And still Thy white-wing'd angels hover dimly in our air.

XII.

CATHERINE ELIZABETH McAULEY.

Miss Catherine Elizabeth McAuley, the foundress of the Order of Sisters of Mercy, ranks high among the notable women whose achievements have enriched the history of the Catholic Church. The religious institution first planted by her in the city of Dublin has spread to such an extent that its branches now spread into at least every quarter of the English-speaking globe. The communities of the Sisters of Mercy in the United States have done excellent work in many fields, but they particularly distinguished themselves as nurses during the unhappy conflict between the North and the South.

Miss McAuley was born September 29, 1878, at Stormanstown, Dublin, Ireland. She was the daughter of pious, well-known and respectable parents. Her father was especially prominent by reason of his goodness to the poor and the unfortunate. One of his regular practices was to have all the poor of the vicinity come to his house on Sundays and holidays for the purpose of instructing them in their religion. Both father and mother died when the subject of this sketch was very young.

Shortly after this unfortunate event Catherine was adopted by Mr. and Mrs. William Callahan, who belonged to a family that was distantly connected with the mother of Miss McAuley. Her foster-parents, although very worthy people, were bitterly prejudiced against the religion practiced by their adopted child. They were so opposed to anything Catholic that they would not permit a crucifix or a pious picture in the house. Despite this, Catherine attended to her religious duties with great regularity and fidelity, and by her gentleness succeeded in disarming any anger or annoyance that they might have otherwise felt regarding her course.

She was a model of all the virtues, and this fact did not escape the attention of her foster-parents. Dean Gaffney, writing of her at this period, says: "Everyone who had distress to be relieved, affliction to be mitigated, troubles to be encountered, came to her, and to the best of her ability she advised them what to do. Her zeal made her a missionary in her district." In these works of charity and usefulness she continued for several years, during which she was rendering herself dearer and dearer to her adopted parents. In the course of a few years both these estimable people died, but not before the gentle foster-child had led both of them into the Catholic Church. Catherine was left the sole heiress of Mr. Callahan, and at once made arrangements for systematically distributing food and clothing to the poor.

Miss McAuley was now in a position to realize her early vision of founding an institution in which servants and other women of good character might, when out of work, find a temporary home and be shielded from the dangers to which the unprotected members of the sex are exposed. She unfolded her plans to the Very Rev. Dr. Armstrong and Very Rev. Dr. Blake, her spiritual advisers.

"It was deemed advisable," says Dean Murphy, writing of this, "not to take a house already built and occupied for other purposes, and which she would have some difficulty in adapting to her own designs, but to secure a plot of ground that had never been built upon, and to erect an edifice for the honor and glory of God that had never been profaned by the vices and folly of the world, and which should be as holy in its creation as in its use, and be dedicated to God from its very foundation." The building was constructed and put into operation within a reasonably short time. When finished it was discovered that the architect had created a building which for all purposes could be used as a convent.

This was regarded as a fortunate mistake. In the beginning Miss McAuley had no thought of founding a religious institute, but in working out the ideas that were near to her heart she imperceptibly and almost unconsciously drifted towards that end. Daniel O'Connell, the great Irish liberator, was a friend a patron of Miss McAuley, and frequently visited her establishment, which he regarded as filling a long-felt want in the Irish capital. In 1827 O'Connell presided over a Christmas dinner given by Miss McAuley to the poor children of Dublin.

In 1828, at the suggestion of the Archbishop of the Diocese, she formed the Order of the Sisters of Mercy. There had been a "Royal, Military and Religious Order of Our Lady of Mercy," dating back to the twelfth century, and this new order, founded by a pious young woman, was largely based upon the old one, except that it was intended for women and not for men. Miss McAuley frequently said that what she desired was to found an order whose members would combine the silence, recollection and prayer of the Carmelite with the active zeal of a Sister of Charity. It seems to be generally conceded that she succeeded in achieving her purpose. Three words, "works of mercy," briefly tell the story of the character of the labors of the Sisters of Mercy. Miss McAuley did not finally complete her laudable plan without having to overcome many obstacles, and set aside some very bitter opposition, part of which came, not only from her own relatives, but from bishops and priests as well.

A few years after the dedication of her institute Miss McAuley and a few chosen companions decided that the high purpose to which they had consecrated their lives could be carried out if they would enter the religious state. They were admitted to one of the convents of the Presentation Order, and after a novitiate lasting one year she and her companions received the religious habit.

In October, 1831, she professed and was canonically appointed by the Archbishop as Superior of the new order. The costume worn by the members of the order was devised by Mother Catherine, as she was thereafter called. The Order grew rapidly in numbers and in prominence. The life of its first Mother and foundress was active and edifying. Her labors were not confined to any particular work, but embraced everything that was in the interest and for the benefit of the poor and unfortunate. In 1832 she won enduring laurels by assuming charge of the cholera hospital in Dublin.

She died on November 11, 1837, resigned and happy, and furnished an example of pious fortitude to the Sisters that crowded about her deathbed. The Order that she founded, as it exists to-day, is her best monument. Beginning in Ireland in 1827 it was afterwards successfully introduced into England, Newfoundland, Australia, New Zealand, South America and the United States of America.

XIII.

CLERICAL VETERANS.

Notre Dame, Indiana, enjoys the distinction of a Grand Army Post composed of Catholic clergymen, most of whom are members of the faculty of Notre Dame University. The organization was officially entered on October 6, 1897 , as Post No. 569, Department of Indiana. Very Rev. William E. Corby, C. S. C., the commander of the new post, was chaplain of the Irish Brigade, and is now the provincial, or head officer, of the order of the Holy Cross in the United States. Dr. Corby is also the chaplain of the Indiana Commandery of the Loyal Legion. To this position he was nominated by General Lew Wallace.

The membership of the new post will be very small, but large enough to have a few famous fighters and great men of the war. With the exception of Colonel William E. Haynes, the only lay member, the post is composed altogether of members of the congregation of the Holy Cross. The following complete the roster:

Very Rev. William Corby, C. S. C., chaplain Eighty-eighth New York Volunteers, Irish Brigade.

Rev. Peter P. Cooney, C. S. C., chaplain Thirty-fifth Medina.

James McLain (Brother Leander), C. S. C., B Company, Twenty-fourth United States Infantry.

William A. Olmsted, C. S. C., captain and lieutenant colonel Second Infantry, New York Volunteers, colonel Fifty-ninth New York Veteran Volunteers; brigadier general by brevet, commandery First Brigade, Second Division, Second Army Corps, Army of the Potomac.

Mark A. Willis (Brother John Chrysostom, C. S. C.(, I Company, Fifty-fourth Pennsylvania Volunteers.

Nicholas A. Bath (Brother Cosmos, C. S. C.), D Company, Second United States Artillery.

James Mantle (Brother Benedict, C. S. C.(, A Company, First Pennsylvania Heavy Artillery and Sixth United States Cavalry.

John McInerny (Brother Eustathius, C. S. C.), H Company, Eighty-third Ohio Volunteers.

Joseph Staley (Brother Agathus, C. S. C.), C Company, Eighth Indiana Regulars.

Ignatz Mayer (Brother Ignatius, C. S. C.), C Company, Seventy-fifth Pennsylvania Volunteers and One Hundred and Fifty-seventh Pennsylvania Volunteers.

James C. Malloy (Brother Raphael, C. S. C.), B Company, One Hundred and Thirty-third Pennsylvania Volunteers.

Colonel William E. Haynes.

General Olmsted, who is studying for the priesthood, is much interested in the little gathering. He is justly proud of the work of his men in the celebrated Hancock's Division. He refers to the Government reports in every case as proof of the bravery of his soldiers. The General said not long ago in an interview: "Very much that is said of me is not true, but to show you that my men were brave, I give you the reports from the department at Washington." The General read "'The losses of the First Brigade, Second Division, Second Corps—my brigade—were greater in the battle of Gettysburg than those that occurred to any one brigade in the army. There was, beside, a total casualty of 763 killed and wounded out of 1246 men at Antietam, a percentage of 61."

Father Corby has the honor of being the only chaplain to give absolution under fire. The event of his giving absolution at Gettysburg to the Irish Brigade is the best known of his achievements in chaplain life. It is said that every man, Catholic and Protestant, knelt before the rock upon which he stood, and the colors were lowered. Then they went out and fought, and how many fell upon that bloody field is too well known to be repeated. Father Corby, although an old man, is hale and hearty, and does all his work as provincial of the order without the aid of a secretary.

Rev. Peter Cooney also has a brilliant war record, but he and Father Corby are by no means the only two who went to war from Notre Dame. In all there were eight priests who went forth to service as chaplains in the war. Beside these Mother Mary Angela, a cousin of James G. Blaine, went forth with a large number of sisters to nurse the wounded and care for the dying. To these also great praise is due.

There was much enthusiasm in Notre Dame over the organization exercises, and among those present or who sent their congratulations were General Lew Wallace, General Mulholland, of Philadelphia; Colonel J. A. Smith, of Indianapolis; General J. A. Golden, of New York; General William J. Sewall, Colonel R. S. Robertson, of Port Wayne; General J. A. Starburg, of Boston; Captain Florence Maccarthy., of New York; Captain Emil A Dapper, of Grand Rapids; Captain J. J. Abercrombie, of Chicago; Department Commander James S. Dodge, with his full staff. The G. A. R. post from Elkhart and two posts from South Bend helped to muster in the clerical veterans. Commendatory messages were also received from a large number of posts and leaders in the G. A. R.

XIV.

CATHOLICS IN THE WAR.

St. Teresa's Church, at the northeast corner of Broad and Catherine streets, was temporarily used as a hospital for wounded soldiers during the war. On July 4, 1897, Rev. Joseph V. O'Connor, one of the eloquent priests of the diocese of Philadelphia, delivered an address in this church, relative to Catholics in the war. A score of Grand Army posts attended the exercises, which were also honored by the presence of the venerable Hugh Lane, who has been pastor of the church during and since the war. Father O'Connor's address deserves a place in this volume. He said:

"The sacred edifice in which you assemble is an appropriate spot for religion and patriotism to meet, for St. Teresa's Church was for a time in the Civil War a military hospital. The old railway station at Broad and Prime streets was the rendezvous of the Union troops from the North and East going to and from the seat of war. The gleaming cross upon the church seemed lifted in benediction over army after army marching past. The poet Byron represents the forest of Ardennes as weeping over the 'unreturning brave' of Waterloo, but the sign of man's redemption may have lifted up many a Catholic soldier's heart destined to be stilled in the next battle. These walls, now bright with light and color, have re-echoed the moans of the dying. The venerable priest whose gracious presence lends dignity and historic interest to this celebration prepared her many a soldier for the last dread fight with death, the universal conqueror. I seem to behold, mingling with your solid phalanx, the shadowy forms of the brave men who were delivered from the storm and earthquake of battle to breathe out their spirits here in the peace of the sanctuary.

"Far be it from me to limit to the Catholic breast that noble fire of the love of country, which with purifying flame burned in the great heart of the nation when war sounded the trumpet call to the children of the republic. It is occasion that shows the man. Our Civil War was an occasion that showed our Church. The legislative code

of England was disgraced, even in Victoria's reign by the
calumny and the imbecility of penal laws against Catholics. To be a Catholic was to be a traitor. In vain did we
appeal to history, which crowns with laurels the brows
of unnumbered Catholic patriots and heroes in every
land of the universal Church. The Thundering Legion
fought for the Roman Emperor, who decreed its martyrdom. The fleet of Protestant England was led against the
Armada of Catholic Spain by a Catholic in the service
of a Queen who sent his fellow-religionists to the stake
on account of their faith. The patriotism of the Catholic is motived by his religion. It rises superior to the
form in which civil government may be embodied. Were
the Pope, as temporal prince, to invade our country we
should be bound in conscience to repel him, nor would
our patriotism conflict one iota with our religious faith.

"Our people, driven by misgovernment from their
native soil, found the portals of the great Republic flung
open to them in friendly welcome. They came to the
North and to the West. Thus the great centres of indus-
try in the Northern States were crowded with Catholics.
Most of us had learned the bitter lessons which tyranny,
bad government and religious rancor have to impart
under the scourge of England's misrule of Ireland. As
Bourke Cockran says, England's treatment of the Irish
people has made the world distrust her. Ireland's love
for America dates from before the Revolution. The
Irish Parliament passed resolutions of sympathy with
the American colonists. The great tides of immigration
from Ireland set in early and continued until, at the outbreak of the Civil War, the North was one-fourth Celtic
in blood.

"The Catholic Church studiously refrained from

any official pronouncement upon the causes of the conflict which she deplored. The first regiment to respond to President Lincoln's initial call for troops was the Sixtyninth New York. It was mainly Irish and Catholic. Within 48 hours it was on its way to the front. New York, preeminently a Catholic State, furnished one-seventh of the military forces in the war for the Union.

"Obviously the Government had no reason for recording the religious faith of its soldiers. Patriotism is at once a natural and a civic virtue. That it may be supernaturalized is evident from the words of St. Paul, bidding us obey the higher powers for conscience sake. The country had to face a condition, not a theory, and whatever abstract reasoning has to say about State rights, the will of the majority of the people, which is the supreme law in a republic, decided for the maintenance of the Federal Union. The best traditions of the country, North and South, identified liberty with union. God appears to have made the country one in geographical formation, in sameness of language, in homogeneity of character.

"Two illustrious Catholic prelates, recognized as leaders in Israel—the Moses and the Joshua of the Church— Archbishop Kendrick, of Baltimore, and Archbishop Hughes, of New York, declared in favor if the Union. The sainted sage of the primatial city flung the starry banner from the pinnacle of his Cathedral. The Archbishop of New York was so thoroughly identified with the cause of the Union that he was invested by the President and his Secretary of State with the authority of envoy extraordinary to the courts of Europe.

"Unroll the military records of our country and you will read column after column of names that are historically Catholic. Read the names on the tombstones of soldiers in the great national cemeteries and you will find in the Christian name alone confirmatory evidence of the faith of the hero that sleeps beneath. The Catholic knows that the Church imposes in baptism the name of a saint. We may safely judge that he is a Catholic who bears the name of Patrick and Michael, of Bernard and Dominic. Not even the conservative spirit of the Church of England could retain the old saintly nomenclature, and Puritanism chose the names of Old Testament worthies or names taken from natural history and even heathen mythology.

"If we reckon our soldiers by their religion, the majority would be Catholic and we should find that we had given our children in far greater number than any one denomination. On the second day of Gettysburg a Catholic priest, ascending an eminence, lifted his hand to give absolution, and as far as the eye could reach rank upon rank of soldiers bent their heads like cornfields swept by the summer breeze. Hancock, the "superb," impressed by the solemnity of the scene, bared his brow. If the poet thought that a tear should fall for Stonewall Jackson because he spared Barbara Frietchie's Union flag, will not a Catholic murmur a prayer for the great general who gave heed to the priest calling upon his people to be contrite for their sins in the hour which for many would be the last?

"The seven successive stormings of the heights of Fredericksburg by the Irish Brigade has long passed into history as surpassing Alma and the Sedan. Keenan's cavalry charge at Chancellorsville saved the Union army at the cost of 300 lives. The charge of the Light Brigade at Balaklava was described by a French officer as magnificent, but unmilitary—'C'est magnifique, mais ce n'est pas la guerre.' But Keenan's charge was both glorious and strategic. His troop rushed like a whirlwind upon 20,000 Confederates. His men were shot down or sabered in the saddle. The steeds maddened by wounds and uncontrolled by their dead riders, plunged into the thick of the Confederate ranks, and so disconcerted and appalled them that the main army of the Union had time to save itself from otherwise inevitable destruction. Perhaps the most critical point of the war was the success or the failure of Sheridan's devastation of the Shenandoah Valley, which was the great base of supplies for the South. Sheridan's historic ride, which saved the day at Winchester, was the exploit of a Catholic. The Republic subsequently conferred upon this son of the Church one of the highest and most responsible positions in her keeping, the generalship of her armies.

"One of the first, if not the first band of trained nurses that offered their services to the Government was the religious society of the Sisters of Charity. Their title is their history. Their services in hospitals and on the field did more than tomes of controversy to make the Catholic Church better known, and consequently loved, by the American people. The convalescing soldier by word and by letter spread the information throughout the land that the ministrations of the Catholic Sisterhood reminded him of a mother's love and a sister's tenderness.

"The heroic devotion to the duty of the Catholic chaplains, who made no distinction of religion when a soldier was to be helped, endeared the Catholic religion to many who met a Catholic priest for the first time in camp or hospital. Our own noble-hearted Archbishop rendered such service to the wounded soldiers in St.

Louis that the Government offered him a chaplaincy. Care of the body was often supplemented with the higher care of the soul. In that parting hour, when mortality leans upon the breast of religion, the example of devoted priest and religious gently led many a soul into the hope and the consolation of divine faith.

"God grant that our country shall never again reel under the shock of war! Yet out of the nettle of danger has come the flower of safety. Calumny, suspicion, distrust of our patriotism were struck dumb. Never again shall we be taunted with secret antipathy to free institutions. The banner of the stars was rebaptized in our blood. To the soldier of the war the Church owes a debt of gratitude. He proved often by his death that the religion which he professed, far from condemning his patriotism, commended it as a virtue, and the faith that sustained him in battle supported him when his heart poured out the blood of supreme sacrifice upon the altar of his country. And though no memorial marks his resting place the Church in every mass pleads for the repose of his soul.

"The soldier stands as the highest value which we place upon our country and her institutions. He says to all: 'My country is worth dying for.' In our thoughtless way we take liberty, security of life and property, the blessings of religion and safeguards of law and all the beauty and amenity of our civilization as a matter of course. Without the soldier all these goods would perish. It is war that preserves and protects peace. The soldier is the guardian of our homes. Honor him; make peaceful and happy his declining years. Thank God with David for preparing our hands for the sword, before whose blinding ray, in the hand of the hero, domestic treason and foreign conspiracy slink into their dens. Bless God for making us a nation of soldiers, as well as of citizens. The war proved that the American soldier, North and South, is without a peer in bravery, in discipline, in self-control. Whilst our Republic gives birth to such heroic sons we may laugh armed Europe to scorn.

"Soldiers, there is another battle, another field, a greater Captain than even the archangel who led the embattled seraphim to war. You divine my meaning. Be soldiers of the cross! Fight the good fight of faith. Be sober, pure, charitable. The laurel that binds the warrior's brow on earth soon fades. The flowers of Decoration Day droop with the setting sun. But the Divine Captain of our salvation will place upon your brow, if you are faithful to the end, a crown that fadeth not away, a wreath which you will receive amid the shout of the heavenly armies."

XV.

THE SANITARY COMMISSION.

The purpose of the writer of this history, as already stated, has been to furnish for the first time a full and detailed story of the labors of the Catholic Sisterhoods in the Civil War, but in doing that he has not had the slightest intention of detracting from the splendid service rendered by other bodies and other persons. One of the most notable organizations that contributed its part in the humane work incident to the war was the Sanitary Commission. It had its rise in a spontaneous movement of the women in New England. It is said that 7000 branch Aid Societies were connected with the Commission at

LINCOLN AT GETTYSBURG.

one time. Charles J. Stille, of Philadelphia, has written a history of the Commission, from which most of the facts embodied in this sketch have been obtained. Committees were sent to Washington, and after much negotiation, involving tedious delay on the part of the Government, the Secretary of War, on the 9th of June, 1861, issued an order appointing Henry W. Bellows, D. D., Professor A. D. Boche, LL. D., Professor Jeffries Wyman, M. D., W. H. Van Buren, M. D., Wolcott Gibbs, M. D., R. C. Wood, surgeon U. S. A.; G. W. Cullom, U. S. A.; Alexander E. Shiras, U. S. A., in connection with such others as they might chose to associate with them, "a commission of inquiry and advice in respect of the sanitary interests of the United States forces." There were to serve without remuneration from the Government and were to be provided with a room for their use in the city of Washington.

They were to direct their inquiries to the principles and practices connected with the inspection of recruits and enlisted men, the sanitary condition of volunteers, to the means of preserving and restoring the health and of securing the general comfort and efficiency of the troops, to the proper provision of cooks, nurses and hospitals, and to other subjects of a like nature. The mode by which they proposed to conduct these inquiries was detailed in the letter of the New York delegation to the Secretary of War on the 22d of May. The order appointing them directed that they should correspond freely with the department and with the Medical Bureau concerning these subjects, and on this footing and within these limits their relations with the official authorities were established. To enable them to carry out fully the purposes of their appointment the Surgeon General issued a circular letter announcing the creation of the Commission, and directing all the officers in his department to grant its agents every facility in the prosecution of their duties.

On the 12th of June the gentlemen named as Commissioners in the order of the Secretary of War (with the exception of Professor Wyman, who had declined his appointment) assembled at Washington. They proceeded to organize the Board by the selection of the Rev. Dr. Bellows as president. Their first care was to secure the services of certain gentlemen as colleagues, who were supposed to possess special qualifications, but whose names had not been included in the original warrant. Accordingly Dr. Elisha Harris and Dr. Cornelius R. Agnew were unanimously chosen Commissioners at the first meeting, and George T. Strong and Dr. J. S. Newberry in like manner at the one next succeeding. At different periods during the war Rt. Rev. Bishop Clark, Hon. R. W. Burnet, Hon. Mark Skinner, Hon. Joseph Holt, Horace Binney, Jr., Rev. J. H. Heywood, Prof. Fairman Rogers, J. Huntingdon Wolcott, Charles J. Stille, E. B. McCagg and F. Law Olmstead were elected by the Board members of the Commission.

At the first meeting a "Plan of Organization," prepared by the president, was presented, discussed and finally adopted. On the 13th the Commission, in a body, waited on the President and Secretary of War, who gave their formal sanction to this plan of organization by affixing to it their signatures. The experiences of the war suggested but little alteration, even in the outline of this report, while to a strict adherence to the general principles it embodied the Sanitary Commission owed much of its wonderful success.

The plan reduced to a practical system and method

the principles laid down in the letters of the New York gentlemen to the Government authorities and endeavored to apply them to the actual existing condition of the army. Confining its proposed operations within the limited sphere of "inquiry" and "advice," which had been assigned to it by the Government, it declared what it proposed to do and by what methods in each of these departments of duty.

In order that its work might be carried on systematically and thoroughly two general committees were created, one respecting "inquiry," the other "advice." The object of the first was to determine by all the light which could be derived from experience what must necessarily be the wants and conditions of troops brought together as ours had been, to ascertain exactly how far evils which had proved the scourge of other armies had already invaded our own, and to decide concerning the best measures to be adopted to remove all causes of removable and preventable disease.

Each branch of "inquiry" under this head was referred to a district sub-committee. From the first was expected such suggestions of preventable measures as experience in former wars had proved to be absolutely essential; to the second was entrusted the actual inspection, by its own members or their agents, of the camps and hospitals, so that the real condition of the army, in a sanitary point of view, concerning which there were many conflicting rumors, could be definitely known. To the third was referred all questions concerning the improvement of the health and efficiency of the army in respect to diet, clothing, quarters, and matters of a similar nature.

In regard to the other branch of duty assigned to the Commission under its appointment, that of "advice," the Board took the same wide and comprehensive views as had guided them in regard to the needful subjects of inquiry. Their purpose was to "get the opinions and conclusions of the Commission approved by the Medical Bureau, ordered by the War Department and carried out by the officers and men."

The interest excited in thousands of homes throughout the land, whose inmates were members of aid societies in favor of the Sanitary Commission, and who looked upon it only as the almoner of their vast offerings for the relief of the army, led to the popular error that it was only a relief association upon a grand scale and quite overshadowed in popular estimation its original purpose, if not the peculiar and exclusive work before it. The Commission itself, however, never departed from the true scientific idea and conception of a preventive system, and always regarded the relief system, vast as was the place occupied by it in the war, as inferior in the importance of its results to those due to well considered and thoroughly executed preventive measures.

The Commission at the close of the war established a pension bureau and war claim agency for the benefit of disabled soldiers and their orphans and widows. The entire money receipts of the Commission from 1862 to 1866 were $4,924,480.99, and the value of supplies furnished is estimated at $15,000,000.

XVI.

"THE BLUE AND THE GRAY."

"By the flow of the inland river,
 Whence the fleets of iron have fled,
Where the blades of the grave-grass quiver,
 Asleep on the ranks of the dead—
Under the sod and the dew,
 Waiting the judgment-day;
Under the one, the Blue;
 Under the other, the Gray.

These in the robings of glory,
 Those in the gloom of defeat,
All with the battle-blood gory
 In the dusk of eternity meet—
Under the sod and the dew,
 Waiting the judgment-day;
Under the laurel, the Blue;
 Under the willow, the Gray.

From the silence of sorrowful hours
 The desolate mourners go,
Lovingly laden with flowers,
 Alike for the friend and the foe—
Under the sod and the dew,
 Waiting the judgment-day;
Under the roses, the Blue;
 Under the lilies, the Gray.

So with an equal splendor
 The morning sun-rays fall,
With a touch impartially tender,
 On the blossoms blooming for all—
Under the sod and the dew,
 Waiting the judgment-day;
Broidered with gold, the Blue;
 Mellowed with gold, the Gray.

So when the summer calleth
    On forest and field of grain,
With an equal murmur falleth
    The cooling drip of the rain—
Under the sod and the dew,
    Waiting the judgment-day;
Wet with the rain, the Blue;
    Wet with the rain, the Gray.

Sadly, but not with upbraiding,
    The generous deed was done:
In the storm of the years that are fading,
    No braver battle was won—
Under the sod and the dew,
    Waiting the judgment-day;
Under the blossoms, the Blue;
    Under the garlands, the Gray.

No more shall the war-cry sever,
    Or the winding rivers be red:
They banish our anger forever
    When they laurel the graves of our dead—
Under the sod and the dew,
    Waiting the judgment-day;
Love and tears for the Blue,
    Tears and love for the Gray.

XVII.

A MIRACLE OF THE WAR.

The following interesting little incident is taken from V. Rev. W. C. Corby's book, entitled "Memoirs of Chaplain Life:"

"On the 29th of November, 1863," says Rev. Constantine L. Egan, O. P., chaplain of the Ninth Massachusetts Volunteers, "we advanced to Mine Run and formed a line of battle and bivouacked for the night. The enemy were posted on the east ridge, about one mile from the stream called Mile Run, on a centre ridge nearly 100 feet above the surface of the stream. Their works could easily be seen by us posted on the west ridge of the run. They were strongly fortified, their works bristling with abatis, infantry parapets and epaulements for batteries. About 3 o'clock on the evening of the 30th the order was given to charge the enemy's line. Seeing the danger of death before us I asked the colonel to form his regiment into a solid square so that I could address the men. He did so. I then spoke to them of their danger, and entreated them to prepare for it by going on their knees and making a sincere act of contrition for their sins, with the intention of going to confession if their lives were spared.

"As the regiment fell on their knees, other Catholic soldiers broke from their ranks and joined us, so that in less than two minutes I had the largest congregation I ever witnessed before, or even since. Having pronounced the words of general absolution to be given in such emergencies and danger, I spoke a few words of encouragement to them.

★ ★ ★ "After talking to the soldiers and finishing my remarks, they arose from their knees, grasping their muskets with a firm clinch, and went back to their respective commands, awaiting the hour to expire to make the assault."

Smith Johnson, taking this as his theme, has written the following poem, entitled "A Miracle of War," and dedicated it to Father Corby:

Two armies stood in stern array
On Gettysburg's historic field—

This side the blue, on that the gray—
 Each side resolved to win the day,
Or life to home and country yield.

"Take arms!" "Fall in!" rang o'er the line
 Of Hancock's ever-valiant corps—
For to the left the cannons chime
 With music terribly sublime,
With death's unceasing, solemn roar.

With spirits ardent, undismayed,
 With flags uplifted toward the sky,
There stands brave Meagher's old brigade
 Those noble laurels ne'er will fade
Upon the page of history.

"All forward, men!" No, pause a while—
 Dead silence follows like parade
At "order arms," for 'long the file
 There moves a priest with holy smile—
The priest of Meagher's old brigade.

All eyes were toward him reverent turned,
 For he was known and loved by all,
And every face with fervor burned,
 And with a glance his mission learned—
A mission of high Heaven's call.

Then spake the priest: "My comrades, friends,
 Ere long the battle fierce will surge,
Ere long the curse of war descends—
 At such a moment God commends
You from the soul all sin to purge.

"Kneel, soldiers; lift your hearts to God,
 In sweet contrition crush the pride
Of human minds; kneel on the sod
 That soon will welter in your blood—
Look up to Christ, who for you died."

And every man, whate'er his creed,
 Kneels down, and whispers pass along
The ranks, and murmuring voices plead

To be from sin's contagion freed
And turned from path of mortal wrong.

Across the vale the gray lines view
     The priest and those who, kneeling now,
For absolution humbly sue,
     And joining hearts, the gray and blue
Together make the holy vow.

*   *   *   *   *

The smoke of battle lifts apace,
     And o'er the field lie forms of men,
With glazen eyes and pallid face—
     Dead—yet alive, for God's sweet grace
Has saved them from the death of sin.

SMITH JOHNSON

XVIII.

LINCOLN AT GETTYSBURG.

It has been aptly said that the battlefield of Gettysburg has become the "Mecca of American Reconciliation." By act of Congress a National Park has been established there, observatories erected and everything possible done to make the battlefield convenient and attractive to tourists.

The National Cemetery at Gettysburg was dedicated November 19, 1863. The oration was by Edward Everett. On this occasion President Lincoln made the famous address that will never die. It was as follows:

"Four-score and seven years ago our fathers brought forth on this continent a new nation, conceived in Lib-

erty, and dedicated to the proposition that all men are
created equal. Now, we are engaged in a great civil war,
testing whether that nation, or any nation, so conceived
and so dedicated, can long endure. We are met on a great
battlefield of that war. We have come to dedicate a portion of that field as a final resting place for those who here
gave their lives that the nation might live. It is altogether
fitting and proper that we should do this. But, in a larger
sense, we cannot dedicate—we cannot consecrate—we
cannot hallow this ground. The brave men, living and
dead, who struggled here, have consecrated it far above
our poor power to add or detract. The world will little
note nor long remember what we say here, but it can
never forget what they did here. It is for us the living,
rather, to be dedicated here to the unfinished work which
they who fought here have thus far so nobly carried on.
It is rather for us to be here dedicated to the great task
remaining before us—that from these honored dead we
take increased devotion to that cause for which they gave
the last full measure of devotion. That we here highly re-
solve that these dead shall not have died in vain; that this
nation, under God, shall have a new birth of freedom;
and that the government of the people, by the people,
and for the people, shall not perish from the earth."

———◆◆———

XIX.

THE FAITH AND THE FLAG.

While the work of the zealous Catholic Sisterhoods
on the battlefield and in the camp and hospital was for
humanity in its broadest sense the effect of their example

and the beauty of their daily lives also had the effect of clearing away the mists of prejudice that sometimes distorted and clouded the views of honorable, well-meaning and worthy non-Catholics. The writer has endeavored to present the history of the labors of the Sisters in a straightforward and dispassionate manner.

He has dealt exclusively in facts and has, as far as possible, avoided comment. It has especially been his aim to keep entirely clear of sectional disputes or religious controversies. Hence it will be found that the story of the work of the Sisters has reference, in the main, to their devotion to suffering humanity. It was inevitable, however, that men living in the atmosphere of sanctity created by these good women should feel the consoling benefit of their silent influence. The result was that non-Catholics began to take a broader and more kindly view of their Catholic comrades and fellow-citizens, and long before the war closed they realized that the faith and the flag were entirely compatible.

A few years ago William J. Onahan, of Chicago, in an address, incidentally touched upon this very point. Speaking of those who were distrustful of the Church and its teachings he said: "If they could realize the harmony and benevolent influence of her teaching, the number of souls redeemed through her efforts and graces from despair and sin, the wounded hearts solaced by her balm—the extent of human misery she has removed or mitigated? Let them but think how that Church has consecrated the marriage tie, sanctified the home, shielded the unfortunate, lifted up the lowly and sorrow-stricken, staying the arm of the oppressor, pleading for the rights of the poor against the power of the tyrant and the greed of capital. Witness the asylums and the refuges the Catholic Church has established all over the world for every condition of infirmity and suffering—for the orphans, the foundlings, the sick, the aged, the wayward and the fallen.

"See the admirable sisterhoods—to which no parallel can be found on earth—the Sisters of Charity and Mercy, the Poor Handmaids of Jesus Christ, the Sisters of St. Joseph, the nuns of the Good Shepherd, the Little Sisters of the Poor and countless others, varying in the admirable diversity of their charitable labors. Watch these sisters at their appointed duties in the hospitals and asylums, in the hovels of the poor, by the bedside of the dying—aye, in pesthouses and small-pox hospitals, as well as on the battlefield, ministering to the dying soldier—all bent on doing God's work for God's sake. Assuredly these facts—these daily examples here before our yes, within reach of our feet in daily walk—assuredly these ought to serve toward dispelling the false glare of prejudice.

"As a preliminary let me say I adopt without reserve or qualification the language of the Baltimore Catholic Congress: 'We rejoice at the marvellous development of our country, and regard with just pride the part taken by Catholics in such development' In the words of the pastoral issued by the Archbishops of the United States, assembled in the third Plenary Council of Baltimore, 'we claim to be acquainted both with the laws, institutions and spirit of our country, and we emphatically declare that there is no antagonism between them.

"We repudiate with equal earnestness the assertion that we need to lay aside any of our devotedness to our Church to be true Americans, and the insinuations that we need abate any of our love for our country's principles to be faithful Catholics. We believe that our country's heroes were the instruments of the God of Nations in establishing this home of freedom; to both the Almighty and to His instruments in the work we look with grateful reverence, and to maintain the inheritance of freedom which they have left us, should it ever—which God forbid—be imperiled, our Catholic citizens will be bound to stand forward as one man, ready to pledge anew their lives, their fortunes and their sacred honor.'

"Before turning to the question of the 'rights and duties' let me first define what I understand by the term 'Catholic Citizen.' An American citizen, whether by birth or adoption, who, having had the grace of Christian baptism, believes and practices the teachings of the Catholic Church—in other words a practical Catholic. Now we come to the question of 'rights and duties.' What are our rights as citizens? No more, no less, precisely, than those possessed by any other American Citizen. What are the rights we in common have with others? In general terms we have the 'right' of enjoying and defending life and liberty, of acquiring, possessing and protecting property and reputation and of pursuing our own happiness.

"We hold, in the language of the Constitution of Illinois, that all men have a natural and indefeasible right to worship Almighty God according to the dictates of their own consciences, that no man can of right be compelled to attend, erect or support any place of worship, or to maintain any ministry against his consent, that no human authority can in any case whatever control or interfere with the rights of conscience. We have a right to be protected in our persons and property; we cannot be deprived of either without due process of law; the right of free elections, to trial by jury, to equality before the law—but I need not enter into detail of the 'Bill of Rights' which specifies the catalogue of a freeman's inheritance. The highest and most precious right, however, is that of religious freedom, liberty to worship God without let or hindrance and free from religious disabilities of any kind, and next to their own rights as free men, to exercise it as shall best promote the welfare of the city, State and nation.

"Catholics, then, are entitled to absolute equality before the law, and this is according to the letter and spirit of the Constitution of the United States, as well as of the several States now, I believe, without exception. There is nevertheless an unwritten law, which operates as a practical discrimination against Catholics in public life as effectually as though it were so expressed in the Constitution. It is the law of public opinion deriving its force and effect from popular prejudice. It is a well-known fact that neither of the great political parties would dare to nominate a Catholic for the Presidency, and the same is true as to the office of Governor in the different States. Surely it would not be claimed that no American Catholic could be found qualified by position and ability for any of these high offices.

"Eternal vigilance, it has been said, is the price of liberty. Probably if Catholics were alert in asserting their rights—in a just and lawful, as well as in a reasonable manner—there would be less disposition shown to infringe upon those rights, and to ignore their claim to representation. Again, the government, whether National or State, has no just claim or authority to deny the rights of conscience to Catholics, whether they be employed in the service of the nation, in the army or naval forces, in penal or reformatory institutions, in asylums, or elsewhere. The State may lawfully and justly deprive a man of his liberty and place him behind prison bars; but it has no right to compel him while there to attend a form of religious worship in which he does not believe; it should not deny or hamper the attendance and ministrations of priest or elder whose services are sought by the prisoner or State's own ward. Justice and sound policy alike demonstrate the wisdom of invoking the services of the Catholic Missionary for Catholics, whether in jail or asylum, or on the frontier.

"General Grant testified that Father De Smet's presence among the Indians was of greater value to the Government than a regiment of cavalry, and recent events on our Northern borders intensify the force of this conclusion. The Catholic missionary is always a peacemaker. Catholics ask nothing in the way of 'privileges.' We have no claim to privileges. We only ask what we are willing to concede to others—equality and fair play. If others are content to minimize religious principles or to abdicate them entirely we must be excused if we insist on holding fast to ours. We are on firm ground in that respect; we do not care to follow others into the "slough of despond." We are persuaded that every vexed question occupying and disturbing the public attention, dividing and distracting the people can be amicably adjusted, provided the wise men of the nation and the States will take these questions out of the hands of fanatics and bigots, who are only too eager and anxious to inaugurate a reign of discord and religious strife.

"Catholics, be assured, will have no part in this warfare, beyond protecting and defending their rights— God-given and Constitutional rights. They would be unworthy of American citizenship were they to be content with less.

"We now come to the question of the 'Duties of Catholics as Citizens.' Let it be understood that in undertaking to answer this, as well as the previous question under consideration, I speak for myself only as a Catholic layman. I express my own thoughts and convictions unreservedly. What are the 'duties' referred to? First, and primarily, I should say to be American, in all that the term broadly implies. How do I define the tem American? It stands in my mind for liberty, order, education and opportunities. It is the duty of the Catholic citizen to love liberty for its own sake, order for the general good and to illustrate the highest type and model of civic virtue. It is a duty to foster and nourish the purity of home life and the domestic virtues, eagerly to promote education and to make every necessary sacrifice for it, and to see to it that Catholic children shall have the benefit of a sound Christian education. Catholics should avail themselves of the material opportunities and advantages offered in this wonderful age and country, and strive to be in the front ranks in the march of progress.

"The field is wide and inviting, the race is open to all. The privilege of American citizenship should be regarded as precious and priceless. Because so easily acquired, perhaps, it is not sufficiently estimated at is true value and worth. Think what American citizenship confers; see what it assures! Equal part and membership in this mighty empire—the equal advantage in its unsurpassed opportunities—the unqualified privileges of its unequaled freedom. No standing armies here to be moved at a monarch's caprice, weighing down and oppressing the nation's energies, draining it of its life blood, sapping its vitality, and, worst evil of all, menacing the peace of the world. No armed 'constabulary' to terrorize over a peasant population and enforce the heartless edict of brutal landlords. No hereditary or favored classes. No obstacle to the unfettered enjoyment of those rights which we possess from God in the natural law, and that are guaranteed to us in the Constitution and laws of the land—the right to life, liberty and the pursuit of happiness.

"What a future opens before us, what possibilities for ourselves and for our children! Justly are the American people jealous of this inheritance. It must be guarded with vigilant care, lest unworthy hands and evil guidance should put it in peril. American liberty and the opportunities of American life are too precious to the human family to permit the one and the other to be wrecked or endangered. I rejoice in every indication of patriotic public spirit, whether shown in devotion and respect for the country's flag or in reverence and admiration for the nation's heroes. We need all these demonstrations to keep alive in this material age the ardor and purity of true patriotism.

"True American patriotism is the inheritance and monopoly of no one class or condition. Its title is not derived from accident of birth or color, is not to be determined by locality. Montgomery, Pulaski, Steuben, De Kalb, Rochambeau, the Moylans and Sullivans, fought for American liberty in the Revolutionary days with an ardor and a fidelity at least equal to that displayed by those "native and to the manner born." Jackson was none the less a typical American because of the accident of his father's foreign birth, or, as is sometimes intimated, of his own. And who shall question the patriotic devotion of General Shields, honorably identified with the early history of your own State; of Meagher, of Mulligan, of Sheridan, of Meade and countless others I might name.

"Apprehension is sometimes expressed at the growth of foreign influence and the display of foreign customs, but this fear is after all puerile. Under our system of government the foreigner who comes to stay is soon assimilated, and while there may be here and there instances and examples, the outgrowth of foreign habits and customs, not welcome to American notions, yet these can be only passing and temporary accidents. The foreigner, I insist, is all right, provided he is loyal to American laws and government. We have no use for any other."

Made in the USA
Charleston, SC
26 January 2011